Drupal 8 Development Cookbook

Over 60 hands-on recipes that get you acquainted with Drupal 8's features and help you harness its power

Matt Glaman

[PACKT] PUBLISHING   open source*
community experience distilled

BIRMINGHAM - MUMBAI

Drupal 8 Development Cookbook

First published: March 2016

Production reference: 1040316

Published by Packt Publishing Ltd.
Livery Place
35 Livery Street
Birmingham B3 2PB, UK.

ISBN 978-1-78588-147-3

www.packtpub.com

Credits

Author
Matt Glaman

Project Coordinator
Shweta H Birwatkar

Reviewer
Todd Zebert

Proofreader
Safis Editing

Commissioning Editor
Amarabha Banerjee

Indexer
Tejal Daruwale Soni

Acquisition Editor
Manish Nainani

Graphics
Jason Monteiro

Content Development Editor
Deepti Thore

Production Coordinator
Manu Joseph

Technical Editor
Naveenkumar Jain

Cover Work
Manu Joseph

Copy Editors
Ting Baker

Rashmi Sawant

About the Author

Matt Glaman is a developer at Commerce Guys. He is an open source developer who has been working with Drupal since 2013. He has also been developing web apps for many years prior to this. Since then, he has contributed to over 60 community projects, including being a co-maintainer of Drupal Commerce. While mostly focusing on Drupal and PHP development, he created `https://contribkanban.com`, an AngularJS application, to provide Kanban boards for the Drupal community to collaborate with.

I would like to thank, and I am grateful to, my beautiful and loving wife for putting up with the late nights split between work, spending time contributing to the Drupal community, and writing this book. I would also like to thank my two sons; thank you for giving up your playtime so that Daddy could write this book.

Thank you, Andy Giles, for helping me get to my first Drupal camp and kicking off my Drupal career. I would also like to thank my mentors Bojan Živanović, David Snopek, Ryan Szrama, and everyone else in the Drupal community!

About the Reviewer

Todd Zebert has been involved with Drupal since version 6. He is a full-stack web developer proficient in a variety of technologies, and he is currently working as a lead web developer for Miles. He has also been a technical reviewer for *Developing with Drush, Packt Publishing*.

He has a diverse background in technology, including infrastructure, network engineering, project management, and IT leadership. His experience with web development started with the original Mosaic graphical web browser, SHTML/CGI, and Perl.

He's an entrepreneur involved with the Los Angeles start-up community. He's a believer in volunteering, open source, the Maker movement, and contributing back. He's also an advocate for Science, Technology, Engineering, Art, and Math (STEAM) education.

> I'd like to thank the Drupal community, which is like no other.
>
> Finally, I'd like to thank my pre-teen son with whom I get to share my interest in technology and program video games and microcontrollers.

www.PacktPub.com

eBooks, discount offers, and more

Did you know that Packt offers eBook versions of every book published, with PDF and ePub files available? You can upgrade to the eBook version at www.PacktPub.com and as a print book customer, you are entitled to a discount on the eBook copy. Get in touch with us at customercare@packtpub.com for more details.

At www.PacktPub.com, you can also read a collection of free technical articles, sign up for a range of free newsletters and receive exclusive discounts and offers on Packt books and eBooks.

https://www2.packtpub.com/books/subscription/packtlib

Do you need instant solutions to your IT questions? PacktLib is Packt's online digital book library. Here, you can search, access, and read Packt's entire library of books.

Why Subscribe?

▸ Fully searchable across every book published by Packt

▸ Copy and paste, print, and bookmark content

▸ On demand and accessible via a web browser

Table of Contents

Preface

Drupal is a content management system used to build websites for small businesses, e-commerce, enterprise systems, and many more. Created by over 4,500 contributors, Drupal 8 provides many new features for Drupal. Whether you are new to Drupal, or an experienced Drupalist, *Drupal 8 Development Cookbook* contains recipes that help you immerse yourself in what Drupal 8 has to offer.

What this book covers

Chapter 1, *Up and Running with Drupal 8*, covers the requirements to run Drupal 8, walks you through the installation process, and extends Drupal.

Chapter 2, *The Content Authoring Experience*, dives into the content management experience in Drupal, including working with the newly bundled CKEditor.

Chapter 3, *Displaying Content through Views*, explores how to use Views to create different ways to list and display your content in Drupal.

Chapter 4, *Extending Drupal*, explains how to work with Drupal's Form API to create custom forms to collect data.

Chapter 5, *Frontend for the Win*, teaches you how to create a theme, work with the new templating system, Twig, and harness Drupal's responsive design features.

Chapter 6, *Creating Forms with the Form API*, teaches you how to write a module for Drupal, the building blocks of functionalities in Drupal.

Chapter 7, *Plug and Play with Plugins*, introduces plugins, one of the newest components in Drupal. This chapter walks you through developing the plugin system to work with fields.

Chapter 8, *Multilingual and Internationalization*, introduces features provided by Drupal 8 to create an internationalized website that supports multiple languages for content and administration.

Chapter 9, Configuration Management – Deploying in Drupal 8, explains the configuration management system, new to Drupal 8, and how to import and export site configurations.

Chapter 10, The Entity API, dives into the Entity API in Drupal, allowing you to create custom configurations and content entities.

Chapter 11, Off the Drupalicon Island, explains how Drupal allows you to embrace the mantra of *proudly built elsewhere* and includes third-party libraries in your Drupal site.

Chapter 12, Web Services, shows you how to turn your Drupal 8 site into a web services API provider through a RESTful interface.

Chapter 13, The Drupal CLI, explores working with Drupal 8 through two command-line tools created by the Drupal community: Drush and Drupal Console.

What you need for this book

In order to work with Drupal 8 and to run the code examples found in this book, the following software will be required:

Web server software stack:

- ▶ Web server: Apache (recommended), Nginx, or Microsoft IIS
- ▶ Database: MySQL 5.5 or MariaDB 5.5.20 or higher
- ▶ PHP: PHP 5.5.9 or higher

Chapter 1, Up and Running with Drupal 8, details all of these requirements and includes a recipe that highlights an out of the box development server setup.

You will also need a text editor. Here is a list of suggested popular editors and IDEs:

- ▶ Atom.io editor: `https://atom.io/`
- ▶ PHPStorm (specific Drupal integration): `https://www.jetbrains.com/phpstorm/`
- ▶ Vim with Drupal configuration: `https://www.drupal.org/project/vimrc`
- ▶ Your operating system's default text editor or command-line file editors

Who this book is for

This book is for those who have been working with Drupal, such as site builders and backend and frontend developers, and who are eager to see what awaits them when they start using Drupal 8.

Conventions

In this book, you will find a number of styles of text that distinguish between different kinds of information. Here are some examples of these styles, and an explanation of their meaning.

Code words in text are shown as follows: "The \Drupal\Core\Url class provides static methods to generate an instance of itself, such as ::fromRoute()."

A block of code is set as follows:

```
/**
 * {@inheritdoc}
 */
public function alterRoutes(RouteCollection $collection) {
if ($route = $collection->get('mymodule.mypage')) {
    $route->setPath('/my-page');
  }
}
```

When we wish to draw your attention to a particular part of a code block, the relevant lines or items are set in bold:

```
/**
 * {@inheritdoc}
 */
public function alterRoutes(RouteCollection $collection) {
if ($route = $collection->get('mymodule.mypage')) {
    $route->setPath('/my-page');
  }
}
```

Any command-line input or output is written as follows:

```
$ php core/scripts/run-tests.sh PHPUnit
```

New terms and **important words** are shown in bold. Words that you see on the screen, in menus or dialog boxes for example, appear in the text like this: "Scroll down the page and click **Install and set as default** under **Bootstrap** to enable and set the theme as default."

Warnings or important notes appear in a box like this.

Tips and tricks appear like this.

Reader feedback

Feedback from our readers is always welcome. Let us know what you think about this book—what you liked or may have disliked. Reader feedback is important for us to develop titles that you really get the most out of.

To send us general feedback, simply send an e-mail to feedback@packtpub.com, and mention the book title via the subject of your message.

If there is a topic that you have expertise in and you are interested in either writing or contributing to a book, see our author guide on www.packtpub.com/authors.

Customer support

Now that you are the proud owner of a Packt book, we have a number of things to help you to get the most from your purchase.

Downloading the example code

You can download the example code files for all Packt books you have purchased from your account at http://www.packtpub.com. If you purchased this book elsewhere, you can visit http://www.packtpub.com/support and register to have the files e-mailed directly to you.

Downloading the color images of this book

We also provide you with a PDF file that has color images of the screenshots/diagrams used in this book. The color images will help you better understand the changes in the output. You can download this file from https://www.packtpub.com/sites/default/files/downloads/Drupal8_Development_Cookbook_ColorImages.pdf.

Errata

Although we have taken every care to ensure the accuracy of our content, mistakes do happen. If you find a mistake in one of our books—maybe a mistake in the text or the code—we would be grateful if you would report this to us. By doing so, you can save other readers from frustration and help us improve subsequent versions of this book. If you find any errata, please report them by visiting http://www.packtpub.com/submit-errata, selecting your book, clicking on the **errata submission form** link, and entering the details of your errata. Once your errata are verified, your submission will be accepted and the errata will be uploaded on our website, or added to any list of existing errata, under the Errata section of that title. Any existing errata can be viewed by selecting your title from http://www.packtpub.com/support.

Piracy

Piracy of copyright material on the Internet is an ongoing problem across all media. At Packt, we take the protection of our copyright and licenses very seriously. If you come across any illegal copies of our works, in any form, on the Internet, please provide us with the location address or website name immediately so that we can pursue a remedy.

Please contact us at copyright@packtpub.com with a link to the suspected pirated material.

We appreciate your help in protecting our authors, and our ability to bring you valuable content.

Questions

You can contact us at questions@packtpub.com if you are having a problem with any aspect of the book, and we will do our best to address it.

1

Up and Running with Drupal 8

In this chapter we'll get familiar with Drupal 8 and cover:

- ▶ Installing Drupal
- ▶ Using a distribution
- ▶ Installing modules and themes
- ▶ Using multisites in Drupal 8
- ▶ Tools for setting up an environment
- ▶ Running Simpletest and PHPUnit

Introduction

This chapter will kick off with an introduction to getting a Drupal 8 site installed and running. We will walk through the interactive installer that most will be familiar with from previous versions of Drupal, and from the command line with Drush.

Once we have installed a standard Drupal 8 site, we will cover the basics of extending Drupal. We will discuss using distributions and installing contributed projects, such as modules and themes. We will also include uninstalling modules, as this has changed in Drupal 8.

The chapter will wrap up with recipes on how to set up a multisite installation in Drupal 8, getting a local development environment configured and running the available test suites.

Installing Drupal

Just like most things, there are many different methods for downloading Drupal and installing it. In this recipe, we will focus on downloading Drupal from `https://www.drupal.org/` and setting it up on a basic Linux, Apache, MySQL, PHP (LAMP) server.

In this recipe, we will set-up the files for Drupal 8 and go through the installation process.

Getting ready

Before we start, you are going to need the below mentioned development environments that meet the new system requirements for Drupal 8:

- Apache 2.0 (or higher) or Nginx 1.1 (or higher) web server.
- PHP 5.5.9 or higher.
- MySQL 5.5 or MariaDB 5.5.20 for your database. You will need a user with privileges to create databases, or a created database with a user that has privileges to make tables in that database.
- Ability to upload or move files to the server!
- Drupal also requires specific PHP extensions and configuration. Generally a default installation of PHP should suffice. See `https://www.drupal.org/requirements/php` for up to date requirements information.

 Drupal 8 ships with Symfony components. One of the new dependencies in Drupal 8, to support the Symfony routing system, is that the Drupal `Clean URL` functionality is required. If the server is using Apache, ensure that `mod_rewrite` is enabled. If the server is using Nginx, the `ngx_http_rewrite_module` must be enabled.

We will be downloading Drupal 8 and placing its files in your web server's document root. Generally, this is the `/var/www` folder. If you used a tool such as XAMPP, WAMP, or MAPP please consult the proper documentation to know your document root.

How to do it...

We need to follow the below steps to install Drupal 8:

1. First we need to head to `Drupal.org` and download the latest release of Drupal 8.x! You can find the most recent and recommended release at the bottom of this page: `https://www.drupal.org/project/drupal`. Extract the archive and place the files to your document root as the folder `drupal8`:

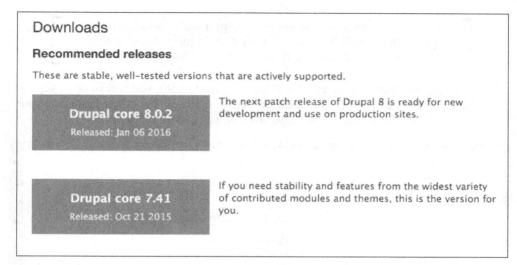

Downloads

Recommended releases

These are stable, well-tested versions that are actively supported.

Drupal core 8.0.2
Released: Jan 06 2016

The next patch release of Drupal 8 is ready for new development and use on production sites.

Drupal core 7.41
Released: Oct 21 2015

If you need stability and features from the widest variety of contributed modules and themes, this is the version for you.

2. Open your browser and visit your web server, for example `http://localhost/drupal8`, to be taken to the Drupal installation wizard. You will land on the new multilingual options install screen. Select your language and click **Save and continue**.

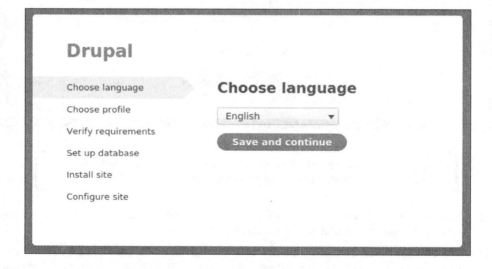

Drupal

Choose language
Choose profile
Verify requirements
Set up database
Install site
Configure site

Choose language

English ▼

Save and continue

3. On the next screen keep the default **Standard** option for the installation profile. This will provide us with a standard configuration with the most commonly used modules installed.

4. The next step will verify your system requirements. If your system does not have any reportable issues, the screen will be skipped.

If you have requirement issues, the installer will report what the specific issues are. Nearly every requirement will link to a `Drupal.org` handbook page with solution steps.

5. Enter the database information for Drupal. In most cases, you only need to supply the username, password, and database name and leave the other defaults. If your database does not exist, the installer will attempt to create the database:

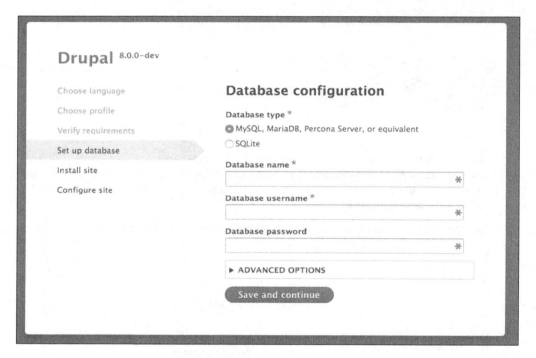

 See the *There's more* section in for information on setting up your database and any possible users.

6. Your Drupal 8 site will begin installing! When it is done installing the base modules, you will be taken to a site configuration screen.

7. The configure site form provides the base configuration for your Drupal site. Enter your site name and the e-mail address for the site. The site email will be used to send administrative notifications and as the originating email for outgoing emails from the Drupal site. The form allows you to set regional information regarding the country and time zone of the site. Setting the timezone ensures time values display correctly.

8. Fill in the site maintenance account information, also known as user 1, which acts in a similar way to root on Unix based systems. The site maintenance account is crucial. As stated, this acts as the first user and resembles the root user in Unix-based systems. In Drupal, the user with the user ID of 1 can bypass permission checks and have global access.

9. Enter the site's regional information and whether the site should check for updates available for modules enabled and Drupal itself. By checking for updates automatically, your site will report anonymous usage statistics to `Drupal.org` along with providing a summary of your version status. You have the option to also opt-in for the site to email you notifications of new releases, including security releases.

10. When satisfied click **Save and continue** and **Congratulations, you installed Drupal!**

How it works...

Drupal 8 supports a multilingual installation. When you visit the installer it reads the language code from the browser. With this language code, it will then select a supported language. If you choose a non-English installation the translation files will be automatically downloaded from `https://localize.drupal.org/`. Previous versions of Drupal did not support automated multilingual installations.

The installation profile instructs Drupal what modules to install by default. Contributed install profiles are termed distributions. The next recipe discusses distributions

When verifying requirements, Drupal is checking application versions and configurations. For example, if your server has the PHP Xdebug extension installed, the minimum `max_nested_value` must be 256 or else Drupal will not install.

There's more...

The Drupal installation process can be very straight forward, but there are a few items worth discussing.

Creating a database user and a database

In order to install Drupal you will need to have access to a database server and an existing (or ability to create) database (or the ability to create one). This process will depend on your server environment setup.

If you are working with a hosting provider, there is more than likely a web based control panel. This should allow you to create databases and users. Refer to your hosting's documentation.

If you are using **phpMyAdmin** on your server, often installed by MAMP, WAMP, and XAMPP, and have root access, you can create your databases and users.

- Sign into `phpMyAdmin` as the root user
- Click **Add a new User** from the bottom of the privileges page
- Fill in the user's information
- Select to create a database for the user with all privileges granted
- You can now use that user's information to connect Drupal to your database

If you do not have a user interface but have command line access, you can set up your database and user using the MySQL command line. These instructions can be found in the `core/INSTALL.mysql.txt` files:

1. Log into MySQL:

   ```
   $ mysql -u username -p
   ```

2. Create the database you will use:

   ```
   $ CREATE DATABASE database CHARACTER SET utf8 COLLATE utf8_
   general_ci;
   ```

3. Create a new user to access the database:

   ```
   $ CREATE USER username@localhost IDENTIFIED BY 'password';
   ```

4. Grant the new user permissions on the database:

   ```
   $ GRANT SELECT, INSERT, UPDATE, DELETE, CREATE, DROP,
   INDEX, ALTER, CREATE TEMPORARY TABLES ON databasename.* TO
   'username'@'localhost' IDENTIFIED BY 'password';
   ```

If you are installing Drupal with a PostgresSQL or SQLite database, see the appropriate installation instructions, either `INSTALL.pgsql.txt` or `INSTALL.sqlite.txt`.

Database prefixes

Drupal, like other content management systems, allows you to prefix its database tables from the database set-up form. This prefix will be placed before table names to help make them unique. While not recommended this would allow multiple installations to share one database. Utilizing table prefixes can, however, provide some level of security through obscurity since the tables will not be their default names.

▼ ADVANCED OPTIONS

Host *

localhost ✳

Port number

3306

Table name prefix

| ✳

If more than one application will be sharing this
database, a unique table name prefix – such as *drupal_* –
will prevent collisions.

Downloading and installing with Drush

You may also install Drupal using the PHP command line tool Drush. Drush is a command line
tool created by the Drupal community and must be installed. Drush is covered in *Chapter 13,
Drupal CLI*.

The pm-download command will download packages from Drupal.org. The site-install
command will allow you to specify an installation profile and other options for installing a Drupal
site. The installation steps in this recipe could be run through Drush as:

```
$ cd /path/to/document/root
$ drush pm-download drupal-8 drupal8
$ cd drupal8
$ drush site-install standard –locale=en-US --account-name=admin
--account-pass=admin –account-email=demo@example.com –db-url=mysql://
user:pass@localhost/database
```

We use Drush to download the latest Drupal 8 and place it in a folder named drupal8. Then
the site-install command instructs Drush to use the standard install profile, configure
the maintenance account, and provides a database URI string so that Drupal can connect to
its database.

Security updates

If you choose to disable the update options, you will have to check manually for module
upgrades. While most upgrades are for bug fixes or features, some are for security updates.
It is highly recommended that you subscribe to the Drupal security team's updates. These
updates are available on Twitter at @drupalsecurity or the feeds on
https://www.drupal.org/security.

See also

- ▸ For more on multilingual, see *Chapter 8, Multilingual and Internationalization*
- ▸ For more on using the command line and Drupal, see *Chapter 13, Drupal CLI*
- ▸ See the `Drupal.org` handbook on installing Drupal https://www.drupal.org/documentation/install
- ▸ Drush site install `http://drushcommands.com/drush-8x/site-install/site-install`

Using a distribution

A distribution is a contributed installation profile that is not provided by Drupal core. Why would you want to use a distribution? Distributions provide a specialized version of Drupal with specific feature sets. On `Drupal.org` when you download an installation profile it not only includes the profile and its modules but a version of Drupal core. Hence the name distribution. You can find a list of all Drupal distributions here `https://www.drupal.org/project/project_distribution`.

How to do it...

We will follow these steps to download a distribution to use as a customized version of Drupal 8:

1. Download a distribution from `Drupal.org`. For this recipe let's use the Demo Framework provided by Acquia `https://www.drupal.org/project/df`.
2. Select the recommended version for the 8.x branch.
3. Extract the folder contents to your web server's document root. You'll notice there is Drupal core and, within the profiles folder, the installation profile's folder `df`.
4. Install Drupal as you would normally, by visiting your Drupal site in your browser.
5. Demo Framework declares itself as an exclusive profile. Distributions which declare this are automatically selected and assumed to be the default installation option.

 The exclusive flag was added with Drupal 7.22 to improve the experience of using a Drupal distribution `http://drupal.org/node/1961012`.

6. Follow the installation instructions and you'll have installed the distribution!

How it works...

Installation profiles work by including additional modules that are part of the contributed project realm or custom modules. The profile will then define them as dependencies to be installed with Drupal. When you select an installation profile, you are instructing Drupal to install a set of modules on installation.

There's more...

Distributions provide a specialized version of Drupal with specific feature sets, but there are a few items worth discussing.

Makefiles

The current standard for generating a built distribution is the utilization of Drush and makefiles. Makefiles allow a user to define a specific version of Drupal core and other projects (themes, modules, third party libraries) that will make up a Drupal code base. It is not a dependency management workflow, like Composer, but is a build tool.

If you look at the Demo Framework's folder you will see `drupal-org.make` and `drupal-org-core.make`. These are parsed by the `Drupal.org` packager to compile the code base and package it as a `.zip` or `.tar.gz`, like the one you downloaded.

Installing with Drush

As shown in the first recipe, you can install a Drupal site through the Drush tool. You can instruct Drush to use a specific installation profile by providing it as the first argument. The following command would install the Drupal 8 site using the Demo Framework.

```
$ drush pm-download df
$ drush site-install df –db-url=mysql://user:pass@localhost/database
```

See also...

- ▶ See *Chapter 13*, *Drupal CLI*, for information on makefiles.
- ▶ Drush documentation page for drush make
  `http://www.drush.org/en/master/make/`
- ▶ Distribution documentation on `Drupal.org`,
  `https://www.drupal.org/documentation/build/distributions`

Installing modules and themes

Drupal 8 provides more functionality out of the box than previous versions of Drupal – allowing you to do more with less. However, one of the more appealing aspects of Drupal is the ability to extend and customize.

In this recipe, we will download and enable the Honeypot module, and tell Drupal to use the Bootstrap theme. The Honeypot module provides honeypot and timestamp anti-spam measures on Drupal sites. This module helps protect forms from spam submissions. The Boostrap theme implements the Bootstrap front-end framework and supports using Bootswatch styles for theming your Drupal site.

Getting ready

If you have used Drupal previously, take note that the folder structure has changed. Modules, themes, and profiles are now placed in their respective folders in the root directory and no longer under sites/all. For more information about the developer experience change, see `https://www.drupal.org/node/22336`.

Downloading the example code

You can download the example code files for all Packt books you have purchased from your account at `http://www.packtpub.com`. If you purchased this book elsewhere, you can visit `http://www.packtpub.com/support` and register to have the files e-mailed directly to you.

How to do it...

Let's install modules and themes:

1. Visit `https://www.drupal.org/project/honeypot` and download the latest 8.x release for Honeypot.

2. Extract the archive and place the `honeypot` folder inside the `modules` folder inside of your Drupal core installation:

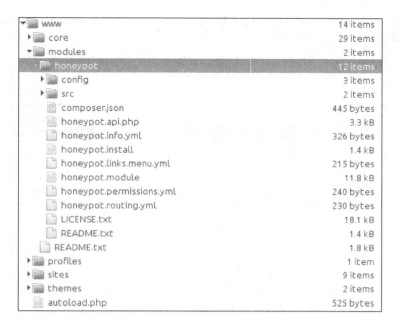

3. In Drupal, log in and select the **Extend** option to access the list of available modules.

4. Using the search text field, type in Honeypot. Check the checkbox and click **Install**.

5. Once enabled, search for it again. Clicking on the module's description will expand the row and expose links to configure permissions and module settings:

6. Visit https://www.drupal.org/project/bootstrap and download the latest 8.x release for Bootstrap.

7. Extract the archive and place the `bootstrap` folder inside the `themes` folder inside your Drupal core installation.

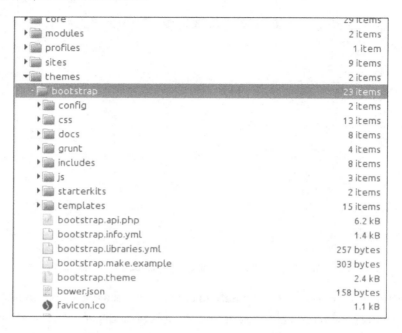

8. In Drupal, select the **Appearance** option to manage your Drupal themes.

9. Scroll down the page and click **Install and set as default** under **Bootstrap** to enable and set the theme as default:

How it works...

The following outlines the procedure for installing a module or theme and how Drupal discovers these extensions.

Discovering modules and themes

Drupal scans specific folder locations to identify modules and themes defined by the `.info.yml` file in their directory. The following is the order in which projects will be discovered:

- ▸ Respective core folder (modules, themes)
- ▸ Current installed profile
- ▸ The root `modules` or `themes` folder
- ▸ The current site directory (default or current domain)

Module installation

By placing the module inside the root `modules` folder, we are allowing Drupal to discover the module and allow it to be installed. When a module is installed, Drupal will register its code with the system through the `module_installer` service. The service will check for required dependencies and prompt for them to be enabled if required. The configuration system will run any configuration definitions provided by the module on install. If there are conflicting configuration items, the module *will not be installed*.

Theme installation

A theme is installed through the `theme_installer` service and sets any default configuration by the theme along with rebuilding the theme registry. Setting a theme to default is a configuration change in `system.theme.default` to the theme's machine name (in the recipe it would be `bootstrap`.)

There's more...

The following outlines the procedure for installing a module or theme and some more information on it.

Installing a module with Drush

Modules can be downloaded and enabled through the command line using `drush`. The command to replicate the recipe would resemble:

```
$ drush pm-download honeypot
$ drush pm-enable honeypot
```

It will prompt you to confirm your action. If there were dependencies for the module, it would ask if you would like to enable those, too.

Uninstalling a module

One of the larger changes in Drupal 8 is the module disable and uninstall process. Previously modules were first disabled and then uninstalled once disabled. This left a confusing process which would disable its features, but not clean up any database schema changes. In Drupal 8 modules cannot just be disabled but must be uninstalled. This ensures that when a module is uninstalled it can be safely removed from the code base.

A module can only be uninstalled if it is not a dependency of another module or does not have a configuration item in use – such as a field type – which could disrupt the installation's integrity.

 With a standard installation, the Comment module cannot be uninstalled until you delete all Comment fields on the article content type. This is because the field type is in use.

See also...

▶ *Chapter 4, Extending Drupal*, to learn about setting defaults on enabling a module

▶ *Chapter 9, Confiuration Management – Deploying in Drupal 8*

Using multisites in Drupal 8

Drupal provides the ability to run multiple sites from one single Drupal code base instance. This feature is referred to as multisite. Each site has a separate database; however, projects stored in *modules*, *profiles*, and *themes* can be installed by all of the sites.

Site folders can also contain their own modules and themes. When provided, these can only be used by that one site.

The default folder is the default folder used if there is not a matching domain name.

Getting ready

If you are going to work with multisite functionality, you should have an understanding of how to setup virtual host configurations with your particular web server. In this recipe, we will use two subdomains under localhost called dev1 and dev2.

How to do it...

We will use multisites in Drupal 8 by two subdomains under localhost:

1. Copy `sites/example.sites.php` to `sites/sites.php`.

2. Create a `dev1.localhost` and a `dev2.localhost` folder inside of the sites folder.

3. Copy the `sites/default/default.settings.php` file into `dev1.localhost` and `dev2.localhost` as `settings.php` in each respective folder:

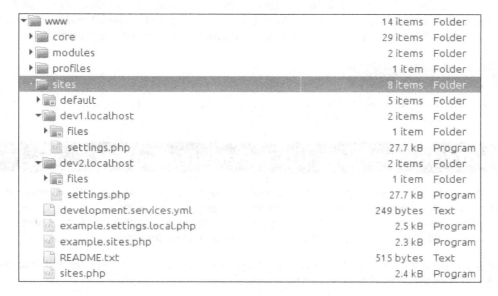

▾ www	14 items	Folder
▸ core	29 items	Folder
▸ modules	2 items	Folder
▸ profiles	1 item	Folder
▾ sites	8 items	Folder
▸ default	5 items	Folder
▾ dev1.localhost	2 items	Folder
▸ files	1 item	Folder
settings.php	27.7 kB	Program
▾ dev2.localhost	2 items	Folder
▸ files	1 item	Folder
settings.php	27.7 kB	Program
development.services.yml	249 bytes	Text
example.settings.local.php	2.5 kB	Program
example.sites.php	2.3 kB	Program
README.txt	515 bytes	Text
sites.php	2.4 kB	Program

4. Visit `dev1.localhost` and run the installation wizard.

5. Visit `dev2.localhost` and see that you still have the option to install a site!

How it works...

The `sites.php` must exist for multisite functionality to work. By default, you do not need to modify its contents. The `sites.php` file provides a way to map aliases to specific site folders. The file contains the documentation for using aliases.

The `DrupalKernel` class provides `findSitePath` and `getSitePath` to discover the site folder path. On Drupal's bootstrap this is initiated and reads the incoming HTTP host to load the proper `settings.php` file from the appropriate folder. The `settings.php` file is then loaded and parsed into a `\Drupal\Core\Site\Settings` instance. This allows Drupal to connect to the appropriate database.

There's more...

Let's understand the security concerns of using multisite:

Security concerns

There can be cause for concern if using multisite. Arbitrary PHP code executed on a Drupal site might be able to affect other sites sharing the same code base. Drupal 8 marked the removal of the `PHP Filter` module that allowed site administrators to use PHP code in the administrative interface. While this mitigates the various ways an administrator had easy access to run PHP through an interface it does not mitigate the risk wholesale. For example, the `PHP Filter` module is now a contributed project and could be installed.

See also...

> ▶ Multi-site documentation on `Drupal.org`, `https://www.drupal.org/documentation/install/multi-site`

Tools for setting up an environment

One of the initial hurdles to getting started with Drupal is a local development environment. This recipe will cover how to set up the DrupalVM project by Jeff Geerling. DrupalVM is a VirtualBox virtual machine run through Vagrant, provisioned and configured with Ansible. It will set up all of your services and build a Drupal installation for you.

Luckily you only need to have VirtualBox and Vagrant installed on your machine and DrupalVM works on Windows, Mac OS X, and Linux.

Getting ready

To get started, you will need to install the two dependencies required for DrupalVM:

> ▶ **VirtualBox**: `https://www.virtualbox.org/wiki/Downloads`
>
> ▶ **Vagrant**: `http://www.vagrantup.com/downloads.html`

How to do it...

Let's set up the DrupalVM project by Jeff Geerling. DrupalVM is a VirtualBox virtual machine run through Vagrant, provisioned and configured with Ansible:

1. Download the DrupalVM archive from `https://github.com/geerlingguy/drupal-vm/archive/master.zip`.

2. Extract the archive and place the project in your directory of choice.

3. Copy `example.drupal.make.yml` to `drupal.make.yml`.

4. Copy `example.config.yml` to `config.yml`

5. Edit `config.yml` and modify the `local_path` setting to be the directory where you've placed the DrupalVM project. This will be synchronized into the virtual machine:

```
vagrant_synced_folders:
  - local_path: /path/to/drupalvm
    destination: /var/www
  type: nfs
  create: true
```

6. Open a terminal and navigate to the directory where you have placed the DrupalVM project.

7. Enter the command `vagrant up` to tell Vagrant to build the virtual machine and begin the provisioning process.

8. While this process is ongoing, modify your hosts file to provide easy access to the development site. Add the line `192.168.88.88 drupalvm.dev` to your hosts file.

9. Open your browser and access `http://drupalvm.dev/`.

10. Login to your Drupal site with the username `admin` and password `admin`.

How it works...

DrupalVM is a development project that utilizes the Vagrant tool to create a VirtualBox virtual machine. Vagrant is configured through the project's `Vagrantfile`. Vagrant then uses Ansible – an open source IT automation platform – to install Apache, PHP, MySQL, and other services on the virtual machine.

The `config.yml` file has been set up to provide a simple way to customize variables for the virtual machine and provisioning process. It also uses Drush to create and install a Drupal 8 site, or whatever components are specified in `drupal.make.yml`. This file is a Drush `make` file, which contains a definition for Drupal core by default and can be modified to include other contributed projects.

The `vagrant up` command tells Vagrant to either launch an existing virtual machine or create one anew in a headless manner. When Vagrant creates a new virtual machine it triggers the provisioning process. In this instance Ansible will read the `provisioning/playbook.yml` file and follow each step to create the final virtual machine. The only files needing to be modified, however, are the `config.yml` and `drupal.make.yml` files.

There's more...

The topic of automating and streamlining a local environment is quite popular right now with quite a few different options. If you are not comfortable with using Vagrant, there are a few other options that provide a server installation and Drupal.

Acquia Dev Desktop

Acquia Dev Desktop is developed by Acquia and can be found at `https://docs.acquia.com/dev-desktop2`. It is an automated environment installer for Windows and Mac. The Dev Desktop application allows you to create a regular Drupal installation or select from a distribution.

XAMPP + Bitnami

XAMPP – Apache + MySQL + PHP + Perl – is a cross platform environment installation. XAMPP is an open source project from Apache Friends. XAMPP has partnered with Bitnami to provide free all-in-one installations for common applications – including Drupal 8! You can download XAMPP at `https://www.apachefriends.org/download.html`.

Kalabox

Kalabox is developed by the Kalamuna group and intends to be a robust workflow solution for Drupal development. Kalabox is cross-platform compatible, allowing you to easily work on Windows machines. It is based for the command line and provides application binaries for you to install. You can learn more about Kalabox at `http://www.kalamuna.com/products/kalabox/`.

See also...

- See *Chapter 13*, *Drupal CLI*, for information on makefiles
- DrupalVM documentation `http://docs.drupalvm.com/en/latest/`
- `Drupal.org` community documentation on local environment set-up `https://www.drupal.org/node/157602`

Running Simpletest and PHPUnit

Drupal 8 ships with two testing suites. Previously Drupal only supported `Simpletest`. Now there are PHPUnit tests as well. In the official change record, PHPUnit was added to provide testing without requiring a full Drupal bootstrap, which occurs with each `Simpletest` test. Read the change record here: `https://www.drupal.org/node/2012184`.

Getting ready

Currently core comes with Composer dependencies prepackaged and no extra steps need to be taken to run PHPUnit. This recipe will demonstrate how to run tests the same way that the QA testbot on `Drupal.org` does.

 The process of managing Composer dependencies may change, but is currently postponed due to Drupal.org's testing and packaging infrastructure. Read more here `https://www.drupal.org/node/1475510`.

How to do it...

1. First enable the `Simpletest` module. Even though you might only want to run PHPUnit, this is a soft dependency for running the test runner script.

2. Open a command line terminal and navigate to your Drupal installation directory and run the following to execute all available PHPUnit tests:

    `php core/scripts/run-tests.sh PHPUnit`

3. Running `Simpletest` tests required executing the same script, however, instead of passing PHPUnit as the argument, you must define the `url` option and `tests` option:

    `php core/scripts/run-tests.sh --url http://localhost --all`

4. Review test output!

How it works...

The `run-tests.sh` script has been shipped with Drupal since 2008, then named `run-functional-tests.php`. The command interacts with the other suites in Drupal to run all or specific tests and sets up other configuration items. We will highlight some of the useful options below:

*   **--help**: This displays the items covered in the following bullets
*   **--list**: This displays the available test groups that can be run
*   **--url**: This is required unless the Drupal site is accessible through `http://localhost:80`
*   **--sqlite**: This allows you to run `Simpletest` without having to have Drupal installed
*   **--concurrency**: This allows you to define how many tests run in parallel

There's more...

Is run-tests a shell script?

The `run-tests.sh` isn't actually a shell script. It is a PHP script which is why you must execute it with PHP. In fact, within core/scripts each file is a PHP script file meant to be executed from the command line. These scripts are not intended to be run through a web server which is one of the reasons for the `.sh` extension. There are issues with discovered PHP across platforms that prevent providing a shebang line to allow executing the file as a normal `bash` or `bat` script. For more info view this `Drupal.org` issue at `https://www.drupal.org/node/655178`.

Running Simpletest without Drupal installed

With Drupal 8, `Simpletest` can be run from SQLite and no longer requires an installed database. This can be accomplished by passing the **sqlite** and **dburl** options to the run-tests.sh script. This requires the PHP SQLite extension to be installed.

Here is an example adapted from the DrupalCI test runner for Drupal core:

```
php core/scripts/run-tests.sh --sqlite /tmp/.ht.sqlite --die-on-fail
--dburl sqlite://tmp/.ht.sqlite --all
```

Combined with the built in PHP webserver for debugging you can run `Simpletest` without a full-fledged environment.

Running specific tests

Each example thus far has used the `all` option to run every `Simpletest` available. There are various ways to run specific tests:

- ▸ **--module**: This allows you to run all the tests of a specific module
- ▸ **--class**: This runs a specific path, identified by a full namespace path
- ▸ **--file**: This runs tests from a specified file
- ▸ **--directory**: This run tests within a specified directory

 Previously in Drupal, tests were grouped inside **module.test** files, which is where the file option derives from. Drupal 8 utilizes the `PSR-4 autoloading` method and requires one class per file.

DrupalCI

With Drupal 8 came a new initiative to upgrade the testing infrastructure on `Drupal.org`. The outcome was DrupalCI. DrupalCI is open source and can be downloaded and run locally. The project page for DrupalCI is `https://www.drupal.org/project/drupalci`.

The test bot utilizes Docker and can be downloaded locally to run tests. The project ships with a Vagrant file to allow it to be run within a virtual machine or locally. Learn more on the testbot's project page: `https://www.drupal.org/project/drupalci_testbot`.

See also...

- ▶ PHPUnit manual: `https://phpunit.de/manual/4.8/en/writing-tests-for-phpunit.html`
- ▶ Drupal PHPUnit handbook: `https://drupal.org/phpunit`
- ▶ `Simpletest` from the command line: `https://www.drupal.org/node/645286`

2
The Content Authoring Experience

In this chapter we will explore what Drupal 8 brings to the content authoring experience:

- ► Configuring the WYSIWYG editor
- ► Adding and editing content
- ► Creating a menu and linking content
- ► Providing inline editing
- ► Creating a custom content type
- ► Applying new Drupal 8 core field types
- ► Customizing the form display of a node
- ► Customizing the display output of a node

Introduction

In this chapter we'll cover the Drupal 8 content authoring experience. We will show you how to configure text formats and set up the bundled CKEditor that ships with Drupal 8. We will look at how to add and manage content, along with utilizing menus for linking to content. Drupal 8 ships with inline editing for per-field modifications from the front-end.

This chapter dives into *creating custom content types* and harnessing different fields to create advanced content. We'll cover the five new fields added to Drupal 8 core and how to use them, along with getting new field types through contributed projects. We will go through customizing the content's display and modifying the new form display added in Drupal 8.

Configuring the WYSIWYG editor

Drupal 8 caused the collaboration between the Drupal development community and the CKEditor development community. Because of this, Drupal now ships with CKEditor out of the box as the default **What You See Is What You Get** (**WYSIWYG**) editor. The new Editor module provides an API for integrating WYSIWYG editors. Even though CKEditor is provided out of the box, contributed modules can provide integrations with other WYSIWYG editors.

Text formats control the formatting of content and WYSIWYG editor configuration for content authors. The standard Drupal installation profile provides a fully configured text format with CKEditor enabled. We will walk through the steps of recreating this text format.

In this recipe we will create a new text format with a custom CKEditor WYSIWYG configuration.

Getting ready

Before starting, make sure that the CKEditor module is enabled, which also requires Editor as a dependency. **Editor** is the module that provides an API to integrate WYSIWYG editors with text formats.

How to do it...

Let's create a new text format with a custom CKEditor WYSIWYG configuration:

1. Visit **Configuration** and head to **Text formats and editors** under the **Content authoring** heading.

2. Click on **Add text format** to begin creating the new text format:

Text formats and editors ☆

Home » Administration » Configuration » Content authoring

Text formats define the HTML tags, code, and other formatting that can be used when entering text. **Improper text format configuration is a security risk**. Learn more on the Filter module help page.

Text formats are presented on content editing pages in the order defined on this page. The first format available to a user will be selected by default.

(**+ Add text format**)

3. Enter a name for the text format, such as **editor format**.

4. Select which roles have access to this format – this allows you to have granular control over what users can use when authoring content.

5. Select **CKEditor** from the **Text editor** select list. The configuration form for CKEditor will then be loaded.

6. You may now use an in-place editor to drag buttons onto the provided toolbar to configure your CKEditor toolbar:

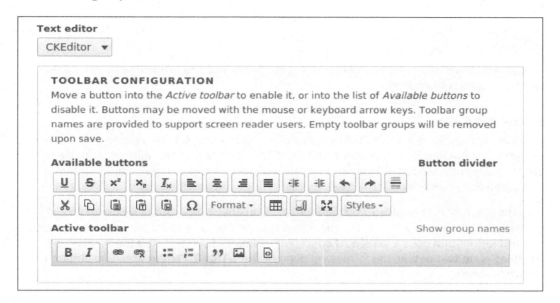

7. Select any of the **Enabled** filters you would like, except for **Display any HTML as Plain text**. That would be counter intuitive to using a WYSIWYG editor!

How it works...

The Filter modules provide text formats that control over how rich text fields are presented to the user. Drupal will render rich text saved in a text area based on the defined text format for the field. Text fields with (formatted) in their title will respect text format settings, others will render in plain text.

The text formats and editors screen warns of a security risk due to improper configuration. That is because you could grant an anonymous user access to a text format that allows full HTML, or allow image sources to be from remote URLs.

The Editor module provides a bridge to WYSIWYG editors and text formats. It alters the text format form and rendering to allow the integration of WYSIWYG editor libraries. This allows each text format to have its own configuration for its WYSIWYG editor.

Out of the box the Editor module alone does not provide an editor. The CKEditor module works with the Editor API to enable usage of that WYSIWYG editor.

Drupal can support other WYSWIG editors, such as MarkItUp or TinyMCE through contributed modules.

There's more...

Drupal provides granular control of how rich text is rendered and extensible ways as well, which we will discuss further.

Filter module

When string data is added to a field that supports text formats, the data is saved and preserved as it was originally entered. Enabled filters for a text format will not be applied until the content is viewed. Drupal works in such a way that it saves the original content and only filters on display.

With the Filter module enabled, you gain the ability to specify how text is rendered based on the roles of the user who created the text. It is important to understand the filters applied to a text format that uses a WYSIWYG editor. For example, if you selected the **Display any HTML as plain text** option, the formatting done by the WYSIWYG editor would be stripped out when viewed.

CKEditor plugins

The CKEditor module provides a plugin type called CKEditorPlugin. Plugins are small pieces of swappable functionality within Drupal 8. Plugins and plugin development are covered in *Chapter 7, Plug and Play with Plugins.* This type provides integration between CKEditor and Drupal 8.

The image and link capabilities are plugins defined within the CKEditor module. Additional plugins can be provided through contributed projects or custom development.

See the \Drupal\ckeditor\Annotation\CKEditorPlugin class for the plugin definition and the suggested \Drupal\ckeditor\Plugin\CKEditorPlugin\ DrupalImage class as a working example.

See also

- ▶ The official blog post from CKEditor about how Drupal adopted it as the official WYSIWYG editor: http://ckeditor.com/blog/CKEditor-Joins-Drupal.
- ▶ *Chapter 7, Plug and Play with Plugins.*

Adding and editing content

The main functionality of a content management system is in the name itself – the ability to manage content; that is, to add, edit, and organize content. Drupal provides a central form that allows you to manage all of the content within your website and allows you to create new content. Additionally, you can view a piece of content and have the ability to click an edit link when viewing it.

Getting ready

This recipe assumes you have installed the standard installation profile and have the default node content types available for use.

How to do it...

Let's manage the content by adding, editing, and organizing the content:

1. Visit **Content** to view the content management overview from.

2. Click **Add content** to view the list of available content types. Select **article** as the piece of content you would like to make.

3. Provide a title for the piece of content. Titles are always required for content.

   Fill in body text for the article:

You may change the text format to customize what kind of text is allowed. If the user only has one format available there will be no select box, but the **About** text formats link will still be present.

4. Once you have added your text, click **Save and publish** at the bottom of the form. You will then be redirected to view the newly created piece of content.

5. Note that the URL for the piece of content is `/node/#`. This is the default path for content and can be changed by editing the content.

6. Click on **Edit** from the tabs right above the content.

7. From the right sidebar, click on **URL Path Settings** to expand the section and enter a custom alias. For example `/awesome-article` (note the required "/".):

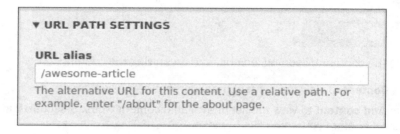

8. Save the content and notice the URL for your article is `/awesome-article`.

9. You could also edit this article from the `Content` table by clicking **Edit** there instead of from viewing the content.

How it works...

The `Content` page is a **View**, which will be discussed in *Chapter 3, Displaying Content through Views*. This creates a table of all the content in your site that can be searched and filtered. From here you can view, edit, or delete any single piece of content.

In Drupal there are content entities that provide a method of creation, editing, deletion, and viewing. Nodes are a form of a content entity. When you create a node it will build the proper form that allows you to fill in the piece of content's data. The same process follows for editing content.

When you save the content, Drupal writes the node's content to the database along with all of its respective field data.

There's more

Drupal 8's content management system provides many features; we will cover some extra information.

Save as draft

New to Drupal 8 is the ability to easily save a piece of content as a draft instead of directly publishing it. Instead of clicking on **Save and publish**, click the arrow next to it to expand the option of **Save as unpublished**.

Pathauto

There is a contributed project called Pathauto that simplifies the process of providing URL aliases. It allows you to define patterns that will automatically create URL aliases for content. This module utilizes tokens to allow for very robust paths for content.

The Pathauto project can be found at `https://www.drupal.org/project/pathauto`.

Bulk moderation

You also have the capability to perform bulk actions on content. The table provides checkboxes at the beginning of each row. For each selected item, you can choose an item from **With selection** to make bulk changes – such as deleting, publishing, and unpublishing content:

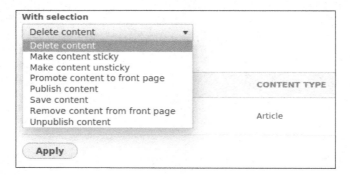

See also

> ► *Chapter 2, The Content Authoring Experience* in recipe *Customizing the Form Display of a Node*

Creating a menu and linking content

Drupal provides a way to link content being authored to a specified menu on the website, generally the main menu. You can, however, create a custom menu for providing links to content. In this recipe we will show you how to create a custom menu and link content to it. We will then place the menu as a block on the page, in the sidebar.

Getting ready

This recipe assumes you have installed the standard installation profile and have the default node content types available for use. You should have some content created to create a link to.

How to do it...

1. Visit **Structure** and click on **Menus**.
2. Click on **Add Menu**.
3. Provide the title **Sidebar** and optional summary and then click on **Save**.
4. Once the menu has saved, click on the **Add link** button.
5. Enter in a link title and then begin typing the title for a piece of content. The form will provide autocomplete suggestions for linkable content:

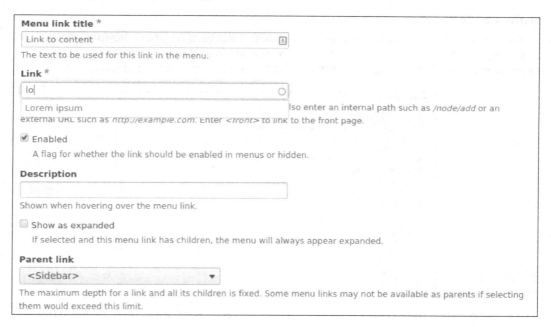

6. Click on **Save** to save the menu link.

7. With the menu link saved, visit **Structure**, and then **Block layout**.

8. Click on **Place block** next to **Sidebar first**. In the modal, search for the **Sidebar** menu and click on **Place block**:

9. Save the following forms and, at the bottom of the block list, click on **Save**. View your Drupal site and you will see the menu:

How it works...

Menus and links are part of Drupal core. The ability to make custom menus and menu links is provided through the **Menu UI** module. This module is enabled on the standard installation profile, but may not be in others.

The **Link** input of the menu link form allows you to begin typing node titles and easily link to existing content. This was a piece of functionality not available in previous versions of Drupal! It will automatically convert the title into the internal path for you. Link input also accepts a regular path, such as /node/1 or an external path.

You must have a valid path; you cannot add empty links to a menu. There is work being done to allow adding empty or ID selector link paths: `https://www.drupal.org/node/1543750`.

There's more...

Managing a contents menu link from its form

A piece of content can be linked to a menu from the **add** or **edit** form. The **menu settings** section allows you to toggle the availability of a menu link. The menu link title will reflect the content's title by default.

The parent item allows you to decide which menu and which item it will appear under. By default content types only have the main menu allowed. Editing a content type can allow multiple menus, or only choosing a custom menu.

This allows you to populate a main menu or complimentary menu without having to visit the menu management screens.

Providing inline editing

A touted feature of Drupal 8 is the ability to provide inline editing. Inline editing is enabled by default with the standard installation profile through the **Quick Edit** module. The Quick Edit module allows for editing individual fields while viewing a piece of content and integrates with the Editor module for WYSIWYG editors!

How to do it...

Let's provide inline editing:

1. Visit a piece of created content.
2. In order to enable inline editing, you must toggle contextual links on the page by clicking **Edit** in the upper right of the administrative toolbar:

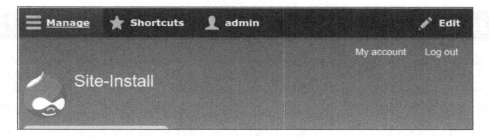

3. This will toggle the contextual links available on the page. Click on the **context link** next to the content and select **Quick edit**:

4. Hover over the body text and click to **Edit**.
5. You can now edit the text with a minimal version of the WYSIWYG editor toolbar.
6. Once you have changed the text, click **Save**.
7. The changes will be saved immediately.

How it works...

The **Contextual links** module provides privileged users with shortcut links to modify blocks or content. The contextual links are toggled by clicking **Edit** in the toolbar. The **Edit** link toggles the visibility of contextual links on the page. Previously, in Drupal 7, contextual links appeared as cogs when a specific region was hovered over.

The Quick Edit module builds on top of the contextual links features. It allows field formatters, which display field data, to describe how they will interact. By default Quick Edit sets this to a form. Clicking on an element will use JavaScript to load a form and save data via AJAX calls.

Quick Edit will not work on administrative pages.

Creating a custom content type

Drupal excels in the realm of content management by allowing different types of content. In this recipe we will walk through creating a custom content type. We will create a **Services** type that has some basic fields and would be used in a scenario that brings attention to a company's provided services.

You will also learn how to add fields to a content type in this recipe; which generally goes hand in hand when making a new content type on a Drupal site.

How to do it...

1. Visit **Structure** and then **Content types**. Click **Add content type** to begin creating a new content type.

2. Enter **Services** as the name and an optional description.

3. Select **Display settings** and uncheck the **Display author and date information** checkbox. This will hide the author and submitted time from services pages.

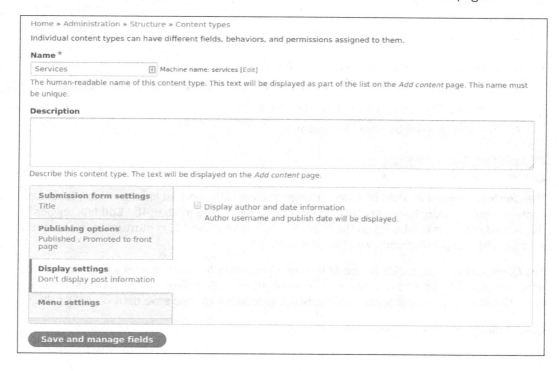

4. Press the **Save and manage fields** button to save our new content type and manage its fields.

5. By default, new content types have a **Body** field automatically added to them. We will keep this field in place.

6. We will add a field that will provide a way to enter a marketing headline for the service. Click on **Add field**.

   Select **Text (plain)** from the drop down and enter **Marketing headline** as the label:

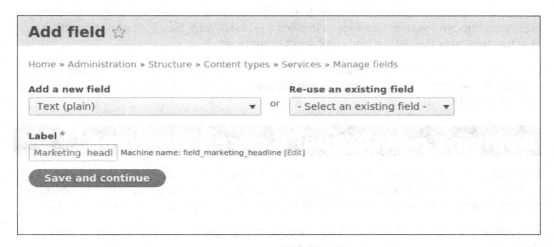

> **Text (plain)** is a regular text field. The **Text (formatted)** option will allow you to use text formats on the displayed text in the field.

7. Save the field settings on the next form. On the next form you may hit **Save settings** to finish adding the field.

   The field has now been added and content of this type can be created:

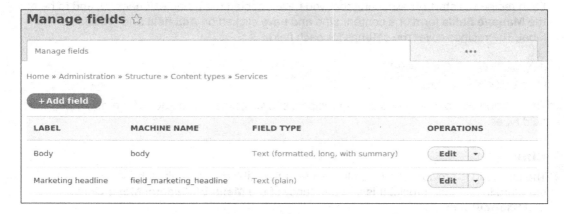

How it works...

In Drupal there are entities that have bundles. A bundle is just a type of entity that can have specific configuration and fields attached. When working with nodes, a bundle is generally referred to as a content type.

Content types can be created as long as the Node module is enabled. When a content type is created through the user interface, it invokes the `node_add_body_field()` function. This function adds the default body field for content types.

Fields can only be managed or added if the Field UI module is enabled. The Field UI module exposes the **Manage Fields**, **Manage Form Display**, and **Manage Display** for entities – such as nodes and blocks.

Applying new Drupal 8 core field types

The field system is what makes creating content in Drupal so robust. With Drupal 8 some of the most used contributed field types have been merged into Drupal core as their own module. In fact, Entity reference is no longer a module but part of the main Field API now.

This recipe is actually a collection of mini-recipes to highlight the new fields: `Link`, `Email`, `Telephone`, `Date`, and `Entity reference`!

Getting ready

The standard installation profile does not enable all of the modules that provide these field types by default. For this recipe you will need to manually enable select modules so you can create the field. The module that provides the field type and its installation status in the standard profile will be highlighted.

Each recipe will start off expecting that you have enabled the module, if needed, and to be at the **Manage fields** form of a content type and have clicked on **Add field** and provided a field label. The recipes cover the settings for each field.

How to do it...

This section contains a series of mini recipes, showing how to use each of the new core field types.

Link

The Link field is provided by the Link module. It is enabled by default with the standard installation profile. It is a dependency of the **Menu UI**, **Custom Menu Links**, and **Shortcut module**.

1. The Link field type does not have any additional field level settings that are used across all bundles.

2. Click **Save field settings** to begin customizing the field for this specific bundle.

3. Using the **Allowed link type** setting, you can control whether provided URLs can be external, internal, or both. Selecting **Internal or Both** will allow linking to content by autocompleting the title.

4. The **Allow link** text defines if a user must provide text to go along with the link. If no text is provided, then the URL itself is displayed.

5. The field formatter for a Link field allows you to specify `rel="nofollow"` or if the link should open in a new window.

The e-mail field

The **Email** field is provided by core and is available without enabling additional modules:

1. The **Email** field type does not have any additional field level settings that are used across all bundles.

2. Click **Save field settings** to begin customizing the field for this specific bundle.

3. There are no further settings for an **Email** field instance. This field uses the HTML5 e-mail input, which will leverage browser input validation.

4. The field formatter for an **Email** field allows you to display the e-mail as plain text or a `mailto:` link.

The Telephone field

The **Telephone** field is provided by the **Telephone** module. It is not enabled by default with the standard installation profile:

1. The **Telephone** field type does not have any additional field level settings that are used across all bundles.

2. Click **Save field settings** to begin customizing the field for this specific bundle.

3. There are no further settings for a **Telephone** field instance. This field uses the HTML5 e-mail input, which will leverage browser input validation.

4. The field formatter for a **Telephone** field allows you to display the telephone number as a plain text item, or using the `tel:` link with an optional replacement title for the link.

Date

The **Date** field is provided by the Datetime module. It is enabled by default with the standard installation profile.

1. The Date module has a setting that defines what kind of data it will be storing: date and time, or date only. This setting cannot be changed once field data has been saved.

2. Click **Save field settings** to begin customizing the field for this specific bundle.

3. The **Date** field has two ways of providing a default value. It can either be the current date or a relative date using PHP's date time modifier syntax.

4. By default, **Date** fields use the HTML5 date and time inputs, resulting in a native date and time picker provided by the browser.

5. Additionally, **Date** fields can be configured to use a select list for each date and time component:

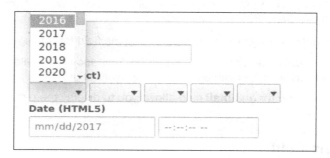

6. The default date field formatter display uses Drupal's time formats to render the time format. These are configured under **Configuration** and **Regional and language** in the **Date and time formats** form.

7. Dates and times can be displayed as **Time ago** to provide a semantic display of how far in the future or past a time is. The formats for both are customizable in the display settings.

8. Finally, dates and times can be displayed using a custom format as specified by the PHP date formats.

The Entity Reference

The Entity Reference field is part of core and is available without enabling additional modules. Unlike other fields, Entity Reference appears as a grouping of specific items when adding a field. That is because you must pick a type of entity to reference!

1. The interface allows you to select a **Content, File, Image, Taxonomy term, User,** or **Other**. Selecting one of the predefined options will preconfigure the field's target entity type.

2. When creating an Entity Reference field using the Other choice, you must specify the type of item to reference. This option cannot be changed once data is saved.

 You will notice there are two groups: **content** and **configuration**. Drupal uses configuration entities. Even though configuration is an option, you may not benefit from referencing those entity types. Only content entities have a way to be viewed. Referencing configuration entities would fall under an advanced use case implementation.

3. Click **Save field settings** to begin customizing the field for this specific bundle.

4. The Entity Reference field has two different methods for allowing users to search for content: using the default autocomplete or a View.

5. Depending on the type of entity you are referencing, there will be different entity properties you may sort the results based on.

6. The default field widget for an Entity Reference field is to use autocomplete, however there is the option to use a select list or checkboxes for the available options.

7. The values of an Entity Reference field can display the referenced entity's label or the rendered output. When rendering a label it can be optionally linked to the entity itself. When displaying a rendered entity you may choose a specific view mode.

How it works...

When working with fields in Drupal 8, there are two steps. When you first create a field you are defining a base field to be saved. This configuration is a base that specifies how many values a field can support and any additional settings defined by the field type. When you attach a field to a bundle it is considered a field storage and contains configuration unique to that specific bundle. If you have the same **Link** field on the **Article** and **Page** content type, the label, link type, and link text settings are for each instance.

Each field type provides a method for storing and presents a specific type of data. The benefit of using these fields comes from validation and data manipulation. It also allows you to utilize HTML5 form inputs. By using HTML5 for telephone, e-mail, and date the authoring experience uses the tools provided by the browser instead of additional third party libraries. This also provides a more native experience when authoring with mobile devices.

There's more...

Having Drupal 8 released with new fields was a large feature and we will cover some additional topics.

Upcoming updates

Each of the recipes covers a field type that was once part of the contributed project space. These projects provided more configuration options than are found in core at the time of writing this book. Over time more and more features will be brought into core from their source projects.

For instance, the Datetime module is based on the contributed date project. However not all of the contributed project's features have made it to Drupal core. Each minor release of Drupal 8 could see more features moved to core.

Views and Entity Reference

Using a View with an Entity Reference field is covered in *Chapter 3, Displaying Content through Views*. Using a View, you can customize the way results are fetched for a reference field.

See also

> ▶ *Chapter 3, Displaying Content through Views*, providing an entity reference result view

Customizing the form display of a node

New in Drupal 8 is the availability of form display modes. Form modes allow a site administrator to configure different field configurations for each content entity bundle edit form. In the case of nodes, you have the ability to rearrange and alter the display of fields and properties on the node edit form.

In this recipe we'll modify the default form for creating the **Article** content type that comes with the standard installation profile.

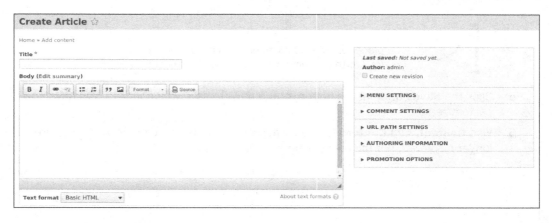

How to do it...

1. To customize the form display mode, visit **Structure** and then **Content Types**.

2. We will modify the **Article** content type's form. Click on the **expand the operations** drop down and select **Manage form display**.

3. First we will modify the **Comments** field. From the **Widget** dropdown choose the **Hidden** option to remove it from the form. Follow the same steps for the **sticky at top of lists** field.

4. Click on the settings cog for the **Body** field. Enter in a placeholder for the field, such as Enter your article text here. Click on **Update**.

Note:

The placeholder will only appear on a `textarea` using a text format that does not provide a WYSIWYG editor.

5. Click the **Save** button at the bottom of the page to save your changes. You have now customized the form display!

6. Visit **Content**, **Add Content**, and then **Article**. Note that the comment settings are no longer displayed, nor the sticky options under promotion options:

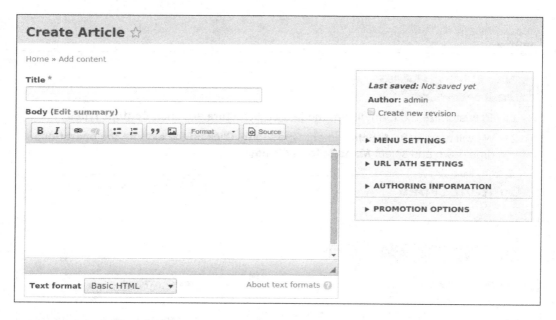

How it works...

Entities in Drupal have various view modes for each bundle. In Drupal 7 there were only display view modes, which are covered in the next recipe. Drupal 8 brings in new form modes to allow for more control of how an entity edit form is displayed.

Form display modes are configuration entities. Form display modes dictate how the `\Drupal\Core\EntityContentEntityForm` class will build a form when an entity is edited. This will always be set to default unless changed or specified specifically to a different mode programmatically.

Since form display modes are configuration entities they can be exported using configuration management.

Hidden field properties will have no value, unless there is a provided default value. For example, if you hide the Authoring information without providing code to set a default value the content will be authored by anonymous (no user).

There's more...

Managing form display modes

Form display modes for all entities are managed under one area and are enabled for each bundle type. You must first create a display mode and then it can be configured through the bundle manage interface.

Programmatically providing a default to hidden form items

In *Chapter 6, Creating Forms with the Form API*, we will have a recipe that details altering forms. In order to provide a default value for an entity property hidden on the form display, you will need to alter the form and provide a default value. The Field API provides a way to set a default value when fields are created.

See also

- ▸ *Chapter 10, The Entity API*
- ▸ *Chapter 6, Creating Forms with the Form API*

Customizing the display output of a node

Drupal provides display view modes that allow for customization of the fields and other properties attached to an entity. In this recipe we will adjust the teaser display mode of an **Article**. Each field or property has a control for displaying the label, the format to display the information in, and additional settings for the format.

Harnessing view displays allows you to have full control over how content is viewed on your Drupal site.

How to do it...

1. Now it is time to customize the form display mode by visiting **Structure** and then **Content Types**.

2. We will modify the **Article** content type's display. Click on the dropdown button arrow and select **Manage display**.

3. Click on the **Teaser** view mode option to modify it. The teaser view mode is used in node listings, such as the default home page.

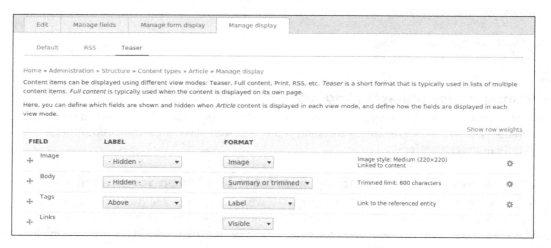

4. Change the format for **Tags** to be **Hidden**. Additionally, this can be accomplished by dragging it to the hidden section. The tags on an article will no longer be displayed when viewing a teaser view mode.

5. Click on the settings cog for the **Body** field to adjust the trimmed limit. The trim limit is a fallback for **Summary or trimmed** when the summary of a `textarea` field is not provided. Modify this from 600 to 300.

6. Press **Save** to save all of your changes that you have made.

7. View the home page and see that your changes have taken affect!

Fusce bibendum finibus risus

Submitted by admin on Sun, 10/04/2015 - 13:16

Lorem ipsum dolor sit amet, consectetur adipiscing elit. Morbi eu dolor vehicula, ullamcorper quam sed, bibendum diam. Proin cursus euismod nisi sit amet ultricies. Suspendisse tincidunt vitae sem nec facilisis. Sed hendrerit risus eros, quis fringilla ligula cursus et.

Read more   Add new comment

How it works...

View display modes are configuration entities. View display modes dictate how the `\Drupal\Core\EntityContentEntityForm` class will build a view display when an entity is viewed. This will always be set to default unless changed or specified as a different mode programmatically.

Since view display modes are configuration entities they can be exported using configuration management.

3
Displaying Content through Views

This chapter will cover the Views module and how to use a variety of its major features:

- ▶ Listing content
- ▶ Editing the default admin interfaces
- ▶ Creating a block from a View
- ▶ Utilizing dynamic arguments
- ▶ Adding a relationship in a View
- ▶ Providing an Entity Reference result View

Introduction

For those who have used Drupal previously, Views is in core for Drupal 8! If you are new to Drupal, Views has been one of the most used contributed projects for Drupal 6 and Drupal 7.

To briefly describe Views, it is a visual query builder, allowing you to pull content from the database and render it in multiple formats. Select administrative areas and content listings provided out of the box by Drupal are all powered by Views. We'll dive into how to use Views to customize the administrative interface, customize ways to display your content, and interact with the entity reference field.

Listing content

Views does one thing, and it does it well: listing content. The power behind the Views module is the amount of configurable power it gives the end user to display content in various forms.

This recipe will cover creating a content listing and linking it in the main menu. We will use the **Article** content type provided by the standard installation and make an articles landing page.

Getting ready

The Views UI module must be enabled in order to manipulate Views from the user interface. By default this is enabled with the standard installation profile.

How to do it...

Let's list the Views listing content:

1. Visit **Structure** and then **Views**. This will bring you to the administrative overview of all the views that have been created:

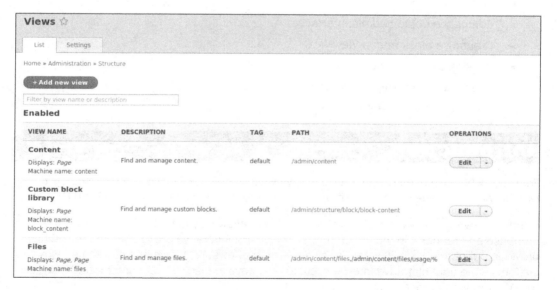

2. Click on **Add new view** to begin creating a new view.

3. The first step is to provide the **View name** of **Articles**, which will serve as the administrative and (by default) displayed title.

4. Next, we modify the **VIEW SETTINGS**. We want to display **Content** of the type Articles and leave the **tagged with** empty. This will force the view to only show content of the **article** content type.

5. Choose to **Create a page**. The **Page title** and **Path** will be auto populated based on the view name and can be modified as desired. For now, leave the display and other settings at their default values.

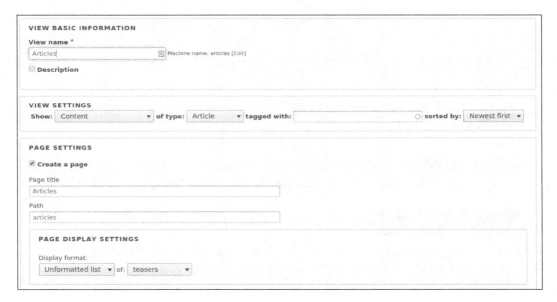

6. Click on **Save and edit** to continue modifying your new view.

7. In the middle column, under the **Page settings** section we will change the **Menu item** settings. Click on **No menu** to change the default.

8. Select **Normal menu entry**. Provide a menu link title and optional description. Keep the **Parent** set to **<Main Navigation>**.

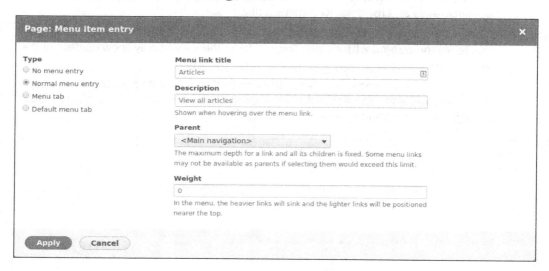

9. Click on **Apply** at the bottom of the form.
10. Once the view is saved you will now see the link in your Drupal site's main menu.

How it works...

The first step for creating a view involves selecting the type of data you will be displaying. This is referred to as the base table, which can be any type of entity or data specifically exposed to Views.

 Nodes are labeled as Content in Views and you will find throughout Drupal this interchanged terminology.

When creating a Views page we are adding a menu path that can be accessed. It tells Drupal to invoke Views to render the page, which will load the view you create and render it.

There are display `style` and `row` plugins that format the data to be rendered. Our recipe used the **unformatted list** style to wrap each row in a simple `div` element. We could have changed this to a table for a formatted list. The row display controls how each row is output.

There's more...

Views has been one of the must-use modules since it first debuted, to the point that almost every Drupal 7 site used the module. In the following section we will dive further into Views.

Views in Drupal Core Initiative

Views has been a contributed module up until Drupal 8. In fact, it was one of the most used modules. Although the module is now part of Drupal core it still has many improvements that are needed and are being committed.

Some of these changes will be seen through minor Drupal releases, such as 8.1x and 8.2.x, as development progresses and probably not through patch releases (8.0.10).

Views and displays

When working with Views, you will see some different terminology. One of the key items to grasp is what a display is. A view can contain multiple displays. Each display is of a certain type. Views comes with the following display types:

▶ **attachment**: This is a display that becomes attached to another display in the same view

▶ **block**: This allows you to place the view as a block

▶ **embed**: The display is meant to be embedded programmatically

▶ **Entity Reference**: This allows Views to provide results for an entity reference field

▶ **feed**: This display returns an XML based feed and can be attached to another display to render a feed icon

▶ **page**: This allows you to display the view from a specific route

Each display can have its own configuration, too. However, each display will share the same base table (content, files, etc.). This allows you to take the same data and represent it in different ways.

Format style plugins: style and row

Within Views there are two types of style plugins that represent how your data is displayed – style and row.

▶ The **style** plugin represents the overall format

▶ The **row** plugin represents each result row's format

For example, the `grid` style will output multiple `div` elements with specified classes to create a responsive `grid`. At the same time, the `table` style creates a tabular output with labels used as table headings.

Row plugins define how to render the row. The default content will render the entity as defined by its selected display mode. If you choose **Fields** you manually choose which fields to include in your view.

Each format style plugin has a corresponding Twig file that the theme layer uses. You can define new plugins in custom modules or use contributed modules to access different options.

Using the Embed display

Each of the available display types has a method to expose itself through the user interface, except for **Embed**. Often, contributed and custom modules use Views to render displays instead of manually writing queries and rendering the output. Drupal 8 provides a special display type to simplify this.

If we were to add an Embed display to the view created in the recipe, we could pass the following render array to output our view programmatically.

```
$view_render = [
  '#type' => 'view',
  '#name' => 'articles',
  '#display_id' => 'embed_1',
];
```

When rendered, the #type key tells Drupal this is a view element. We then point it to our new display embed_1. In actuality, the Embed display type has no special functionality, in fact it is a simplistic display plugin. The benefit is that it does not have additional operations conducted for the sake of performance.

See also

> ▸ VDC Initiative:
> https://www.drupal.org/community-initiatives/drupal-core/vdc

> ▸ *Chapter 7, Plug and Play with Plugins*, to learn more about plugins

Editing the default admin interfaces

With the addition of Views in Drupal core, many of the administrative interfaces are powered by Views. This allows customization of default admin interfaces to enhance site management and content authoring experiences.

In Drupal 7 and 6 there was the administrative Views module, which provided a way to override administrative pages with Views. This module is no longer required, as the functionality comes with Drupal core out of the box!

In this recipe we will modify the default content overview form that is used to find and edit content. We will add the ability to filter content by the user who authored it.

How to do it...

1. Visit **Structure** and then **Views**. This will bring you to the administrative overview of all existing views.

2. From the **Enabled** section, select the **Edit** option for the **Content** view. This is the view displayed on /admin/content when managing content.

3. In order to filter by the content author, we must add a **FILTER CRITERIA** to our view, which we will expose the following for users to modify:

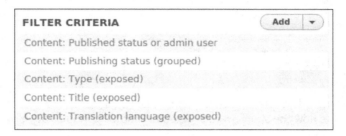

4. Click on **Add** to add a new filter. In the search text box type **Authored by** to search the available options. Select **Content: Authored by** and click **Apply (all displays)**:

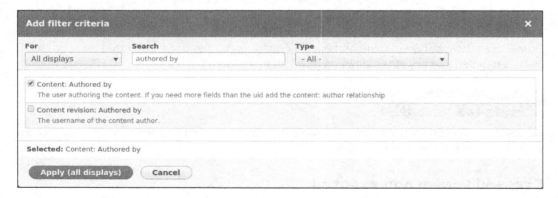

5. Check **Expose this filter to visitors**, to allow them to change it via checkbox. This will allow users to modify the data for the filter.

6. You may modify the **Label** and add a **Description** to improve the usability of the filter option for your use case.

7. Click on **Apply (all displays)** once more to finish configuring the filter. It will now show up in the list as filter criteria active. You will also see the new filter in the preview below the form.

8. Click on **Save** to commit all changes to the view.

9. View `/admin/content` and you will have your filter. Content editors will be able to search for content authored by a user through autocompleted username searches:

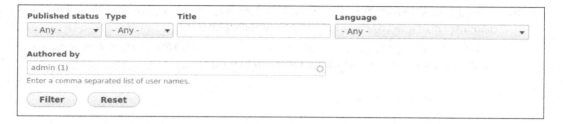

How it works...

When a view is created that has a path matching an existing route, it will override it and present itself. That is how the `/admin/content` and other administrative pages are able to be powered by Views.

 If you were to disable the Views module you can still manage content and users. The default forms are tables that do not provide filters or other extra features.

Drupal uses the overridden route and uses Views to render the page. From that point on the page is handled like any other Views page would be rendered.

There's more...

We will dive into additional features available through Views that can enhance the way you use Views and present them on your Drupal site.

Exposed versus non-exposed

Filters allow you to narrow the scope of the data displayed in a view. Filters can either be exposed or not; by default a filter is not exposed. An example would be using the **Content: Publishing status** set to **Yes (published)** to ensure a view always contains published content. This is an item you would configure for displaying content to site visitors. However, if it were for an administrative display, you may want to expose that filter. This way content editors have the ability to view, easily, what content has not been published yet or has been unpublished.

All filter and sort criteria can be marked as exposed.

Filter identifiers

Exposed filters work by parsing query parameters in the URL. For instance, on the content management form, changing the `Type` filter will add `type=Article` amongst others to the current URL.

With this recipe the author filter would show up as **uid** in the URL. Exposed filters have a **Filter identifier** option that can change the URL component.

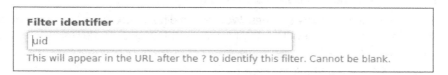

This could be changed to `author` or some other value to enhance the user experience behind the URL, or mask the Drupal-ness of it.

Overriding routes with Views

Views is able to replace administrative pages with enhanced versions due to the way the route and module system works in Drupal. Modules are executed in order of the module's weight or alphabetical order if weights are the same. Naturally, in the English alphabet, the letter *V* comes towards the end of the alphabet. That means any route that Views provides will be added towards the end of the route discovery cycle.

If a view is created and it provides a route path, it will override any that exist on that path. There is not a collision checking mechanism (and there was not in Views before merging into Drupal core) that prevents this.

This allows you to easily customize most existing routes. But, beware that you could easily have conflicting routes and Views will normally override the other.

Creating a block from a View

Previous recipes have shown how to create and manipulate a page created by a view. Views provides different display types that can be created, such as a block. In this recipe we will create a block powered by Views. The Views block will list all Tag taxonomy terms that have been added to the Article content type.

Getting ready

This recipe assumes you have installed the standard installation profile and have the default node content types available for use.

How to do it...

1. Visit **Structure** and then **Views**. This will bring you to the administrative overview of all the views that have been created.

2. Click on **Add new** view to begin creating a new view.

3. The first step is to provide the View name of `Tags`, which will serve as the administrative and (by default) displayed title.

4. Next, we modify the **View** settings. We want to display Taxonomy terms of the type Tags. This will make the view default to only displaying taxonomy terms created under the Tags vocabulary

5. Check the **Create a block** checkbox.

6. Choose the **HTML List** option from the **Display** format choices. Leave the **row style** as **Fields**.

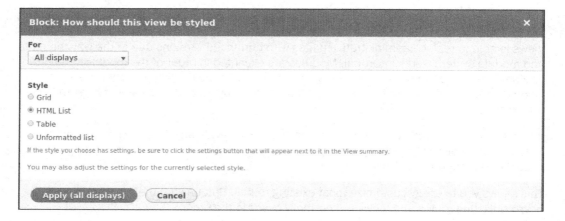

7. We want to display all of the available tags. To change this, click the current pager style link. Pick the **Display all items** radio and click **Apply (all displays)**. On the next model, click **Save** to keep the offset at 0.

8. Next we will sort the view by tag name instead of order of creation. Click **Add** on the **Sort criteria** section. Add **Taxonomy term: Name** and click **Apply (all displays)** to use the default **sort by ascending**.

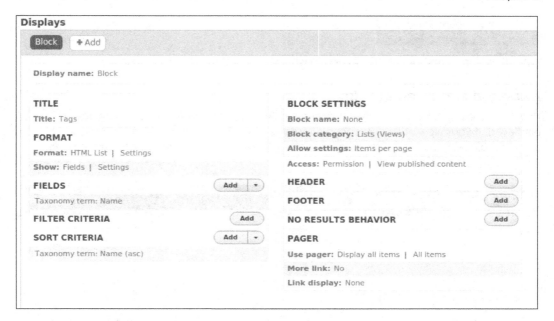

9. Press **Save** to save the view.

10. Visit **Structure** and **Block layout** to place the block on your Drupal site. Press **Place block** for the **Sidebar** region in the **Bartik** theme.

11. Filter the list by typing your view's name. Press **Place block** to add your view's block to the block layout.

12. Finally click on **block** to commit your changes!

How it works...

In the Drupal 8 plugin system there is a concept called **Derivatives**. Plugins are small pieces of swappable functionality within Drupal 8. Plugins and plugin development are covered in *Chapter 7, Plug and Play with Plugins*. A derivative allows a module to present multiple variations of a plugin dynamically. In the case of Views, it allows the module to provide variations of a `ViewsBlock` plugin for each view that has a block display. Views implements the `\Drupal\views\Plugin\Block\ViewsBlock\ViewsBlock` class, providing the base for the dynamic availability of these blocks. Each derived block is an instance of this class.

When Drupal initiates the block, Views passes the proper configuration required. The view is then executed and the display is rendered whenever the block is displayed.

There's more...

We will explore some of the other ways in which Views interacts with blocks.

Exposed forms as blocks

Pages and feeds have the ability to provide blocks, however not for the actual content displayed. If your view utilizes exposed filters you have the option to place the exposed form in a block. With this option enabled you may place the block anywhere on the page, even pages not for your view!

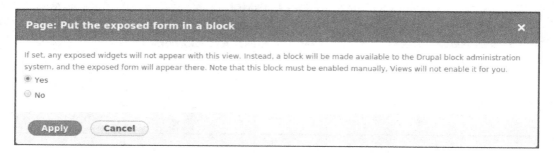

To enable the exposed filters as a block, you must first expand the **Advanced** section on the right side of the Views edit form. Click on the **Exposed form in block** option from the **Advanced** section. In the options modal that opens, select the **Yes** radio button and click **Apply**. You then have the ability to place the block from the **Block layout** form.

An example for using an exposed form in a block is for a search result view. You would add an exposed filter for keywords that control the search results. With the exposed filters in a block you can easily place it in your site's header. When an exposed `filters` block is submitted, it will direct users to your view's display.

See also

> ▶ Chapter 7, *Plug and Play with Plugins*, to learn more about derivatives

Utilizing dynamic arguments

Views can be configured to accept **contextual filters**. Contextual filters allow you to provide a dynamic argument that modifies the view's output. The value is expected to be passed from the URL; however, if it is not present there are ways to provide a default value.

In this recipe we will create a new page called `My Content`, which will display a user's authored content on the route `/user/%/content`.

How to do it...

1. Visit **Structure** and then **Views**. This will bring you to the administrative overview of all the views created. Click on **Add new view** to begin creating a new view.

2. Set the **View name** to **My Content**.

3. Next, we modify the **View** settings. We want to display **Content of the type All** and leave the **Tagged** with empty. This will allow all content to be displayed.

4. Choose to **Create** a page. Keep the page title the same. We need to change the path to be `user/%/content`. Click **Save and edit** to move to the next screen and add the contextual filter.

 When building a views page, adding a percentage sign to the path identifies a route variable.

5. Toggle the Advanced portion of the form on the right hand side of the page. Click on **Add in the Contextual filters** section.

6. Select **Content: Authored by and then click Apply (all displays)**.

7. Change the default value When the filter is not in the URL to **Display "Access Denied"** to prevent all content from being displayed with a bad route value.

▼ WHEN THE FILTER VALUE IS *NOT* IN THE URL

Default actions
- ○ Display all results for the specified field
- ○ Provide default value
- ○ Show "Page not found"
- ○ Display a summary
- ○ Display contents of "No results found"
- ● Display "Access Denied"

▸ EXCEPTIONS

---

8. Click **Apply (all displays)** and save the form.

9. Visit `/user/1/content` and you will see content created by the root admin!

How it works...

Contextual filters mimic the route variables found in the Drupal routing system. Variables are represented by percentage signs as placeholders in the view's path. Views will match up each placeholder with contextual filters by order of their placement. This allows you to have multiple contextual filters; you just need to ensure they are ordered properly.

Views is aware of how to handle the placeholder because the type of data is selected when you add the filter. Once the contextual filter is added there are extra options available for handling the route variable.

There's more...

We will explore extra options available when using contextual filters.

Previewing with contextual filters

You are still able to preview a view from the edit form. You simply add the contextual filter values in to the text form concatenated by a forward slash (/). In this recipe you could replace visiting /user/1/content with simply inputting 1 into the preview form and updating the preview.

Displaying as a tab on the user page

Even though the view created in the recipe follows a route under /user, it will not show up as a local task tab until it has a menu entry defined. From the **Page settings** section you will need to change **No menu** from the **Menu** option. Clicking on that link will open the menu link settings dialog.

Select **Menu tab** and provide a **Menu link title**, such as **My Content**. Click on **Apply** and save your view.

Altering the page title

With contextual filters you have the ability to manipulate the current page's title. When adding or editing a contextual filter you can modify the page title. From the When the filter value is present in the URL or a default is provided section, you may check the Override title option.

This text box allows you to enter in a new title that will be displayed. Additionally, you can use the information passed from the route context using the format of %# where the # is the argument order.

Validation

Contextual filters can have validation attached. Without specifying extra validation, Views will take the expected argument and try to make it *just work*. You can add validation to help limit this scope and filter out invalid route variables.

You can enable validation by checking **Specify validation criteria** from the When the filter value is present in the URL or a default is provided section. The default is set to – Basic Validation – which allows you to specify how the view should react if the data is invalid; based on our recipe, if the user was not found.

The list of **Validator** options is not filtered by the contextual filter item you selected, so some may not apply. For our recipe one might want **User ID** and select the **Validate user has access to the User**. This validator would make sure the current user is able to view the route's user's profile. Additionally, it can be restricted further based on role.

This gives you more granular control over how the view operates when using contextual filters for route arguments.

Multiple and exclusion

You may also configure the contextual filter to allow AND or OR operations along with exclusion. These options are under the **More** section when adding or editing a contextual filter.

The Allow multiple values option can be checked to enable AND or OR operations. If the contextual filter argument contains a series of values concatenated by plus (+) signs it acts as an OR operation. If the values are concatenated by commas (,) it acts as an AND operation.

When the **Exclude** option is checked the value will be excluded from the results rather than the view being limited by it.

Adding a relationship in a View

As stated at the beginning of the chapter, Views is a visual query builder. When you first create a view, a base table is specified to pull data from. Views automatically knows how to join tables for field data, such as body text or custom attached fields.

When using an entity reference field, you have the ability to display the value as the raw identifier, the referenced entity's label, or the entire rendered entity. However, if you add a Relationship based on a reference field you will have access to display any of that entity's available fields.

In this recipe, we will update the Files view, used for administering files, to display the username of the user who uploaded the file.

How to do it...

1. Visit **Structure** and then **Views**. This will bring you to the administrative overview of all the views that have been created

2. Find the **Files** view and click **Edit**.

3. Click on **Advanced** to expand the section and then click **Add** next to **Relationships**.

4. Search for **user**. Select the **User** who uploaded **relationship option** and click **Apply (this display)**.

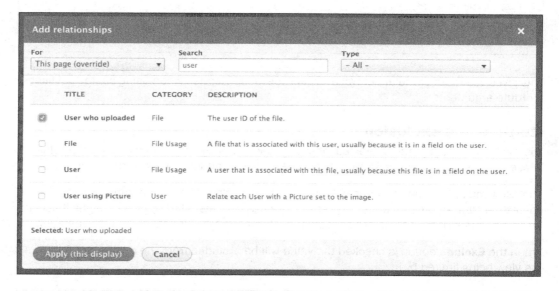

5. Next we will be presented with a configure form for the relationship. Click **Apply (this display)** to use the defaults.

6. Add a new field by clicking **Add** in the **Fields** section.

7. Search for **name** and select the **Name** field and click **Apply (this display)**.

8. This view uses aggregation, which presents a new configuration form when first adding a field. Click **Apply and continue** to use the defaults.

 We will discuss Views and aggregation in the _There's more..._ section.

9. We will use the default field settings that will provide the label **Name** and format it as the username and link to the user's profile. Click **Apply (all displays).**

10. Click on **Save** to finish editing the view and commit your changes.

How it works...

Drupal stores data in a normalized format. Database normalization, in short, involves the organization of data in specific related tables. Each entity type has its own database table and all fields have their own database table. When you create a view and specify what kind of data will be shown, you are specifying a base table in the database that Views will query. Views will automatically associate fields that belong to the entity and the relationship to those tables for you.

When an entity has an Entity reference field you have the ability to add a relationship to the referenced entity type's table. This is an explicit definition, whereas fields are implicit. When the relationship is explicitly defined all of the referenced entity type's fields come into scope. The fields on the referenced entity type can then be displayed, filtered, and sorted by.

There's more...

Using relationships in Views allows you to create some powerful displays. We will discuss aggregation and additional information about relationships.

Relationships provided by entity reference fields

Views uses a series of hooks to retrieve data that it uses to represent ways to interact with the database. One of these is the `hook_field_views_data` hook, which processes a field storage configuration entity and registers its data with Views. The Views module implements this on behalf of Drupal core to add relationships, and reverse relationships, for Entity reference fields.

Since Entity reference fields have set schema information, Views can dynamically generate these relationships by knowing the field's table name, destination entity's table name, and the destination entity's identifier column.

Relationships provided through custom code

There are times where you would need to define a relation on your own with custom code. Typically, when working with custom data in Drupal, you would more than likely create a new entity type, covered in *Chapter 9, Confiuration Management – Deploying in Drupal 8*. This is not always the case, however, and you may just need a simple method of storing data. An example can be found in the Database Logging module. The Database Logging module defines schema for a database table and then uses `hook_views_data` to expose its database table to Views.

The `dblog_schema` hook implementation returns a `uid` column on the watchdog database table created by the module. That column is then exposed to Views with the following definition:

```
$data['watchdog']['uid'] = array(
  'title' => t('UID'),
  'help' => t('The user ID of the user on which the log entry
    was written..'),
  'field' => array(
    'id' => 'numeric',
  ),
  'filter' => array(
    'id' => 'numeric',
  ),
  'argument' => array(
    'id' => 'numeric',
```

```
    ),
  'relationship' => array(
    'title' => t('User'),
    'help' => t('The user on which the log entry as written.'),
    'base' => 'users',
    'base field' => 'uid',
    'id' => 'standard',
  ),
);
```

This array tells Views that the `watchdog` table has a column named `uid`. It is `numeric` in nature for its display, filtering capabilities and sorting capabilities. The `relationship` key is an array of information that instructs Views how to use this to provide a relationship (`LEFT JOIN`) on the `users` table. The `User` entity uses the `users` table and has the primary key of `uid`.

Using Aggregation and views.

There is a view setting under the **Advanced** section that allows you to enable aggregation. This feature allows you to enable the usage of SQL aggregate functions, such as MIN, MAX, SUM, AVG, and COUNT. In this recipe, the Files view uses aggregation to SUM the usage counts of each file in the Drupal site.

Aggregation settings are set for each field and when enabled have their own link to configure the settings.

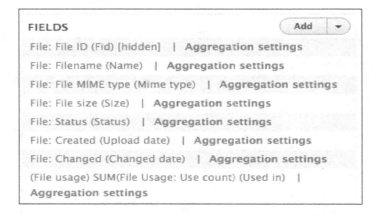

Providing an Entity Reference result View

The Entity reference field, covered in *Chapter 2, The Content Authoring Experience*, can utilize a custom view for providing the available field values. The default entity reference field will display all available entities of the type it is allowed to reference. The only available filter is based on the entity bundle, such as only returning Article nodes. Using an entity reference view you can provide more filters, such as only content that user has authored.

In this recipe we will create an entity reference view that filters content by the author. We will add the field to the user account form, allowing users to select their favorite contributed content.

How to do it...

1. Visit **Structure** and then **Views**. This will bring you to the administrative overview of all the views that have been created. Click on **Add new view** to begin creating a new view.

2. Set the **View name** to **My Content Reference View**. Modify the **View** settings. We want to display **Content of the type All** and leave the Tagged with empty.

3. Do not choose to create a page or block. Click **Save and edit** to continue working on your view.

4. Click on the **Add** button to create a new display. Select the **Entity Reference** option to create the display.

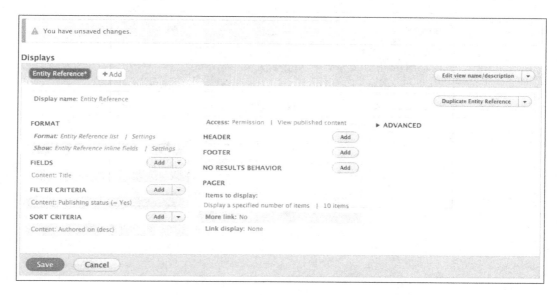

5. The **Format** will be automatically set to **Entity Reference List**, which utilizes fields. Click on **Settings** next to it to modify the style format.

6. For **Search Fields**, check the **Content:Title** option then click **Apply**. This is what the field will autocomplete search on.

7. You will need to modify the **Content: Title** field to stop it from wrapping the result as a link. Click on the field label and uncheck **Link to the Content**. Click **Apply (all displays)** to save.

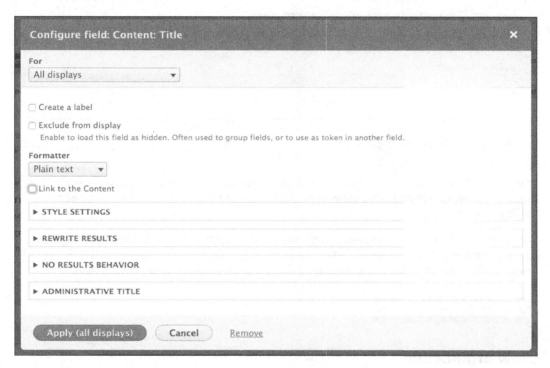

8. Click on **Save** to save the view.

9. Go to **Configuration** and then **Account settings** to be able to **Manage fields** on user accounts.

10. Add a new **Entity Reference** field that references **Content**, call it Highlighted contributions, and allow it to have unlimited values. Click the **Save field settings** button.

11. Change the **Reference type** method to use **View: Filter by an entity reference view** and select the view we have just created:

▼ REFERENCE TYPE

Reference method *
Views: Filter by an entity reference view ▼

View used to select the entities *
my_content_reference_view - Entity Reference ▼

Choose the view and display that select the entities that can be referenced.
Only views with a display of type "Entity Reference" are eligible.

View arguments

Provide a comma separated list of arguments to pass to the view.

How it works...

The entity reference field definition provides selection plugins. Views provides an entity reference selection plugin. This allows entity reference to feed data into a view to receive available results.

The display type for Views requires you to select which fields will be used to search against when using the autocomplete widget. If not using the autocomplete widget and using the select list or checkboxes and radio buttons, then it will return the view's entire results.

There's more...

View arguments

Entity reference view displays can accept contextual filter arguments. These are not dynamic, but can be passed manually through the field's settings. The **View arguments** field allows you to add a comma separated list of arguments that are passed to the view. The order should match the order of the contextual filters as configured.

In this recipe we could have added a **Content: type** contextual filter that fell back to **Display all results** if the argument was missing. This allows the view to be reused in multiple references. Perhaps there is one view that should limit the available references to all Articles created by the current user. You would then add **Article** to the text field and pass the argument to the view.

See also

▶ Chapter 7, *Plug and Play with Plugins*, to learn more about plugins

4
Extending Drupal

This chapter dives into extending Drupal using a custom module:

- ▶ Creating a module
- ▶ Defining a custom page
- ▶ Defining permissions
- ▶ Providing the configuration on installation or update
- ▶ Using Features 2.x

Introduction

A feature of Drupal that makes it desirable is the ability to customize it through modules. Whether custom or contributed, modules extend the functionalities and capabilities of Drupal. Modules can be used to not only extend Drupal, but also to create a way to provide configuration and reusable features.

This chapter will discuss how to create a module and allow Drupal to discover it, allowing it to be installed from the extend page. Permissions, custom pages, and default configurations all come from modules. We will explore how to provide these through a custom module.

In addition to creating a module, we will discuss the Features module that provides a set of tools for exporting the configuration and generating a module.

Creating a module

The first step to extend Drupal is to create a custom module. Although the task sounds daunting, it can be accomplished in a few simple steps. Modules can provide functionalities and customizations to functionalities provided by other modules, or they can be used as a way to contain the configuration and a site's state.

In this recipe, we will create a module by defining an `info` file, a file containing information that Drupal uses to discover extensions, and enabling the module.

How to do it...

1. Create a folder named `mymodule` in the `modules` folder in the base directory of your Drupal site. This will be your module's directory.

2. Create a `mymodule.info.yml` file in your module's directory. This contains metadata that identifies the module to Drupal.

3. Add a line to the `name` key to provide a name for the module:

   ```
   name: My Module!
   ```

4. We need to provide the `type` key to define the type of extension. We provide the value `module`:

   ```
   type: module
   ```

5. The `description` key allows you to provide extra information about your module, which will be displayed on the module's list page:

   ```
   description: This is an example module from the Drupal 8 Cookbook!
   ```

6. All modules need to define the `core` key in order to specify a major release compatibility:

   ```
   core: 8.x
   ```

7. Save the `mymodule.info.yml` file, which resembles the following code:

   ```
   name: My Module!
   type: module
   description: This is an example module from the Drupal 8 Cookbook!
   core: 8.x
   ```

8. Log in to your Drupal site and visit **Extend** from the administrative toolbar.

9. Search for **My Module** to filter the list of options.

10. Check the checkbox and click on **Install** to enable your module.

Home » Administration

Download additional contributed modules to extend your site's functionality.

Regularly review available updates to maintain a secure and current site. Always run the update script each time a module is updated. Enable the Update Manager module to update and install modules and themes.

> mymodule

Enter a part of the module name or description

▼ OTHER

☑   **My Module!**

How it works...

Drupal utilizes `info.yml` files to define extensions. Drupal has a discovery system that locates these files and parses them to discover modules. The `info_parser` service, provided by the `\Drupal\Core\Extension\InfoParser` class, reads the `info.yml` file. The parser guarantees that the required type, core, and name keys are present.

When a module is installed, it is added to the `core.extension` configuration object, which contains a list of installed modules and themes. The collection of modules in the `core.extension` module array will be installed and will have PHP namespaces resolved, services loaded, and hooks registered.

When Drupal prepares to execute a hook or register services, it will iterate across the values in the `module` key in `core.extension`.

There's more...

There are more details that we can explore about module `info` files.

Module namespaces

Drupal 8 uses the PSR-4 standard developed by the PHP Framework Interoperability Group. The PSR-4 standard is for package-based PHP namespace autoloading. It defines a standard to understand how to automatically include classes based on a namespace and class name. Drupal modules have their own namespaces under the Drupal root namespace.

Using the module from the recipe, our PHP namespace will be `Drupal\mymodule`, which represents the `modules/mymodule/src` folder.

With PSR-4, files need to contain only one class, interface, or trait. These files need to have the same filename as the containing class, interface, or trait name. This allows a class loader to resolve a namespace as a directory path and know the class's filename. The file can then be automatically loaded when it is used in a file.

Module discovery locations

Drupal supports multiple module discovery locations. Modules can be placed in the following directories and discovered:

- `/profiles/CURRENT PROFILE/modules`
- `/sites/all/modules`
- `/modules`
- `/sites/default/modules`
- `/sites/example.com/modules`

The `\Drupal\Core\Extension\ExtensionDiscovery` class handles the discovery of extensions by types. It will iteratively scan each location and discover modules that are available. The discovery order is important. If the same module is placed in `/modules` but also in the `sites/default/modules` directory, the latter will take precedence.

Defining a package group

Modules can define a `package` key to group modules on the module list page:

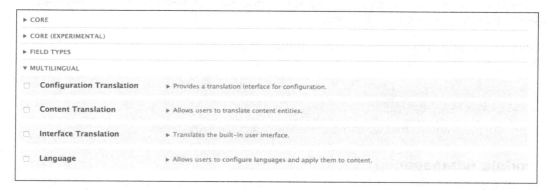

Projects that include multiple submodules, such as Drupal commerce, specify packages to normalize the modules' list form. Contributed modules for the Drupal commerce project utilize a package name, `Commerce (contrib)`, to group on the module list page.

Module dependencies

Modules can define dependencies to ensure that those modules are enabled before your module can be enabled.

Here is the `info.yml` for the `Responsive Image` module:

```
name: Responsive Image
type: module
description: 'Provides an image formatter and breakpoint mappings to
output responsive images using the HTML5 picture tag.'
package: Core
version: VERSION
core: 8.x
dependencies:
  - breakpoint
  - image
```

The `dependencies` key specifies that the Breakpoint and Image modules need to be enabled first before the Responsive Image module can be enabled. When enabling a module that requires dependencies that are disabled, the installation form will provide a prompt asking you if you would like to install the dependencies as well. If a dependency module is missing, the module cannot be installed. The dependency will show a status of (`missing`).

A module that is a dependency of another module will state the information in it's description, along with the other module's status. For example, the Breakpoint module will show that the Responsive Image module requires it as a dependency and is disabled:

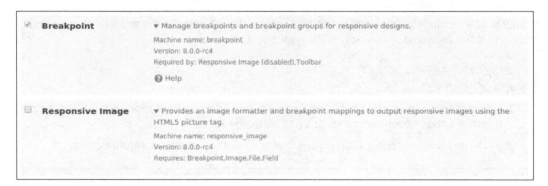

Specifying the module's version

There is a `version` key that defines the current module's version. Projects on Drupal.org do not specify this directly, as the packager adds it when a release is created. However, this key can be important for private modules to track the release information.

Versions are expected to be single strings, such as `1.0-alpha1`, `2.0.1`. You can also pass `VERSION`, which will resolve to the current version of Drupal core.

> Drupal.org does not currently support semantic versioning for contributed projects. There is an ongoing policy discussion in the issue queue, which can be found at `https://www.drupal.org/node/1612910`.

See also...

► Refer to the PSR-4: Autoloader specification at `http://www.php-fig.org/psr/psr-4/`

Defining a custom page

In Drupal, there are routes that represent URL paths that Drupal interprets to return content. Modules have the ability to define routes and methods that return data to be rendered and then displayed to the end user.

In this recipe, we will define a controller that provides an output and a route. The route provides a URL path that Drupal will associate with our controller to display the output.

Getting ready

Create a new module like the one in the first recipe. We will refer to the module as `mymodule` throughout the recipe. Use your module's name as appropriate.

How to do it...

1. Firstly, we'll set up the controller. Create a `src` folder in your module's base directory and another folder named `Controller` inside it.

2. Create `MyPageController.php` that will hold the route's controller class.

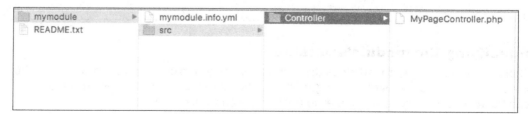

3. The PSR-4 standard states that filenames match the class names they hold, so we will create a `MyPageController` class:

```php
<?php
/**
 * @file
 * Contains \Drupal\mymodule\Controller\MyPageController class.
 */

namespace Drupal\mymodule\Controller;

use Drupal\Core\Controller\ControllerBase;

/**
 * Returns responses for My Module module.
 */
class MyPageController extends ControllerBase {

}
```

This creates the `MyPageController` class, which extends the `\Drupal\Core\Controller\ControllerBase` class. This base class provides a handful of utilities for interacting with the container.

The `Drupal\mymodule\Controller` namespace allows Drupal to automatically load the file from `/modules/mymodule/src/Controller`.

4. Next, we will create a method that returns a string of text in our class:

```php
/**
 * Returns markup for our custom page.
 */
public function customPage() {
  return [
  '#markup' => t('Welcome to my custom page!'),
  ];
}
```

The `customPage` method returns a render array that the Drupal theming layer can parse. The `#markup` key denotes a value that does not have any additional rendering or theming processes.

5. Create a `mymodule.routing.yml` in the base directory of your module so that a route can be added to this controller and method.

6. The first step is to define the route's internal name for the route to be referenced by:

```
mymodule.mypage:
```

7. Give the route a path (mypage):

```
mymodule.mypage:
  path: /mypage
```

8. The defaults key allows us to provide the controller through a fully qualified class name, the method to use, and the page's title:

```
mymodule.mypage:
  path: /mypage
  defaults:
    _controller: '\Drupal\mymodule\Controller\
MyPageController::customPage'
    _title: 'My custom page'
```

You need to provide the initial \ when providing the fully qualified class name.

9. Lastly, define a requirements key to set the access callback:

```
mymodule.mypage:
  path: /mypage
  defaults:
    _controller: '\Drupal\mymodule\Controller\
MyPageController::customPage'
    _title: 'My custom page'
  requirements:
    _permission: 'access content'
```

Defining _access to TRUE for the requirements means that access is always granted.

10. Visit **Configuration** and then **Development** to rebuild Drupal's caches.

11. Visit /mypage on your Drupal site and view your custom page:

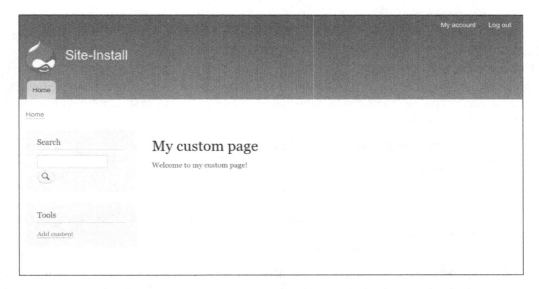

How it works...

Drupal uses routes, which define a path, that return content. Each route has a method in a controller class that generates the content, in the form of a render array, to be delivered to the user. When a request comes to Drupal, the system makes an attempt to match the path to known routes. If the route is found, the route's definition is used to deliver the page. If the route cannot be found, the 404 page is displayed.

The HTTP kernel takes the request and loads the route. It will invoke the defined controller method or procedural function. The result of the invoked method or function is then handed to the presentation layer of Drupal to be rendered into the content that can be delivered to the user.

Drupal 8 builds on top of the Symfony HTTP kernel to provide the underlying functionality of its route system. It has added the ability to provide access requirements, casting placeholders into loaded objects, and partial page responses.

Routes have extra capabilities that can be configured; we will explore those in the next section.

Parameters in routes

Routes have the ability to accept dynamic arguments that can be passed to the route controller's method. Placeholder elements can be defined in the route using curly brackets in the URL that denote dynamic values.

An example of a route might look like the following code:

```
mymodule.cats:
  path: '/cat/{name}'
  defaults:
    _controller: '\Drupal\mymodule\Controller\MyPageController::cats'
  requirements:
    _permission: 'access content'
```

This route specifies the /cat/{name} path. The {name} placeholder will accept dynamic values and pass them to the controller's method:

```
class MyPageController {
  // ...
  public function cats($name) {
    return [
      '#markup' => t('My cats name is: @name', [
        '@name' => $name,
      ]),
    ];
  }
}
```

This method accepts the name variable from the route and substitutes it into the render array to display it as text.

Drupal's routing system provides a method of upcasting a variable into a loaded object. There are a set of parameter converter classes under the \Drupal\Core\ParamConverter namespace. The EntityConverter class will read options defined in the route and replace a placeholder value with a loaded entity object.

If we have an entity type called **cat**, we can turn the name placeholder into a method to be provided the loaded the cat object in our controller's method:

```
mymodule.cats:
  path: '/cat/{name}'
  defaults:
```

```
    _controller: '\Drupal\mymodule\Controller\MyPageController::cats'
  requirements:
    _permission: 'access content'
  options:
    parameters:
      name:
        type: entity:cat
```

 This is not required for entities as the defined entity route handler can automatically generate this. Entities are covered in *Chapter 10, The Entity API*.

Validating parameters in routes

Drupal provides regular expression validation against route parameters. If the parameter fails the regular expression validation, a 404 page will be returned. Using the recipe's example route, we can add the validation to ensure that only alphabetical characters are used in the route parameter:

```
mymodule.cats:
  path: '/cat/{name}'
  defaults:
    _controller: '\Drupal\mymodule\Controller\MyPageController::cats'
  requirements:
    _permission: 'access content'
    name: '[a-zA-z]+'
```

Under the `requirements` key, you can add a new value that matches the name of the placeholder. You then set it to have the value of the regular expression you would like to use.

Route requirements

Routes can define different access requirements through the `requirements` key. Multiple validators can be added. However, there must be one that provides a true result or else the route will return **403, access denied**. This is true if the route defines no requirement validators.

Route requirement validators are defined by implementing `\Drupal\Core\Routing\Access\AccessInterface`. Here are some of the common requirement validators defined throughout Drupal core:

▶ `_entity_access` validates that the current user has the ability to perform `entity_type.operation`, such as `node.view`

▶ `_permission` checks whether the current user has the provided permission

▶ `_user_is_logged_in` validates that the current user is logged in, which is defined with a Boolean value in the `routing.yml`

Providing dynamic routes

The routing system allows modules to define routes programmatically. This can be accomplished by providing a `routing_callbacks` key that defines a class and method that will return an array of the `\Symfony\Component\Routing\Route` objects.

 If you are working with entities, refer to *Chapter 10*, *The Entity API*, to learn about overriding the default route handler to create dynamic routes.

In the module's `routing.yml`, you will define the routing callbacks key and related class:

```
route_callbacks:
  - '\Drupal\mymodule\Routing\CustomRoutes::routes'
```

The `\Drupal\mymodule\Routing\CustomRoutes` class will then have a method named routes, which returns an array of Symfony route objects:

```php
<?php

namespace Drupal\mymodule\Routing;
use Symfony\Component\Routing\Route;

class CustomRoutes {
  public function routes() {
    $routes = [];

    // Create mypage route programmatically
    $routes['mymodule.mypage'] = new Route(
        // Path definition
        'mypage',
        // Route defaults
        [
          '_controller' => '\Drupal\mymodule\Controller\
MyPageController::customPage',
          '_title' => 'My custom page',
        ],
        // Route requirements
        [
          '_permission' => 'access content',
        ]
    );
    return $routes;
  }
}
```

If a module provides a class that interacts with routes, the best practice is to place it in the Routing portion of the module's namespace. This helps you identify it's purpose.

The invoked method is expected to return an array of initiated Route objects. The Route class takes the following arguments:

- **Path**: This represents the route
- **Defaults**: This is an array of default values
- **Requirements**: This is an array of required validators
- **Options**: This is an array that can be passed and its used optionally

Altering existing routes

When Drupal's route system is rebuilt due to a module being enabled or caches being rebuilt, an event is fired that allows modules to alter routes defined statically in YAML or dynamically. This involves implementing an event subscriber by extending \Drupal\Core\Routing\ RouteSubscribeBase, which subscribes the RoutingEvents::ALTER event.

Create src/Routing/RouteSubscriber.php in your module. It will hold the route subscriber class:

```php
<?php

namespace Drupal\mymodule\Routing;

use Drupal\Core\Routing\RouteSubscriberBase;
use Symfony\Component\Routing\RouteCollection;

class RouteSubscriber extends RouteSubscriberBase {

  /**
   * {@inheritdoc}
   */
  public function alterRoutes(RouteCollection $collection) {
    // Change path of mymodule.mypage to use a hyphen
    if ($route = $collection->get('mymodule.mypage')) {
      $route->setPath('/my-page');
    }
  }

}
```

The preceding code extends `RouteSubscribeBase` and implements the `alterRoutes()` method. We make an attempt to load the `mymodule.mypage` route and, if it exists, we change it's path to `my-page`. Since objects are always passed by reference, we do not need to return a value.

For Drupal to recognize the subscriber, we need to describe it in the module's `services.yml` file. In the base directory of your module, create a `mymodule.services.yml` file and add the following code:

```
services:
  mymodule.route_subscriber:
    class: Drupal\mymodule\Routing\RouteSubscriber
    tags:
      - { name: event_subscriber }
```

This registers our route subscriber class as a service to the container so that Drupal can execute it when the event is fired.

See also

- ▸ Refer to the Symfony routing documentation at `http://symfony.com/doc/current/book/routing.html`
- ▸ *Chapter 10, The Entity API*
- ▸ Refer to access checking on routes community documentation at `https://www.drupal.org/node/2122195`

Defining permissions

In Drupal, there are roles and permissions used to define robust access control lists for users. Modules use permissions to check whether the current user has access to perform an action, view specific items, or other operations. Modules then define the permissions used so that Drupal is aware of them. Developers can then construct roles, which are made up of enabled permissions.

In this recipe, we will define a new permission to view custom pages defined in a module. The permission will be added to a custom route and restrict access to the route path to users who have a role containing the permission.

Getting ready

Create a new module like the one in the first recipe. We will refer to the module as `mymodule` throughout the recipe. Use your module's name as appropriate.

This recipe also modifies a route defined in the module. We will refer to this route as `mymodule.mypage`. Modify the appropriate path in your module's `routing.yml` file.

How to do it...

1. Permissions are stored in a `permissions.yml` file. Add a `mymodule.permissions.yml` to the base directory of your module.

2. First, we need to define the internal string used to identify this permission, such as `view mymodule pages`:

   ```
   view mymodule pages:
   ```

3. Each permission is a YAML array of data. We need to provide a `title` key that will be displayed on the permissions page:

   ```
   view mymodule pages:
     title: 'View my module pages'
   ```

4. Permissions have a `description` key to provide details of the permission on the permissions page:

   ```
   view mymodule pages:
     title: 'View my module pages'
     description: 'Allows users to view pages provided by My Module'
   ```

5. Save your `permissions.yml`, and edit the module's `routing.yml` to add the permission.

6. Modify the route's `requirements` key to have a `_permissions` key that is equal to the defined permission:

   ```
   mymodule.mypage:
     path: /mypage
     defaults:
       _controller: '\Drupal\mymodule\Controller\MyPageController::customPage'
       _title: 'My custom page'
     requirements:
       _permission: 'view mymodule pages'
   ```

7. Visit **Configuration** and then **Development** to rebuild Drupal's caches.

8. Visit **People** and then **Permissions** to add your permission to the authenticated user and anonymous user roles.

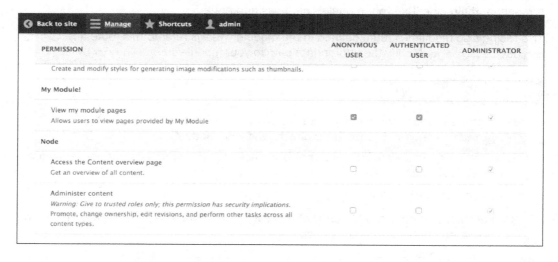

9. Log out of your Drupal site, and view the /mypage page. You will see the content and not receive an access denied page.

How it works...

Permissions and Roles are provided by the User module. The user.permissions service discovers permissions.yml defined in installed modules. By default, the service is defined through the \Drupal\user\PermissionHandler class.

Drupal does not save a list of all permissions that are available. The permissions for a system are loaded when the permissions page is loaded. Roles contain an array of permissions.

When checking a user's access for a permission, Drupal checks all of the user's roles to see whether they support that permission.

 You can pass an undefined permission to a user access check and not receive an error. The access check will simply fail, unless the user is UID 1, which bypasses access checks.

There's more...

Restrict access flag for permissions

Permissions can be flagged as having a security risk if enabled. This is the `restrict access` flag. When this flag is set to `restrict access: TRUE`, it will add a warning to the permission description.

This allows module developers to provide more context to the amount of control a permission may give a user:

PERMISSION	ANONYMOUS USER	AUTHENTICATED USER	ADMINISTRATOR
Administer content *Warning: Give to trusted roles only; this permission has security implications.* *Promote, change ownership, edit revisions, and perform other tasks across all* *content types.*	☐	☐	✓

Defining permissions programmatically

Permissions can be defined by a module programmatically or statically in a `YAML` file. A module needs to provide a `permission_callbacks` key in its `permissions.yml` that contains an array of classes and their methods or a procedural function name.

For example, the Filter module provides granular permissions based on the different text filters created in Drupal:

```
permission_callbacks:
 - Drupal\filter\FilterPermissions::permissions
```

This tells the `user_permissions` service to execute the permissions method of the `\Drupal\Filter\FilterPermissions` class. The method is expected to return an array that matches the same structure as that of the `permissions.yml` file.

 Dynamically defined permissions cannot use the restrict access flag and need to manually add the security warning to the description, just as `\Drupal\Filter\FilterPermissions` does.

Checking whether a user has permissions

The user account interface provides a method for checking whether a user entity has a permission. To check whether the current user has a permission, you will get the current user, and you need to invoke the `hasPermission` method:

```
\Drupal::currentUser()->hasPermission('my permission');
```

The `\Drupal::currentUser()` method returns the current active user object. This allows you to check whether the active user has permissions to perform some sort of actions.

Providing the configuration on installation or update

Drupal provides a configuration management system, which is discussed in *Chapter 9, Confiuration Management – Deploying in Drupal 8*, and modules are able to provide configuration on an installation or through an update system. Modules provide the configuration through YAML files when they are first installed. Once the module is enabled, the configuration is then placed in the configuration management system. Updates can be made to the configuration, however, in code through the Drupal update system.

In this recipe, we will provide configuration YAMLs that create a new contact form and then manipulate them through a schema version change in the update system.

Getting ready

Create a new module like the one in the first recipe. We will refer to the module as `mymodule` throughout the recipe. Use your module's appropriate name.

How to do it...

1. Create a `config` folder in your module's base directory. All configuration YAMLs should be in a subfolder of `config`.

2. Create a folder named install in the `config` folder. Configuration YAMLs in this folder will be imported on module installation.

3. In the install folder, create a `contact.form.contactus.yml` to store the YAML definition of the contact form, **Contact Us**:

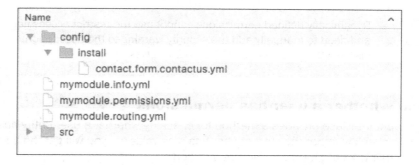

4. We will define the configuration of a contact form based on the `contact.schema.yml` file provided by the Contact module:

```
langcode: en
status: true
dependences: {}
id: contactus
label: 'Contact Us'
recipients:
  - webmaster@example.com
reply: ''
weight: 0
```

The configuration entry is based on a schema definition, which we will cover in *Chapter 9, Confiuration Management – Deploying in Drupal 8*. The langcode, status, and dependencies are the required configuration management keys.

The `id` is the contact form's machine name and the label is the human display name. The `recipients` key is a YAML array of valid e-mail addresses. The reply key is a string of text for the **Auto-reply** field. And, finally, the weight defines the form's weight in the administrative list.

5. Visit **Extend** and enable your module to import the configuration item.

6. The **Contact Us** form will now be located on the **Contact** forms overview page, located under `Structure`:

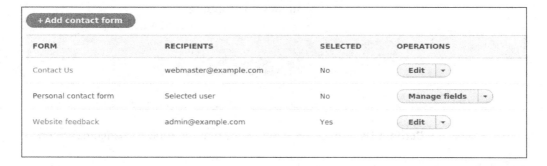

7. Create a `mymodule.install` file in the module's base directory. We will create an update hook to set a reply message for the contact form.

8. We will create a function called `mymodule_update_8001()` that will be read by the update system and make our configuration changes:

```php
<?php

/**
 * Update "Contact Us" form to have a reply message.
```

```
 */
function mymodule_update_8001() {
  $contact_form = \Drupal\contact\Entity\
ContactForm::load('contact_us');
  $contact_form->setReply(t('Thank you for contacting us, we will
reply shortly'));
  $contact_form->save();
}
```

This function uses the entity's class to load our configuration entity object. It loads `contact_us`, which our module has provided, and sets the reply property to a new value.

9. Visit `/update.php` in your browser to run the Drupal's database update system:

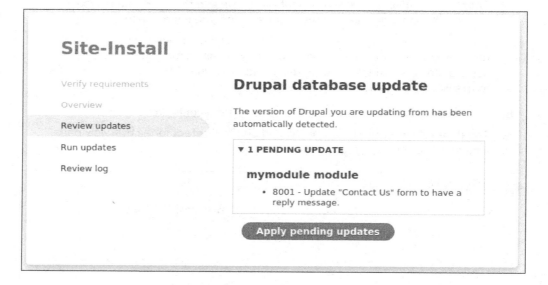

10. Review the **Contact Us** form settings and verify that the reply message has been set.

How it works...

Drupal's `moduler_installer` service, provided through `\Drupal\Core\Extension\ModuleInstaller`, ensures that configuration items defined in the module's `config` folder are processed on installation. When a module is installed, the `config.installer` service, provided through `\Drupal\Core\Config\ConfigInstaller`, is called to process the module's default configuration.

In the event, the `config.installer` service makes an attempt to import the configuration from the `install` folder that already exists and an exception will be thrown. Modules cannot provide changes made to the existing configuration through static YAML definitions.

Since modules cannot adjust configuration objects through static YAML definitions provided to Drupal, modules can utilize the database update system to modify the configuration. Drupal utilizes a schema version for modules. The base schema version for a module is `8000`. Modules can provide update hooks in the form of `hook_update_N`, where N represents the next schema version. When Drupal's updates are run, they will execute the proper update hooks and update the module's schema version.

Configuration objects are immutable by default. In order to edit a configuration, a mutable object needs to be loaded through the configuration factory service.

There's more...

We will discuss the configuration in _Chapter 9, Confiuration Management – Deploying in Drupal 8_, however, we will now dive into some important notes when working with modules and configurations.

Configuration subdirectories

There are three directories that the configuration management system will inspect in a module's `config` folder, which are as follows:

- `install`
- `optional`
- `schema`

The `install` folder specifies the configuration that will be imported. If the configuration object exists, the installation will fail.

The `optional` folder contains the configuration that will be installed if the following conditions are met:

- The configuration does not already exist
- It is a configuration entity
- Its dependencies can be met

If any one of the conditions fail, the configuration will not be installed, but it will not halt the module's installation process.

The `schema` folder provides definitions of configuration object definitions. This uses YAML definitions to structure configuration objects and is covered in depth in _Chapter 9, Configuration Management_.

Modifying the existing configuration on installation

The configuration management system does not allow modules to provide configuration on an installation that already exists. For example, if a module tries to provide `system.site` and defines the site's name, it would fail to install. This is because the System module provides this configuration object on installation.

Drupal provides `hook_install()` that modules can implement in their `.install` file. This hook is executed during the module's installation process. The following code will update the site's title to *Drupal 8 Cookbook*! on the module's installation:

```
/**
 * Implements hook_install().
 */
function mymodule_install() {
  // Set the site name.
  \Drupal::configFactory()
    ->getEditable('system.site')
    ->set('name', 'Drupal 8 Cookbook!')
    ->save();
}
```

Configurable objects are immutable by default when loaded by the default `config` service. In order to modify a configuration object, you need to use the configuration factory to receive a mutable object. The mutable object can have set and `save` methods that are executed to update the configuration in a configuration object.

See also

▸   *Chapter 9, Confiuration Management – Deploying in Drupal 8*

Using Features 2.x

Many Drupal users create custom modules to provide specific sets of features that they can reuse across multiple sites. In fact, there is a module for the sole purpose of providing a means to export configuration and create modules that provide features. This is how the Features modules received its name, in fact.

The Features module has two sub-modules. The main Features module provides all the functionalities. The Features UI module provides a user interface for creating and managing features.

We will use Features to export a module with a configuration that contains the default page and article content types provided by the standard installation, so they can be used on other installation profiles.

How to do it...

1. The Features module requires **Configuration Update Manager** as a dependency. Visit `https://www.drupal.org/project/config_update` and download the latest Drupal 8 release and place it in your Drupal site's `/modules` folder.

2. Now, visit `https://www.drupal.org/project/features` and download the latest Drupal 8 release and place it in your Drupal site's `/modules` folder.

3. Visit **Extend** and install the Features UI module, confirming the requirements to install Features and Configuration Update Manager as well.

4. Visit **Configuration** and then **Configuration Synchronization**. The user interface for **Features** is accessed as a tab from this page:

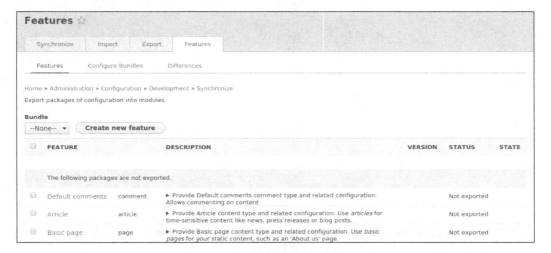

5. Click on **Create new feature** to start making a custom Feature module.

6. Provide a `Name` for the feature, such as **Content Authoring**.

7. Optionally, you can provide a description. This acts as the `description` key in the module's `info.yml`.

8. Toggle the **Content types** grouping and check **Article** and **Basic Page** to mark them for export.

9. The features module will automatically add detected dependencies or important configuration items to also be exported, such as fields and view modes.

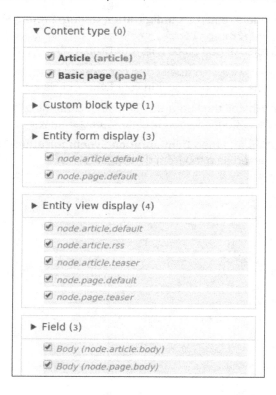

10. Click on **Write** to write the module to export the module and configuration to the / `modules/custom` directory in your Drupal site.

11. Visit **Extend** to enable your newly created module.

How it works...

Features exports static YAML configuration files into the module's `config/install` folder. Features modifies the standard configuration management workflow by ensuring that a specific kind of configuration exists. Configuration management does not allow modules to overwrite existing configuration objects but Features manages and allows this to happen.

To accomplish this, Features provides `\Drupal\features\FeaturesConfigInstaller`, which extends the default `config.install` service class. It then alters the services definition to use it's `FeaturesConfigInstaller` class instead of the default `\Drupal\Core\Config\ConfigInstaller` class.

Beyond adjusting the `config.install` service, Features harnesses all the functionalities of the configuration management system to provide a simpler way to generate modules.

 Any module can be considered a Feature's module by adding the `features: true` key to it's `info.yml`. This will allow it to be managed through the Features UI.

There's more...

Suggested feature modules

The features module provides an intelligent bundling method that reviews the current Drupal site's configuration and suggests feature modules that should be created to preserve the configuration. These are provided through package assignment plugins. These plugins use logic to assign configurations to specific packages.

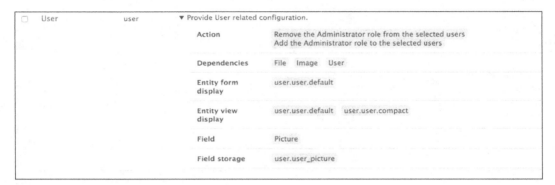

When you visit the Features UI, it will present you with suggested feature modules to be exported. Expanding the items will list the configuration items that will be bundled. Clicking on the suggested feature's link opens the creation form. Or the checkbox can be used in conjunction with the `download archive` or `write` buttons at the bottom of the form.

 The unpackaged section shows a configuration, which has not met any of the packaging rules to group the configuration into a specified module. This will need to be manually added to a created feature module.

Features bundles

In the Features module, there are bundles and bundles have their own assignment method configurations. The purpose of bundles inside Features is to provide an automatic assignment of configuration that can be grouped into exported modules:

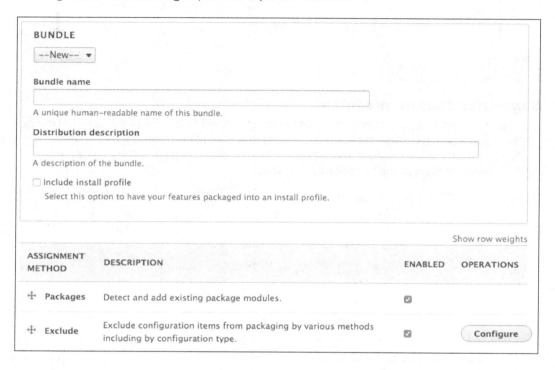

A bundle has a human display name and machine name. The bundle's machine name will be prefixed on all feature modules generated under this bundle. You also have the ability to specify the bundle to act as an install profile. Features UI was heavily used in Drupal 7 to construct distributions and spawn the concept of the bundle functionality.

Assignment methods can be rearranged and configured to your liking.

Managing the configuration state of Features

The Features UI provides a means to review changes to the feature's configuration that may have been made. If a configuration item controlled by a Feature module has been modified, it will show up under the differences section of the Features UI. This will allow you to import or update the Feature module with the change.

The `Import` option will force the site to use the configuration defined in the module's configuration `YAML` files. For example, we have an exported content type whose description was modified in the user interface after being exported.

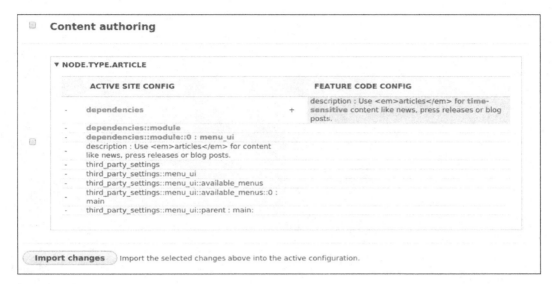

The difference created by the Feature module is highlighted. If the difference was checked, and if you click on **Import changes**, the content type's description would be reset to that defined in the configuration.

From the main features overview table, the Feature module can be reexported to include the change and update the exported YAML files.

See also

> ► Refer to Features for the Drupal 8 session by Mike Potter at DrupalCon Los Angeles at https://events.drupal.org/losangeles2015/sessions/features-drupal-8

5
Frontend for the Win

In this chapter, we will explore the world of frontend development in Drupal 8:

- ▶ Creating a custom theme based on Classy
- ▶ Using the new asset management system
- ▶ Twig templating
- ▶ Using the Breakpoint module
- ▶ Using the Responsive Image module module

Introduction

Drupal 8 brings many changes with regard to the frontend. It is now focused on the mobile-first responsive design. Frontend performance has been given a high priority, unlike in the previous versions of Drupal. There is a new asset management system based around libraries that will deliver only the minimum required assets for a page that comes with Drupal 8.

In Drupal 8, we have a new feature, the Twig templating engine, that replaces the previously used PHPTemplate engine. Twig is part of the large PHP community and embraces more of Drupal 8's *made elsewhere* initiative. Drupal 7 supported libraries to define JavaScript and CSS resources. However, it was very rudimentary and did not support the concept of library dependencies.

There are two modules provided by Drupal core that implement the responsive design with server-side components. The Breakpoint module provides a representation of media queries that modules can utilize. The Responsive Image module implements the HTML5 picture tag for image fields.

This chapter dives into harnessing Drupal 8's frontend features to get the most out of them.

Creating a custom theme based on Classy

Drupal 8 ships with a new base theme that is intended to demonstrate the best practice and CSS class management. The Classy theme is provided by Drupal core and is the base theme for the default frontend theme, Bartik, and the administrative theme, Seven.

Unlike the previous versions of Drupal, Drupal 8 provides two base themes: Classy and Stable as a means to jump start Drupal theming. Stable provides a more lean approach to frontend theming with fewer classes and wrapping elements. In this recipe, we will create a new theme called `mytheme` that uses Classy as its base.

How to do it...

1. In the `root` directory of your Drupal site, create a folder called `mytheme` in the `themes` folder.

2. Inside the `mytheme` folder, create a `mytheme.info.yml` file so that Drupal can discover the `theme`. We will then edit this file:

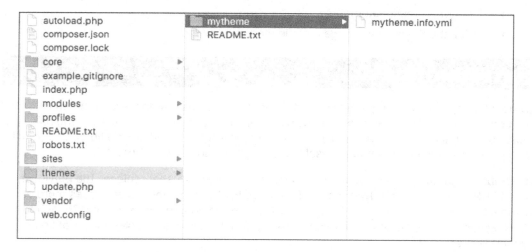

3. First, we need to define the `themes` name using the `name` key:

```
name: My Theme
```

4. All the themes need to provide a `description` key, which will be displayed on the **Appearance** page:

```
description: My custom theme
```

5. Next, we need to define the type of extension, that is, a theme, and the version of core that is supported:

```
type: theme
core: 8.x
```

6. The `base theme` call allows us to instruct Drupal to use a specific theme as a base:

```
base theme: classy
```

7. The last item is a `regions` key that is used to define the regions of the blocks that can be placed, which is a YAML-based array of key/value pairs:

```
regions:
  header: Header
  primary_menu: 'Primary menu'
  page_top: 'Page top'
  page_bottom: 'Page bottom'
  breadcrumb: Breadcrumb
  content: Content
```

8. Regions are rendered in the page `template` file, which will be covered in the next recipe, Twig templates.

9. Log in to your Drupal site, and go to **Appearance** from the administrative toolbar.

10. Click on **Install and set default** in the **My theme** entry in order to enable and use the new custom theme:

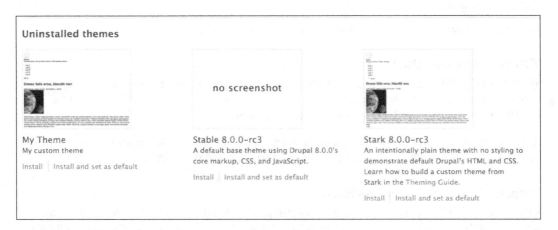

How it works...

In Drupal 8, the `info.yml` files define Drupal themes and modules. The first step to create a theme is to provide the `info.yml` file so that the theme can be discovered. Drupal will parse these values and register the theme.

The following keys are required, as a minimum, when you define a theme:

- `name`
- `description`
- `type`
- `base theme`
- `core`

The `name` key defines the human-readable name of the theme that will be displayed on the **Appearance** page. The `description` will be shown under the `themes` display name on the **Appearance** page. All Drupal projects need to define the `type` key to indicate the kind of extension that is being defined. For themes, the type must always be `theme`. You need to also define which version of Drupal the project is compatible with using the core value. All Drupal 8 projects will use the `core: 8.x` value. When you define a theme, you need to also provide the base `theme` key. If your theme does not use a base theme, then you need to set the value to `false`.

The `libraries` and `region` keys are optional, but these are keys that most themes provide. Drupal's asset management system parses a theme's `info.yml` and adds those libraries, if required. Regions are defined in an `info.yml` file and provide the areas into which the Block module may place blocks.

There's more...

Next, we will dive into some additional information about themes.

Theme screenshots

Themes can provide a screenshot that shows up on the **Appearance** page. A theme's screenshot can be provided by placing a `screenshot.png` in the `theme` folder or a file specified in the `info.yml` file under the screenshot key.

If the screenshot is missing, a `default` is used, as seen with the Classy and Stark themes. Generally, a screenshot is a Drupal site with generic content using the theme.

Themes, logos, and favicons

Drupal controls the site's favicon and logo settings as a theme setting. Theme settings are active on a theme-by-theme basis and are not global. Themes have the ability to provide a default logo by providing a `logo.svg` in the `theme` root folder. A `favicon.ico` placed in a `theme` folder will also be the default value of the `favicon` for the website.

Currently, there is no way to specify a logo of a different file type for a theme. Previous versions of Drupal looked for `logo.png`. A feature has been postponed for Drupal 8.1 to allow the `themes` to have the ability to define the logo's filename and extension. Refer to the core issue for more information at `https://www.drupal.org/node/1507896`.

You can change the site's logo and favicon by going to **Appearance** and then clicking on **Settings** for your current theme. Unchecking the `use default` checkboxes for the favicon and logo settings allows you to provide custom files.

▼ LOGO IMAGE SETTINGS

☐ Use the default logo supplied by the theme

Path to custom logo

[   ]

Examples: `logo.svg` (for a file in the public filesystem), `public://logo.svg`, or `core/themes/seven/logo.svg`.

Upload logo image

[Choose File] No file chosen

If you don't have direct file access to the server, use this field to upload your logo.

▼ SHORTCUT ICON SETTINGS

Your shortcut icon, or 'favicon', is displayed in the address bar and bookmarks of most browsers.

☐ Use the default shortcut icon supplied by the theme

Path to custom icon

[   ]

Examples: `favicon.ico` (for a file in the public filesystem), `public://favicon.ico`, or `core/themes/seven/favicon.ico`.

Upload icon image

[Choose File] No file chosen

If you don't have direct file access to the server, use this field to upload your shortcut icon.

Base themes and shared resources

Many content management systems that have a theme system support base (or parent) themes differ mostly in the terminology used. The concept of a base theme is used to provide established resources that are shared, reducing the amount of work required to create a new theme.

All libraries defined in the base theme will be inherited and used by default, allowing subthemes to reuse existing styles and JavaScript. This allows frontend developers to reuse work and only create specific changes that are required for the subtheme.

The `Subthemes` will also inherit all Twig template overrides provided by the base theme. This was one of the initiatives used for the creation of the Classy theme. Drupal 8 makes many fewer assumptions compared to previous version as to what class names to provide on elements. Classy overrides all of the core's templates and provides sensible default classes, giving themes the ability to use them and accept those class names or be given a blank slate.

CKEditor stylesheets

As discussed in *Chapter 2*, *The Content Authoring Experience*, Drupal ships with the WYSIWYG support and CKEditor as the default editor. The CKEditor module will inspect the active theme, and its base theme if provided, and loads any stylesheets defined in the `ckeditor_stylesheets` key as an array of values.

For example, the following code can be found in `bartik.info.yml`:

```
ckeditor_stylesheets:
  - css/base/elements.css
  - css/components/captions.css
  - css/components/table.css
```

This allows themes to provide style sheets that will style elements within the CKEditor module to enhance the *what you see is what you get* element of the editor.

See also

▸ To define a theme with an `info.yml` file, refer to https://www.drupal.org/node/2349827

▸ To use Classy as a base theme, refer to the community documentation at https://www.drupal.org/theme-guide/8/classy

▸ To create a Drupal 8 subtheme, refer to the community documentation at https://www.drupal.org/node/2165673

Using the new asset management system

New to Drupal 8 is the asset management system. The asset management system allows modules and themes to register libraries. Libraries define CSS stylesheets and JavaScript files that need to be loaded with the page. Drupal 8 takes this approach for the frontend performance. Rather than loading all CSS or JavaScript assets, only those required for the current page in the specified libraries will be loaded.

In this recipe, we will define a `libraries.yml` file that will define a CSS stylesheet and JavaScript file provided by a custom theme.

Getting ready

This recipe assumes that you have a custom theme created, such as the one you created in the first recipe. When you see `mytheme`, use the machine name of the theme that you have created.

How to do it...

1. Create a folder named `css` in your `themes` base directory.

2. In your `css` folder, add a `style.css` file that will hold the theme's CSS declarations. For demonstration purposes, add the following CSS declaration to `style.css`:

```css
body {
    background: cornflowerblue;
}
```

3. Then, create a `js` folder, and add a `scripts.js` file that will hold the `themes` JavaScript items.

4. In your theme folder, create a `mytheme.libraries.yml` file and edit it, as shown in the following screenshot:

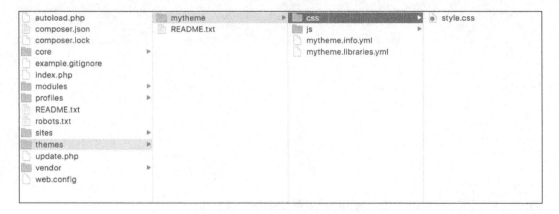

5. Add the following `YAML` text to define the `global-styling` library for your theme that will load the CSS file and JavaScript file:

```yaml
global-styling:
  version: VERSION
  css:
    theme:
      css/style.css: {}
  js:
    js/scripts.js: {}
```

6. This tells Drupal that there is a `global-styling` library. You have the ability to specify a library version and use the VERSION defaults for your themes. It also defines the `css/styles.css` stylesheet as part of the library under the `theme` group.

7. Edit your `mytheme.info.yml`, and we need to add the declaration to our `global-styling` library:

```
libraries:
    - mytheme/global-styling
```

8. Themes are able to specify a `libraries` key that defines the libraries that should always be loaded. This YAML array lists libraries to be loaded for each page.

9. Go to **Configuration** and then to **Development** to rebuild Drupal's caches.

10. With your theme set to the default, go to your Drupal site.

11. Your theme's `global-styling` library will be loaded and the page's background color will be styled appropriately:

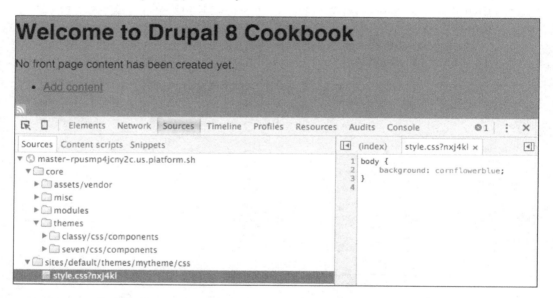

How it works...

Drupal aggregates all the available `library.yml` files and passes them to the `library.discovery.parser` service. The `default` class for this service provider is `\Drupal\Core\Asset\LibraryDiscoveryParser`. This service reads the library definition from each `library.yml` and returns its value to the system. Before parsing the file, the parser allows themes to provide overrides and extensions to the library.

Libraries are enqueuers as they are attached to rendered elements. Themes have the ability to generically add libraries through their `info.yml` files via the `libraries` key. These libraries will always be loaded on the page when the theme is active.

CSS stylesheets are added to the data, which will build the head tag of the page. JavaScript resources, by default, are rendered in the footer of the page for performance reasons.

There's more...

We will explore the options surrounding libraries in Drupal 8 in more detail.

CSS groups

With libraries, you have the ability to specify CSS by different groups. Drupal's asset management system provides the following CSS groups:

- `base`
- `layout`
- `component`
- `state`
- `theme`

Stylesheets are loaded in the order in which the groups are listed. Each one of them relates to a PHP constant defined in `/core/includes/common.inc`. This allows separation of concerns when working with stylesheets. Drupal 8's CSS architecture borrows concepts from the SMACSS system to organize CSS declarations.

Library asset options

Library assets can have configuration data attached to them. If there are no configuration items provided, a simple set of empty brackets is added. This is why, in each example, files end with `{}`.

The following example, taken from `core.libraries.yml`, adds HTML5shiv:

```
assets/vendor/html5shiv/html5shiv.min.js: { weight: -22, browsers: {
IE: 'lte IE 8', '!IE': false }, minified: true }
```

Let's take a look at the attributes of `html5shiv.min.js`:

- The `weight` key ensures that the script is rendered earlier than other libraries
- The `browser` tag allows you to specify conditional rules to load the scripting
- You should always pass `minified` as `true` if the asset has already been minified

For CSS assets, you can pass a media option to specify a media query for the asset. Reviewing classes which implement `\Drupal\Core\Asset\AssetCollectionRendererInterface`.

Library dependencies

Libraries have the ability to specify other libraries as dependencies. This allows Drupal to provide a minimum footprint on the frontend performance.

 jQuery is only loaded if a JavaScript library specifies it as a dependency. Refer to `https://www.drupal.org/node/1541860`.

Here's an example from the Quick Edit module's `libraries.yml` file:

```
quickedit:
  version: VERSION
  js:
    ...
  css:
    ...
  dependencies:
    - core/jquery
    - core/jquery.once
    - core/underscore
    - core/backbone
    - core/jquery.form
    - core/jquery.ui.position
    - core/drupal
    - core/drupal.displace
    - core/drupal.form
    - core/drupal.ajax
    - core/drupal.debounce
    - core/drupalSettings
  - core/drupal.dialog
```

The Quick Edit module defines jQuery, the jQuery Once plugin, Underscore, and Backbone, and selects other defined libraries as dependencies. Drupal will ensure that these are present whenever the `quickedit/quickedit` library is attached to a page.

A complete list of the default libraries provided by Drupal core can be found in `core.libraries.yml`, which is in `core/core.libraries.yml`.

Overriding and extending other libraries

Themes have the ability to override libraries using the `libraries-override` and `libraries-extend` keys in their `info.yml`. This allows themes to easily customize the existing libraries without having to add the logic for conditionally removing or adding their assets when a particular library has been attached to a page.

The `libraries-override` key can be used to replace an entire library, replace selected files in a library, remove an asset from a library, or disable an entire library. The following code will allow a theme to provide a custom jQuery UI theme:

```
libraries-override:
  core/jquery.ui:
    css:
      component:
        assets/vendor/jquery.ui/themes/base/core.css: false
      theme:
        assets/vendor/jquery.ui/themes/base/theme.css: css/jqueryui.
css
```

The override declaration mimics the original configuration. Specifying `false` will remove the asset or else a supplied path will replace that asset.

The `libraries-extend` key can be used to load additional libraries with an existing library. The following code will allow a theme to associate a CSS stylesheet with selected jQuery UI declaration overrides, without always having them included in the rest of the theme's assets:

```
libraries-extend:
  core/jquery.ui:
- mytheme/jqueryui-theme
```

Using a CDN or external resource as a library

Libraries also work with external resources, such as assets loaded over a CDN. This is done by providing a URL for the file location along with selected file parameters.

Here is an example to add the `FontAwesome` font icon library from the `BootstrapCDN` provided by MaxCDN:

```
mytheme.fontawesome:
  remote: http://fontawesome.io/
  version: 4.4.0
  license:
    name: SIL OFL 1.1
    url: http://fontawesome.io/license/
    gpl-compatible: true
  css:
    base:
      https://maxcdn.bootstrapcdn.com/font-awesome/4.4.0/css/font-
awesome.min.css: { type: external, minified: true }
```

Remote libraries require additional meta information to work properly:

```
remote: http://fontawesome.io/
```

The `remote` key describes the library as using external resources. While this key is not validated beyond its existence, it is best to define it with the external resource's primary website:

```
version: 4.4.0
```

Like all libraries, a version is required. This should match the version of the external resource being added:

```
license:
  name: SIL OFL 1.1
  url: http://fontawesome.io/license/
  gpl-compatible: true
```

If a library defines the `remote` key, it needs to also define the `license` key. This defines the license name, the URL for the license, and checks whether it is GPL compatible. If this key is not provided, a `\Drupal\Core\Asset\Extension\LibraryDefinitionMissingLicenseException` will be thrown:

```
css:
  base:
      https://maxcdn.bootstrapcdn.com/font-awesome/4.4.0/css/font-
  awesome.min.css: { type: external, minified: true }
```

Finally, specific external resources are added as normal. Instead of providing a relative file path, the external URL is provided.

Manipulating libraries from hooks

Modules have the ability to provide dynamic library definitions and alter libraries. A module can use the `hook_library_info()` hook to provide a library definition. This is not the recommended way to define a library, but it is provided for edge use cases.

Modules do not have the ability to use `libraries-override` or `libraries-extend`, and need to rely on the `hook_library_info_alter()` hook. The hook is documented in `core/lib/Drupal/Core/Render/theme.api.php` or at `https://api.drupal.org/api/drupal/core!lib!Drupal!Core!Render!theme.api.php/function/hook_library_info_alter/8`.

Placing JavaScript in the header

By default, Drupal ensures that JavaScript is placed last on the page. This improves the page, load performance by allowing the critical portions of the page to load first. Placing JavaScript in the header is now an opt-in option.

In order to render a library in the header, you need to add the `header: true` key/value pair:

```
js-library:
  header: true
```

```
js:
   js/myscripts.js: {}
```

This will load a custom JavaScript library and its dependencies into the header of a page.

See also

▸ Refer to the CSS architecture for Drupal 8: Separate concerns at
   `https://www.drupal.org/node/1887918#separate-concerns`

▸ SMACSS(`http://smacss.com/book/`)

Twig templating

Drupal 8's theming layer is complemented by Twig, a component of the Symfony framework. Twig is a template language that uses a syntax similar to Django and Jinja templates. The previous version of Drupal used PHPTemplate that required frontend developers to have a rudimentary understanding of PHP.

In this recipe, we will override the Twig template to provide customizations for the e-mail form element. We will use the basic Twig syntax to add a new class and provide a default placeholder.

Getting ready

This recipe assumes that you have a custom theme created, such as the one you created in the first recipe. When you see `mytheme`, use the machine name of the theme you created.

 At the time of writing this book, the Classy theme does not provide a template suggestion for the e-mail input nor any customizations to the input template that differ from core.

How to do it...

1. Create a `template` folder in your theme's base directory to hold your Twig templates.

2. To begin, you need to copy the `input.html.twig` file from `core/modules/system/templates/input.html.twig` to your theme's `template` folder.

3. Rename the `input.html.twig` file to `input--email.html.twig` in order to use the proper theme hook suggestion, as shown in the following screenshot:

4. We will use the `addClass` `twig` function to add an `input__email` class:

```
<input{{ attributes.addClass('input__email') }}/>{{ children }}
```

5. Above the previous line, we will create a Twig variable using ternary operators to provide a customer placeholder:

```
{% set placeholder = attributes.placeholder ? attributes.
placeholder : 'email@example.com' %}
```

This creates a new variable called `placeholder` using the set operator. The question mark (?) operator checks whether the `placeholder` property is empty in the `attributes` object. If it is not empty, it uses the existing value. If the value is empty, it provides a default value.

6. Go to the **Configuration** tab and then to **Development** to rebuild Drupal's cache. We need to do this because Drupal caches the generated Twig output. Any changes made to a Twig template require a cache rebuild.

7. View an `email` field or `form` element and find the modification:

```
<!-- END OUTPUT from 'core/themes/classy/templates/form/form-element-label.html.twig' -->
<!-- THEME DEBUG -->
<!-- THEME HOOK: 'input__email' -->
<!-- FILE NAME SUGGESTIONS:
   x input--email.html.twig
   x input--email.html.twig
   * input.html.twig
-->
<!-- BEGIN OUTPUT from 'sites/default/themes/mytheme/templates/input--email.html.twig' -->
<input data-drupal-selector="edit-field-email-0-value" type="email" id="edit-field-email-0-value" name="field_email[0]
[value]" value size="60" maxlength="254" placeholder="email@example.com" class="form-email input__email">
<!-- END OUTPUT from 'sites/default/themes/mytheme/templates/input--email.html.twig' -->
```

How it works...

Drupal's theme system is built around hooks and hook suggestions. The element definition of the e-mail input element defines the `input__email` theme hook. If there is no `input__email` hook implemented through a Twig template or PHP function, it will step down to just input.

 Drupal theme hooks are defined with underscores (_) but use hyphens (-) when used in Twig template files.

A processor, such as Drupal's theme layer, passes variables to Twig. Variables or properties of objects can be printed by wrapping the variable name with curly brackets. All of core's default templates provide information in the file's document block that details the available Twig variables.

Twig has a simplistic syntax with basic logic and functions. The `addClass` method will take the `attributes` variable and add the class provided in addition to the existing contents.

When providing a theme hook suggestion or altering an existing template, you will need to rebuild Drupal's cache. The compiled Twig template, as PHP, is cached by Drupal so that Twig does not need to compile each time the template is invoked.

There's more...

Security first

Twig automatically escapes the output by default, making Drupal 8 one of the most secure versions yet. For Drupal 7, as a whole, most security advisors were for **cross-site scripting** (**XSS**) vulnerabilities in contributed projects. With Drupal core, using Twig, these security advisories should be severely reduced.

Theme hook suggestions

Drupal utilizes theme hook suggestions as ways to allow output variations based on different conditions. It allows site themes to provide a more specific template for certain instances.

When a theme hook has double underscores (__), Drupal's theme system understands this, and it can break apart the theme hook to find a more generic template. For instance, the e-mail element definition provides `input__email` as its theme hook. Drupal understands this as follows:

- ▸ Look for a Twig template named `input--email.html.twig` or a theme hook that defines `input__email`

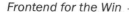

> ▸ If you are not satisfied, look for a Twig template named `input.html.twig` or a theme hook that defines the input

Theme hook suggestions can be provided by the `hook_theme_suggestions()` hook in a `.module` or `.theme` file.

Debugging template file selection and hook suggestions

Debugging can be enabled to inspect the various template files that make up a page and their theme hook suggestions, and check which are active. This can be accomplished by editing the `sites/default/services.yml` file. If a `services.yml` file does not exist, copy the `default.services.yml` to create one.

You need to change `debug: false` to `debug: true` under the `twig.config` section of the file. This will cause the Drupal theming layer to print out the source code comments containing the template information. When debug is on, Drupal will not cache the compiled versions of Twig templates and render them on the fly.

There is another setting that prevents you from having to rebuild Drupal's cache on each template file change, but do not leave debug enabled. The `twig.config.auto_reload` boolean can be set to `true`. If this is set to `true`, the Twig templates will be recompiled if the source code changes.

The Twig logic and operators

The Twig has ternary operators for logic. Using a question mark (`?`), we can perform a basic *is true or not empty* operation, whereas a question mark and colon (`? :`) performs a basic *is false or is empty* operation.

You may also use the `if` and `else` logic to provide different outputs based on variables.

See also

> ▸ Refer to the Twig documentation at `http://twig.sensiolabs.org/documentation`
>
> ▸ Refer to the API documentation for `hook_theme_suggestions` at `https://api.drupal.org/api/drupal/core%21lib%21Drupal%21Core%21Render%21theme.api.php/function/hook_theme_suggestions_HOOK/8`

Using the Breakpoint module

The Breakpoint module provides a method for creating media query breakpoint definitions within Drupal. These can be used by other components, such as the responsive image and toolbar modules, to make Drupal responsive.

Breakpoints are a type of plugin that can be defined in a module's or theme's `breakpoints.yml` in its directory. In this recipe, we will define three different breakpoints under a custom group.

 Breakpoints are defined solely in YAML files from installed modules and themes and are not configurable through the user interface.

Getting ready

Ensure that the Breakpoint module is enabled. If you have used the standard Drupal installation, the module is enabled.

This recipe assumes that you have a custom module created. When you see `mymodule`, use the machine name of the module that you created.

How to do it...

1. Create `mymodule.breakpoints.yml` in your module's base directory. This file will hold the breakpoint configurations.

2. Firstly, we will add a standard mobile breakpoint that does not have a media query, following mobile first practices:

```
mymodule.mobile:
  label: Mobile
  mediaQuery: ''
  weight: 0
```

3. Secondly, we will create a standard breakpoint that will run on a larger viewport:

```
mymodule.standard:
  label: Standard
  mediaQuery: 'only screen and (min-width: 60em)'
  weight: 1
```

4. Thirdly, we will create a wide breakpoint for devices that have a large viewport:

```
mymodule.wide:
  label: Wide
```

```
        mediaQuery: 'only screen and (min-width: 70em)'
        weight: 2
```

5. Go to the **Configuration** tab and then to **Development** to rebuild Drupal's cache and make the system aware of the new breakpoints.

How it works...

The Breakpoint module defines the breakpoint configuration entity. Breakpoints do not have any specific form of direct functionalities beyond providing a way to save media queries and grouping them.

The Breakpoint module provides a default manager service. This service is used by other modules to discover breakpoint groups and then all of the breakpoints within a group.

There's more...

Caveat for providing breakpoints from themes

Themes have the ability to provide breakpoints; however, they cannot be automatically discovered if new ones are added once they have been installed. Drupal only reads breakpoints provided by themes when a theme is either installed or uninstalled.

Inside `breakpoint.manager`, there are two hooks: one for the `theme install` and one for the `theme uninstall`. Each hook retrieves the breakpoint manager service and rebuilds the breakpoint definitions. Without any extra deployment steps, new breakpoints added to a theme will not be discovered unless these hooks are fired.

Accessing breakpoints programmatically

Breakpoints are utility configurations for other modules. Breakpoints can be loaded by using the breakpoint manager service and specifying a group. For example, the following code returns all breakpoints used by the Toolbar module:

```
\Drupal::service('breakpoint.manager')
    getBreakpointsByGroup('toolbar');
```

This code invokes the Drupal container to return the service to manage breakpoints, which, by default, is `\Drupal\breakpoint\BreakpointManager`. The `getBreakpointsByGroup` method returns all breakpoints within a group, which are initiated as the `\Drupal\breakpoint\BreakpointInterface` objects.

The Toolbar element class utilizes this workflow to push the breakpoint media query values as JavaScript settings for the JavaScript model to interact with.

Multipliers

The multipliers value is used to support pixel resolution multipliers. This multiplier is used in coordination with *retina* displays. It is a measure of the viewport's device resolution as a ratio of the device's physical size and independent pixel size. The following is an example of standard multipliers:

- ▶ 1x is normal
- ▶ 1.5x supports Android
- ▶ 2x supports Mac retina devices

See also

- ▶ To work with breakpoints in Drupal 8, refer to the community documentation at `https://www.drupal.org/documentation/modules/breakpoint`

Using the Responsive Image module

The Responsive Image module provides a field formatter for image fields that use the HTML5 picture tag and source sets. Utilizing the Breakpoint module, mappings to breakpoints are made to denote an image style to be used at each breakpoint.

The responsive image field formatter works with using a defined responsive image style. Responsive image styles are configurations that map image formats to specific breakpoints and modifiers. First, you need to define a responsive image style, and then you can apply it to an image field.

In this recipe, we will create a responsive image style set called `Article image` and apply it to the `Article` content type's image field.

Getting ready

You will need to enable the `Responsive Image` module as it is not automatically enabled with the standard installation.

How to do it...

1. Go to **Configuration** and then to **Responsive image styles** under the **Media** section. Click on **Add responsive image style** to begin creating a new style set.

2. Provide a `label` that will be used to administratively identify the **Responsive image style** set.

3. Select a breakpoint group that will be used as a source of breakpoints to define the image style map.

4. Each breakpoint will have a `fieldset`. Expand the `fieldset` and **select a single image style**, and then, pick an appropriate image style:

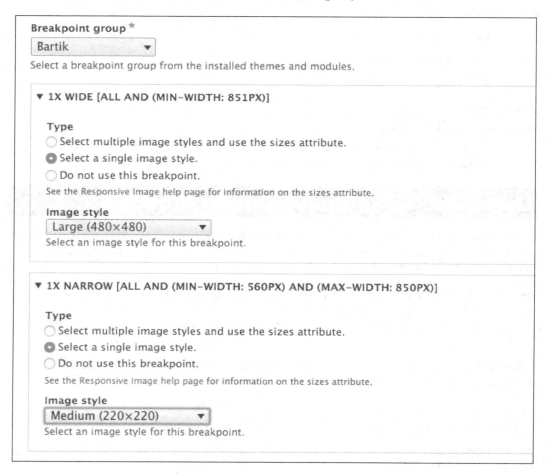

5. Additionally, choose a fallback image style in the event of a browser that doesn't support source sets, such as Internet Explorer 8.

6. Click on **Save** to save the configuration, and add the new style set:

7. Go to **Structure** and **Content types**, and select **Manage Display** from the **Article** content type's drop-down menu.

8. Change the **Image** field's formatter to **Responsive image**.

9. Click on the **Settings** tab of the field formatter to choose your new **Responsive image style** set. Select **Article image** from the **Responsive image style** dropdown:

10. Click on **Update** to save the field formatter settings, and then click on **Save** to save the field display settings.

How it works...

The **Responsive image style** provides three components: a responsive image element, the responsive image style configuration entity, and the responsive image field formatter. The configuration entity is consumed by the field formatter and displayed through the responsive image element.

The responsive image style entity contains an array of breakpoints to image style mappings. The available breakpoints are defined by the selected breakpoint groups. Breakpoint groups can be changed anytime; however, the previous mappings will be lost.

The responsive image element prints a `picture` element with each breakpoint defining a new `source` element. The breakpoint's media query value is provided as the `media` attribute for the element.

 For Internet Explorer 9, Drupal 8 ships with the `picturefill` `polyfill`. Internet Explorer 9 does not recognize source elements wrapped by a `picture` element. The `polyfill` wraps the sources around a video element within the `picture` element.

There's more...

Performance first delivery

A benefit of using the responsive image formatter is performance. Browsers will only download the resources defined in the `srcset` of the appropriate `source` tag. This not only allows you to a deliver a more appropriate image size but also a smaller payload on smaller devices.

Removing picturefill polyfill

The Responsive Image module attaches the `picturefill` library to the responsive image element definition. The element's template also provides HTML to implement the `polyfill`. The `polyfill` can be removed by overriding the element's template and overriding the `picturefill` library to be disabled.

The following snippet, when added to a theme's `info.yml`, will disable the `picturefill` library:

```
libraries-override:
  core/picturefill: false
```

Then, the `responsive-image.html.twig` must be overridden by the theme to remove the extra HTML generated in the template for the `polyfill`:

1. Copy `responsive-image.html.twig` from `core/modules/responsive_image/templates` to the `theme` templates folder.

2. Edit `responsive-image.html.twig` and delete the Twig comment and IE conditional to output the initial video tag.

3. Remove the last conditional, which provides the closing video tag.

See also

- ▶ Refer to the picture element on the Mozilla Developer Network at `https://developer.mozilla.org/en-US/docs/Web/HTML/Element/picture`

- ▶ Refer to `picturefill` for IE9 at `http://scottjehl.github.io/picturefill/#ie9`

6

Creating Forms with the Form API

In this chapter, we will explore the various recipes to work with forms in Drupal:

- ▸ Creating a form
- ▸ Using new HTML5 elements
- ▸ Validating form data
- ▸ Processing submitted form data
- ▸ Altering other forms

Introduction

Drupal provides a robust API for creating and managing forms without writing any HTML. Drupal handles form building, validation, and submission. Drupal handles the request to either build the form or process the HTTP POST request. This allows developers to simply define the elements in a form, provide any additional validation if needed, and then handle a successful submission through specific methods.

This chapter contains various recipes to work with forms in Drupal through the Form API. In Drupal 8, forms and form states are objects.

Creating a form

In this recipe, we will create a form, which will be accessible from a menu path. This will involve creating a route that tells Drupal to invoke our form and display it to the end user.

Forms are defined as classes, which implement \Drupal\Core\Form\FormInterface. The \Drupal\Core\Form\FormBase serves as a utility class that is intended to be extended. We will extend this class to create a new form.

Getting ready

Since we will be writing the code, you will want to have a custom module. Creating a custom module in Drupal is simply creating a folder and an info.yml file. For this recipe, we will create a folder under /modules in your Drupal folder called drupalform.

In the drupalform folder, create drupalform.info.yml. The info.yml file is what Drupal will parse to discover modules. An example of a module's info.yml file is as follows:

```
name: Drupal form example
description: Create a basic Drupal form, accessible from a route
type: module
version: 1.0
core: 8.x
```

The name will be your module's name, and the description will be listed on the Extend page. Specifying the core tells Drupal what version of Drupal it is built for. *Chapter 4, Extending Drupal* covers how to create a module in depth.

How to do it...

1. Create an src folder in your module directory. In this directory, create a Form directory, which will hold the class that defines your form.

2. Next, create a file called ExampleForm.php in your module's src/Form directory.

 Drupal utilizes PSR4 to discover and autoload classes. For brevity, this defines that there should be one class per file, with each filename matching the class name. The folder structure will also mimic the namespace expected.

3. We will edit the `ExampleForm.php` file and add the proper PHP namespace, classes used, and the class itself:

```php
<?php

/**
 * @file
 * Contains \Drupal\drupalform\Form\ExampleForm.
 **/

namespace Drupal\drupalform\Form;

use Drupal\Core\Form\FormBase;
use Drupal\Core\Form\FormStateInterface;

class ExampleForm extends FormBase {

}
```

The `namespace` defines the class in your module's `Form` directory. The `autoloader` will now look into the `drupalform` module path and load the `ExampleForm` class from the `src/Form` directory.

The `use` statement allows us to use just the class name when referencing `FormBase` and, in the next steps, `FormStateInterface`. Otherwise, we would be forced to use the fully qualified namespace path for each class whenever it is used.

4. `\Drupal\Core\Form\FormBase` is an abstract class and requires us to implement four remaining interface methods: `getFormId`, `buildForm`, `validateForm`, and `submitForm`. The latter two are covered in their own recipes; however, we will need to define the method stubs:

```php
class ExampleForm extends FormBase {

  /**
   * {@inheritdoc}
   */
  public function getFormId() {
    return 'drupalform_example_form';
  }

  /**
   * {@inheritdoc}
   */
  public function buildForm(array $form, FormStateInterface $form_
state) {
```

```
    // Return array of Form API elements.
}

/**
 * {@inheritdoc}
 */
public function validateForm(array &$form,  FormStateInterface
$form_state) {
    // Validation covered in later recipe, required to satisfy
interface
}

/**
 * {@inheritdoc}
 */
public function submitForm(array &$form,  FormStateInterface
$form_state) {
    // Validation covered in later recipe, required to satisfy
interface
}
}
```

- ❑ This code flushes out the initial class definition from the previous step. `FormBase` provides `utility` methods and does not satisfy the interface requirements for `FormStateInterface`. We define those here, as they are unique across each form definition.

- ❑ The `getFormId` method returns a unique string to identify the form, for example, `site_information`. You may encounter some forms that append `_form` to the end of their form ID. This is not required, and it is just a naming convention often found in previous versions of Drupal.

- ❑ The `buildForm` method is covered in the following steps. The `validateForm` and `submitForm` methods are both called during the Form API processes and are covered in later recipes.

5. The `buildForm` method will be invoked to return Form API elements that are rendered to the end user. We will add a simple text field to ask for a company name and a submit button:

```
/**
 * {@inheritdoc}
 */
public function buildForm(array $form, FormStateInterface $form_
state) {
```

```
$form['company_name'] = array(
  '#type' => 'textfield',
  '#title' => $this->t('Company name'),
);
$form['submit'] = array(
  '#type' => 'submit',
  '#value' => $this->t('Save'),
);
return $form;
}
```

We have added a form element definition to the `form` array. Form elements are defined with a minimum of a type to specify what the element is and a title to act as the label. The title uses the `t` method to ensure that it is translatable.

Adding a **submit** button is done by providing an element with the type submit.

6. To access the form, we will create `drupalform.routing.yml` in the module's folder. A route entry will be created to instruct Drupal to use `\Drupal\Core\Form\FormBuilder` to create and display our form:

```
drupalform.form:
  path: '/drupal-example-form'
  defaults:
    _title: 'Example form'
    _form: '\Drupal\drupalform\Form\ExampleForm'
  requirements:
    _access: 'TRUE'
```

In Drupal, all routes have a name, and this example defines it as `drupalform.form`. Routes then define a path attribute and override default variables. This route definition has altered the route's title, specified it as a form, and given the fully qualified namespace path to this form's class.

Routes need to be passed a `requirements` property with specifications or else the route will be denied access.

7. Visit the **Extend** page and enable the Drupal form example module that we created.

8. Visit `/drupal-example-form` and the form is now visible, as shown in the following screenshot:

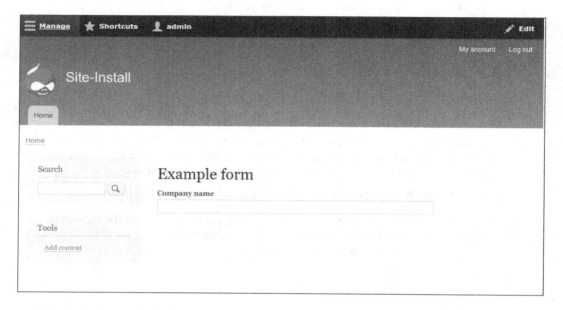

How it works...

This recipe creates a route to display the form. By passing the `_form` variable in the defaults section of our route entry, we are telling the route controller how to render our route's content. The fully qualified class name, which includes the namespace, is passed to a method located in the form builder. The route controller will invoke `\Drupal::formBuilder()->getForm(\Drupal\drupalform\Form\ExampleForm)` based on the recipe. At the same time, this can be manually called to embed the form elsewhere.

A form builder instance that implements `\Drupal\Core\Form\FormBuilderInterface` will then process the form by calling `buildForm` and initiate the rendering process. The `buildForm` method is expected to return an array of form elements and other API options. This will be sent to the render system to output the form as HTML.

There's more...

Many components make up a form created through Drupal's Form API. We will explore a few of them in depth.

Form element definitions

A form is a collection of form elements, which are types of plugin in Drupal 8. Plugins are small pieces of swappable functionalities in Drupal 8. Plugins and plugin development are covered in *Chapter 7, Plug and Play with Plugins*. At the time of writing this book, the Drupal. org Form API reference table was severely out of date and did not reflect all of the form element types available.

Here are some of the most common element properties that can be used:

- ▶ `weight`: This is used to alter the position of a form element in a form. By default, elements will be displayed in the order in which they were added to the form array. Defining a weight allows a developer to control element positions.

- ▶ `default_value`: This gives a developer the ability to prefill the element with a value. For example, when building configuration forms that have existing data or when editing an entity.

- ▶ `placeholder`: This is new to Drupal 8. Drupal 8 provides a new HTML5 support, and this attribute will set the placeholder attribute on the HTML input.

The form state

The `\Drupal\Core\Form\FormStateInterface` object represents the current state of the form and its data. The form state contains user-submitted data for the form along with build state information. Redirection after form submission is handled through the form state as well. You will interact more with the form state during the validation and submission recipes.

The form cache

Drupal utilizes a cache table for forms. This holds the build table, as identified by form build identifiers. This allows Drupal to validate forms during AJAX requests and easily build them when required. It is important to keep the form cache in persistent storage; otherwise, there may be repercussions, such as loss of form data or invalidating forms.

See also

- ▶ Form API in Drupal 8 at `https://www.drupal.org/node/2117411`
- ▶ The Drupal 8 Form API reference at `https://api.drupal.org/api/drupal/developer!topics!forms_api_reference.html/8`
- ▶ *Chapter 4, Extending Drupal*
- ▶ *Chapter 7, Plug and Play with Plugins*, to learn more about derivatives

Using new HTML5 elements

With the release of Drupal 8, Drupal has finally entered into the realm of HTML5. The Form API now allows utilization of HTML5 input elements out of the box. These include the following element types:

- `tel`
- `email`
- `number`
- `date`
- `url`
- `search`
- `range`

This allows your forms in Drupal to leverage native device input methods along with native validation support.

Getting ready

This recipe will walk you through adding elements to a Drupal form. You will need to have a custom form implemented through a module, such as the one created in the *Creating a form* section.

How to do it...

1. In order to use the telephone input, you need to add a new `form` element definition of the `tel` type to your `buildForm` method:

    ```
    $form['phone'] = array(
      '#type' => 'tel',
      '#title' => t('Phone'),
    );
    ```

2. In order to use the e-mail input, you need to add a new `form` element definition of the `email` type to your `buildForm` method. It will validate the format of e-mail addresses in the Form API:

    ```
    $form['email'] = array(
        '#type' => 'email',
        '#title' => t('Email'),
      );
    ```

3. In order to use the number input, you need to add a new `form` element definition of the number type to your `buildForm` method. It will validate the range and format of the number:

```
$form['integer'] = array(
  '#type' => 'number',
  '#title' => t('Some integer'),
  // The increment or decrement amount
  '#step' => 1,
  // Miminum allowed value
  '#min' => 0,
  // Maxmimum allowed value
  '#max' => 100,
);
```

4. In order to use the date input, you need to add a new `form` element definition of the date type to your `buildForm` method. You can also pass the `#date_date_format` option to alter the format used by the input:

```
$form['date'] = array(
  '#type' => 'date',
  '#title' => t('Date'),
  '#date_date_format' => 'Y-m-d',
);
```

5. In order to use the URL input, you need to add a new `form` element definition of the `url` type to your `buildForm` method. The element has a validator to check the format of the URL:

```
$form['website'] = array(
  '#type' => 'url',
  '#title' => t('Website'),
);
```

6. In order to use the search input, you need to add a new `form` element definition of the `search` type to your `buildForm` method. You can specify a route name that the search field will query for autocomplete options:

```
$form['search'] = array(
  '#type' => 'search',
  '#title' => t('Search'),
  '#autocomplete_route_name' => FALSE,
);
```

7. In order to use the `range` input, you need to add a new `form` element definition of the `range` type to your `buildForm` method. It is an extension of the number element and accepts a `min`, `max`, and `step` property to control the values of the range input:

```
$form['range'] = array(
  '#type' => 'range',
  '#title' => t('Range'),
  '#min' => 0,
  '#max' => 100,
  '#step' => 1,
);
```

How it works...

Each type references an extended class of `\Drupal\Core\Render\Element\FormElement`. It provides the element's definition and additional functions. Each element defines a `prerender` method in the class that defines the `input` type attribute along with other additional attributes.

Each input defines its theme as `input__TYPE`, allowing you to copy the `input.html.twig` base to `input.TYPE.html.twig` for templating. The template then parses the attributes and renders the HTML.

Some elements, such as e-mails, provide validators for the element itself. The e-mail element defines the `validateEmail` method. Here is an example of the code from `\Drupal\Core\Render\Element\Email::valdateEmail`:

```
/**
 * Form element validation handler for #type 'email'.
 *
 * Note that #maxlength and #required is validated by _form_
validate() already.
 */
  public static function validateEmail(&$element, FormStateInterface
$form_state, &$complete_form) {
    $value = trim($element['#value']);
    $form_state->setValueForElement($element, $value);

    if ($value !== '' && !\Drupal::service('email.validator')-
>isValid($value)) {
      $form_state->setError($element, t('The email address %mail is
not valid.', array('%mail' => $value)));
    }
  }
```

This code will be executed on form submission and validate the provider's e-mail. It does this by taking the current value and trimming any whitespaces and using the form state object to update the value. The `email.validator` service is invoked to validate the e-mail. If this method returns `false`, the form state is invoked to mark the element as the one that has an error. If the element has an error, the form builder will prevent form submission, returning the user to the form to fix the value.

There's more...

Elements are provided through Drupal's plugin system and are explored in detail in the next section.

Specific element properties

Elements can have their own unique properties along with individual validation methods. At the time of writing, the Drupal 8 Form Reference table is incomplete and does not highlight these new elements nor their properties. However, the classes can be examined and the definition method can be read to learn about the properties of each element. These classes are under the `\Drupal\Core\Render\Element` namespace located in `/core/lib/Drupal/Core/Render/Element`:

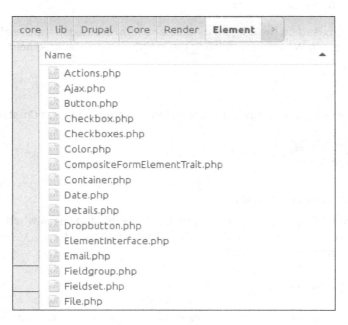

Creating new elements

Each element used in the Form API extends the `\Drupal\Core\Render\Element\FormElement` class, which is a plugin. Modules can provide new element types by adding classes to their Plugins/Element namespace. Refer to *Chapter 7, Plug and Play with Plugins* for more information on how to implement a plugin.

See also

▸   Form API in Drupal 8 at `https://www.drupal.org/node/2117411`

▸   *Chapter 7, Plug and Play with Plugins*

Validating form data

The Form API requires all form classes to implement the `\Drupal\Core\Form\FormInterface`. The interface defines a `validation` method. The `validateForm` method is invoked once a form has been submitted and provides a way to validate the data and halt the processing of the data if required. The form state object provides methods for marking specific fields as having the error, providing a user experience tool to alert your users specifically to the problem input.

This recipe will be based on the custom module and form created in the *Creating a form* section of this chapter. We will be validating the length of the submitted field.

Getting ready

This recipe will be using the module and custom form created in the first *Creating a form* recipe.

How to do it...

1.   Open and edit the `\Drupal\drupalform\Form\ExampleForm` class in the `src/Form` directory of the module.

2.   Before validating the `company_name` value, we need to check whether the value is empty using the `isValueEmpty()` method from the `\Drupal\Core\Form\FormStateInterface` object:

    ```
    /**
     * {@inheritdoc}
     */
    public function validateForm(array &$form,  FormStateInterface
    $form_state) {
        if (!$form_state->isValueEmpty('company_name')) {
    ```

```
        // Value is set, perform validation
    }
}
```

3. The `\Drupal\Form\FormStateInterface::isValueEmpty` method takes the key name of the form element. For example, `$form['company_name']` from the `buildForm` method is referenced through `company_name` in the `isValueEmpty` method.

4. Next, we will check whether the value's length is greater than five:

```
/**
 * {@inheritdoc}
 */
public function validateForm(array &$form,  FormStateInterface $form_state) {
    if (!$form_state->isValueEmpty('company_name')) {
        if (strlen($form_state->getValue('company_name')) <= 5) {
            // Set validation error.
        }
    }
}
```

The `getValue` takes a form element's key and returns the value. Since we have already verified that the value is not empty, we can retrieve the value.

 If you had any experience with previous versions of Drupal, note that the form state is now an object and not an array.

5. If the logic check finds a value with a length of five or fewer characters, it will throw a form error to prevent submission:

```
$form_state->setErrorByName('company_name', t ('Company name is less than 5 characters'));
```

We can place the `setErrorByName` method in our `strlen` logic check. If the string is fewer than five characters, an error is set on the element. The first parameter is the element's key and the second parameter is the message to be presented to the user.

6. The entire validation method will resemble the following code:

```
/**
 * {@inheritdoc}
 */
public function validateForm(array &$form,  FormStateInterface $form_state) {
    if (!$form_state->isValueEmpty('company_name')) {
```

```
      if (strlen($form_state->getValue('company_name')) <= 5) {
        $form_state->setErrorByName('company_name', t('Company
name is less than 5 characters'));
      }
    }
  }
```

7. When the form is submitted, the **Company name** text field will have to have more than five characters or be empty in order to be submitted.

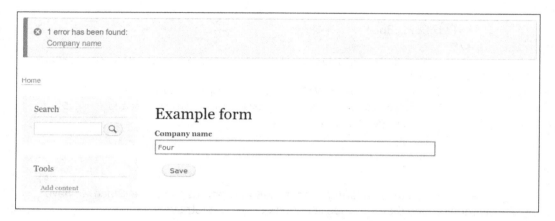

How it works...

Before the form builder service invokes the form object's submitForm method, it invokes the object's validateForm method. In the validation method, the form state can be used to check values and perform logic checks. In the event that an item is deemed *invalid* and an error is set on an element, the form cannot submit and will show errors to the user.

When an error is added to an element, an overall counter for the number of errors on the form is incremented. If the form has any errors, the form builder service will not execute the submit method.

This process is executed through the \Drupal\Core\Form\FormValidator class, which is run through the form builder service.

There's more...

Multiple validation handlers

A form can have multiple validation handlers. By default, all forms come with at least one validator, which is its own `validateForm` method. There is more that can be added. However, by default, the form will merely execute `::validateForm` and all element validators. This allows you to invoke static methods on other classes or other forms.

If a class provides `method1` and `method2`, which it would like to execute as well, the following code can be added to the `buildForm` method:

```
$form_state->setValidateHandlers([
    ['::validateForm'],
    ['::method1'],
    [$this, 'method2'],
]);
```

This sets the validator array to execute the default `validateForm` method and the two additional methods. You can reference a method in the current class using two colons (`::`) and the method name. Or, you can use an array consisting of a class instance and the method to invoke.

Accessing multidimensional array values

Forms support nested form elements in the form array. The default `\Drupal\Core\Form\FormStateInterface` implementation, `\Drupal\Core\Form\FormState`, supports accessing multidimensional array values. Instead of passing a string, you can pass an array that represents the parent array structure in the form array.

If the element is defined in `$form['company']['company_name']`, then we will pass `array('company', 'company_name')` to the form state's methods.

Element validation methods

Form elements can have their own validators. The form state will aggregate all of the element validation methods and pass them to the form validation service. This will run with the form's validation.

There is a `limit_validation_errors` option, which can be set to allow selected invalid errors to be passed. This option allows you to bypass validation on specific elements in your form. This attribute is defined in the submit button, also known as the **triggering** element in the form state. It is an array value consisting of form element keys.

> The triggering element value does not operate in the same fashion as the form state's methods in order to access multidimensional array values. In order to access a nested value, you need to provide a partially constructed string, representing the nested value. For example, `$form['company']['company_name']` will have to be added as `company][company_name`.

Processing submitted form data

A form's purpose is to collect data and do something with the data that was submitted. All forms need to implement the `\Drupal\Core\Form\FormInterface`. The interface defines a submit method. Once the Form API has invoked the class's validation method, the submit method can be run.

This recipe will be based on the custom module and form created in the *Creating a form* recipe of this chapter. We will convert the form to `\Drupal\Core\FormConfigBaseForm`, allowing easy storage of the field element.

Getting ready

In this recipe, we will be using the module and custom form created in the first *Creating a form* recipe.

How to do it...

1. In your module's directory, create a `config` directory, and then create a directory inside it named `install`.

2. Create a file named `drupalform.schema.yml`; this file will tell Drupal about the configuration item that we want to save.

3. Add the following configuration schema definition to `drupalform.schema.yml`:

```
drupalform.company:
  type: config_object
  label: 'Drupal form settings'
  mapping:
    company_name:
      type: string
      label: 'A company name'
```

This tells Drupal that we have the configuration with the name `drupalform.company` and it has a valid option of `company_name`. We will cover this in more detail in *Chapter 9, Confiuration Management – Deploying in Drupal 8.*

4. Replace the `FormBase` use statement to use the `ConfigFormBase` class:

```php
<?php

/**
 * @file
 * Contains \Drupal\drupalform\Form\ExampleForm.
 **/
```

```
namespace Drupal\drupalform\Form;

use Drupal\Core\Form\ConfigFormBase;
use Drupal\Core\Form\FormStateInterface;
```

5. Update the `ExampleForm` class to extend `ConfigFormBase` instead to harness its implementations:

```
class ExampleForm extends ConfigFormBase
```

This allows us to reuse methods from the `ConfigFormBase` class and write less about our own implementation.

6. For `ExampleForm` to implement `ConfigFormBase`, the `getEditableConfigNames` method needs to be implemented to satisfy the `\Drupal\Core\Form\ConfigBaseTrait` trait:

```
/**
 * {@inheritdoc}
 */
protected function getEditableConfigNames() {
    return ['drupalform.company'];
}
```

This function defines the configuration names, which will be editable by the form. This brings all the configurations under `drupalform[company]` to be editable when accessed through the form with the `config` method provided by `ConfigFormBaseTrait`.

7. Remove the submit form element. Update the `buildForm` method to return data from the parent's method rather than from `$form` itself. We also need to add a `#default_value` option to `company_name` so that it uses an existing value the next time our form is loaded:

```
/**
 * {@inheritdoc}
 */
public function buildForm(array $form, FormStateInterface $form_
state) {
    $form['company_name'] = array(
        '#type' => 'textfield',
        '#title' => t('Company name'),
        '#default_value' => $this->config('drupalform.company')-
>get('company_name'),
    );
    return parent::buildForm($form, $form_state);
}
```

The `ConfigFormBase` class implements the `buildForm` method to provide a reusable submit button. It also unifies the presentation across Drupal configuration forms:

8. The `ConfigFormBase` provides a configuration factory method. We will add a `default_value` property to our element with the currently saved item:

    ```
    /**
     * {@inheritdoc}
     */
    public function buildForm(array $form, FormStateInterface $form_
    state) {
        $form['company_name'] = array(
          '#type' => 'textfield',
          '#title' => t('Company name'),
          '#default_value' => $this->config('drupalform.company')-
    >get('name'),
        );
        return parent::buildForm($form, $form_state);
    }
    ```

    The `#default_value` key is added to the element's definition. It invokes the `config` method provided by `ConfigFormBaseTrait` to load our configuration group and access a specific configuration value.

9. The final step is to save the configuration in the `submitForm` method:

    ```
    /**
     * {@inheritdoc}
     */
    public function submitForm(array &$form, FormStateInterface
    $form_state) {
        parent::submitForm($form, $form_state);
        $this->config('drupalform.company')
          ->set('name', $form_state->getValue('company_name'));
    }
    ```

The `config` method is invoked by specifying our configuration group. We then use the set method to define name as the value from the `company name` text field.

10. When you edit your form and click on the **submit** button, the value that you entered in the **Company name** field will now be saved in the configuration.

How it works...

The `ConfigFormBase` utilizes the `ConfigFormBaseTrait` to provide easy access to a configuration factory. The class's implementation of `buildForm` also adds a `submit` button and theme styling to forms. The submit handler displays a configuration saved message but relies on implementing a module to save the configuration.

The form saves its data under the `drupalform.company` namespace. The company name value is stored as `name` and can be accessed as `drupalform.company.name`. Note that the configuration name does not have to match the form element's key.

There's more...

Multiple submit handlers

A form can have multiple submit handlers. By default, all forms implement a submit handler, which is its own `submitForm` method. The form will `execute ::submitForm` automatically and any defined on the triggering element. There is more that can be added. However, this allows you to invoke `static` methods on other classes or other forms.

If a class provides `method1` and `method2`, which it would like to execute as well, the following code can be added to the `buildForm` method:

```
$form_state->setSubmitHandlers([
    ['::submitForm'],
    ['::method1'],
    [$this, 'method2']
]);
```

This sets the submit handler array to execute the default `submitForm` method and two additional methods. You can reference a method in the current class using two colons (`::`) and the method name. Or, you can use an array consisting of a class instance and the method to be invoked.

See also

▶   *Chapter 9, Configuration Management- Deploying in Drupal 8*

Altering other forms

Drupal's Form API does not just provide a way to create forms. There are ways to alter forms through a custom module that allows you to manipulate the core and contributed forms. Using this technique, new elements can be added, default values can be changed, or elements can even be hidden from view to simplify the user experience.

The altering of a form does not happen in a custom class; this is a hook defined in the module file. In this recipe, we will use the `hook_form_FORM_ID_alter()` hook to add a telephone field to the site's configuration form.

Getting ready

This recipe assumes that you have a custom module to add the code to.

How to do it...

1. In the `modules` folder of your Drupal site, create a folder named `mymodule`.

2. In the `mymodule` folder, create a `mymodule.info.yml`, containing the following code:

```
name: My module
description: Custom module that uses a form alter
type: module
core: 8.x
Next, create a .module file in your module's directory:
<?php

/**
 * @file
 * Custom module that alters forms.
 */
```

As a best practice, files have document block headers that describe the purpose of the file and what it pertains to.

3. Add the `mymodule_form_system_site_information_settings_alter()` hook. The form ID can be found by viewing the form's class and reviewing the `getFormId` method:

```
/**
 * Implements hook_form_FORM_ID_alter().
 **/
```

```
function mymodule_form_system_site_information_settings_
alter(&$form, \Drupal\Core\Form\FormStateInterface $form_state) {
  // Code to alter form or form state here
}
```

Drupal will call this hook and pass the current form array and its form state object. The form array is passed by reference, allowing our hook to modify the array without returning any values. This is why the $form parameter has the ampersand (&) before it. In PHP, all objects are passed by reference.

> When calling a class in a normal file, such as the module file, you need to either use the fully qualified class name or add a use statement at the beginning of the file. In this example, we can add \Drupal\Core\ Form\FormStateInterface.

4. Next, we add our telephone field to the form so that it can be displayed and saved:

```
/**
 * Implements hook_form_FORM_ID_alter().
 */
function mymodule_form_system_site_information_settings_
alter(&$form, \Drupal\Core\Form\FormStateInterface $form_state) {
  $form['site_phone'] = array(
    '#type' => 'tel',
    '#title' => t('Site phone'),
    '#default_value' => Drupal::config('system.site')-
>get('phone'),
  );
}
```

We retrieve the current phone value from system.site so that it can be modified if already set.

5. Visit the **Extend** page and enable the module **My module** that we created.

6. Review the **Site Information** form under **Configuration** and test setting the site telephone number:

▼ **ERROR PAGES**

Default 403 (access denied) page

This page is displayed when the requested document is denied to the current user. Leav
page.

Default 404 (not found) page

This page is displayed when no other content matches the requested document. Leave

Site phone

Save configuration

7. We need to add a submit handler in order to save the configuration for our new field. We will need to add a submit handler to the form and a submit handler callback:

```
/**
 * Implements hook_form_FORM_ID_alter().
 */
function mymodule_form_system_site_information_settings_
alter(&$form, \Drupal\Core\Form\FormStateInterface $form_state) {
  $form['site_phone'] = array(
    '#type' => 'tel',
    '#title' => t('Site phone'),
    '#default_value' => Drupal::config('system.site')-
>get('phone'),
  );
  $form['#submit'][] = 'mymodule_system_site_information_phone_
submit';
}


/**
 * Form callback to save site_phone
 * @param array $form
 * @param \Drupal\Core\Form\FormStateInterface $form_state
 */
function mymodule_system_site_information_phone_submit(array
&$form,  \Drupal\Core\Form\FormStateInterface $form_state) {
```

```
$config = Drupal::configFactory()->getEditable('system.site');
$config
->set('phone', $form_state->getValue('site_phone'))
->save();
}
```

The `$form['#submit']` modification adds our callback to the form's submit handlers. This allows our module to interact with the form once it has been submitted.

The `mymodule_system_site_information_phone_submit` callback is passed the form array and form state. We load the current configuration factory to receive the configuration that can be edited. We then load `system.site` and save phone based on the value from the form state.

8. Submit the form and verify that the data has been saved.

How it works...

The `\Drupal\system\Form\SiteInformationForm` class extends `\Drupal\Core\Form\ConfigFormBase` to handle the writing of form elements as individual configuration values. However, it does not write the values automatically to the form state. In this recipe, we need to add a submit handler to manually save our added field.

The form array is passed by reference, allowing modifications to be made in the hook to alter the original data. This allows us to add an element or even modify existing items, such as titles or descriptions.

There's more...

Adding additional validate handlers

Using a form alter hook, we can add additional validators to a form. The proper way to do this is to load the current validators and add the new one to the array and reset the validators in the form state:

```
$validators = $form_state->getValidateHandlers();
$validators[] = 'mymodule_form_validate';
$form_state->setValidateHandlers($validators);
```

First, we receive all of the currently set validators from the form state as the `$validators` variable. We then append a new callback to the end of the array. Once the `$validators` variable has been modified, we override the form state's validator array by executing the `setValidateHandlers` method.

You can also use PHP array manipulation functions to add your validators in different execution orders. For example, `array_unshift` will place your validator at the beginning of the array so that it can run first.

Adding additional submit handlers

Using a form alter hook, we can add additional submit handlers to a form. The proper way to do this is to load the current submit handlers, add the new one to the array, and reset the validators in the form state:

```
$submit_handlers = $form_state->getSubmitHandlers();
$submit_handlers [] = 'mymodule_form_submit';
$form_state->setSubmitHandlers($submit_handlers );
```

First, we receive all of the currently set submit handlers from the form state as the `$submit_handlers` variable. We then append a new callback to the end of the array. Once the `$submit_handlers` variable has been modified, we override the form state's submit handler array by executing the `setSubmitHandlers` method.

You can also use PHP array manipulation functions to add your callback in different execution orders. For example, `array_unshift` will place your callback at the beginning of the array so that it can run first.

7
Plug and Play with Plugins

In this chapter, we will dive into the new Plugin API provided in Drupal 8:

- ► Creating blocks using plugins
- ► Creating a custom field type
- ► Creating a custom field widget
- ► Creating a custom field formatter
- ► Creating a custom plugin type

Introduction

Drupal 8 introduces plugins. Plugins power many items in Drupal, such as blocks, field types, field formatters, and many more. Plugins and plugin types are provided by modules. They provide a swappable and specific functionality. Breakpoints, as discussed in *Chapter 5, Front End for the Win*, are plugins. In this chapter, we will discuss how plugins work in Drupal 8 and show you how to create blocks, fields, and custom plugin types.

Each version of Drupal has had subsystems, which provided pluggable components and even contributed modules. A problem arose in the implementation and management of these. Blocks, fields, and image styles each had an entirely different system to learn and understand. The Plugin API exists in Drupal 8 to mitigate this problem and provide a base API to implement pluggable components. This has greatly improved the developer experience when working with Drupal core's subsystems. In this chapter, we will implement a block plugin. We will use the Plugin API to provide a custom field type along with a widget and formatter for the field. The last recipe will show you how to create and use a custom plugin type.

Creating blocks using plugins

In Drupal, a block is a piece of content that can be placed in a region provided by a theme. Blocks are used to present specific kinds of content, such as a user login form, a snippet of text, and many more.

Blocks are configuration entities, and the block module uses the Drupal plugin system as a way to define blocks for modules. Custom blocks are defined in the PHP code in the module's `Plugin` class namespace. Each class in the `Plugin/Block` namespace will be discovered by the block module's plugin manager.

In this recipe, we will define a block that will display a copyright snippet and the current year, and place it in the footer region.

Getting ready

Create a new module like the one shown in this recipe. We will refer to the module as `mymodule` throughout the recipe. Use your module's appropriate name.

How to do it...

1. Create the `src/Plugin/Block` directory in your module. This will translate the `\Drupal\mymodule\Plugin\Block` namespace and allow a block plugin discovery.

2. Create a `Copyright.php` file in the newly created folder so that we can define the `Copyright` class for our block:

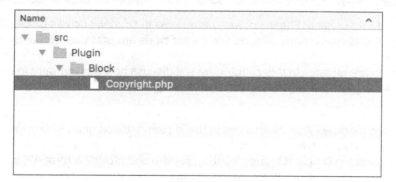

3. The `Copyright` class will extend `\Drupal\Core\Block\BlockBase`:

```php
<?php

/**
 * @file
```

```
 * Contains \Drupal\mymodule\Plugin\Block\Copyright.
 */
namespace Drupal\mymodule\Plugin\Block;
use Drupal\Core\Block\BlockBase;
class Copyright extends BlockBase {
}
```

4. We extend the `BlockBase` class, which implements `\Drupal\Core\Block\ BlockPluginInterface` and provides us with an implementation of nearly all of its methods.

5. Blocks are annotated plugins. Annotated plugins use documentation blocks to provide details of the plugin. We will provide the block's identifier, administrative label, and category:

```php
<?php

/**
 * @file
 * Contains \Drupal\mymodule\Plugin\Block\Copyright.
 */

namespace Drupal\mymodule\Plugin\Block;

use Drupal\Core\Block\BlockBase;
/**
 * @Block(
 *   id = "copyright_block",
 *   admin_label = @Translation("Copyright"),
 *   category = @Translation("Custom")
 * )
 */
class Copyright extends BlockBase {

}
```

6. The annotation document block of the class identifies the type of plugin through `@Block`. Drupal will parse this and initiate the plugin with the properties defined inside it. The `id` is the internal machine name, the `admin_label` is displayed on the block listing page, and `category` shows up in the block select list.

7. We need to provide a `build` method to satisfy the `\Drupal\Core\Block\ BlockPluginInterface` interface. This creates the output to be displayed:

```php
<?php
/**
 * @file
```

```
 * Contains \Drupal\mymodule\Plugin\Block\Copyright
 */

namespace Drupal\mymodule\Plugin\Block;

use Drupal\Core\Block\BlockBase;

/**
 * @Block(
 *   id = "copyright_block",
 *   admin_label = @Translation("Copyright"),
 *   category = @Translation("Custom")
 * )
 */
class Copyright extends BlockBase {
  /**
   * {@inheritdoc}
   */
  public function build() {
    $date = new \DateTime();
    return [
      '#markup' => t('Copyright @year&copy; My Company', [
          '@year' => $date->format('Y'),
      ]),
    ];
  }
}
```

The build method returns a render array that uses Drupal's t function to substitute @year for the \DateTime object's output that is formatted as a full year.

 Since PHP 5.4, a warning will be displayed if you have not explicitly set a timezone in your PHP's configuration.

8. Rebuild Drupal's cache so that the new plugin can be discovered.

9. In the **Footer fourth** region, click on **Place block**.

10. Review the block list and add the custom block to your regions, for instance, the footer region. Find the **Copyright** block, and click on **Place block**:

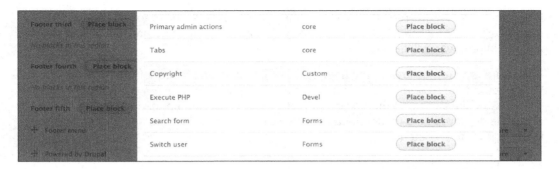

Primary admin actions	core	Place block
Tabs	core	Place block
Copyright	Custom	Place block
Execute PHP	Devel	Place block
Search form	Forms	Place block
Switch user	Forms	Place block

11. Uncheck the **Display title** checkbox so that only our block's content can be rendered.

12. Review the copyright statement that will always keep the year dynamic:

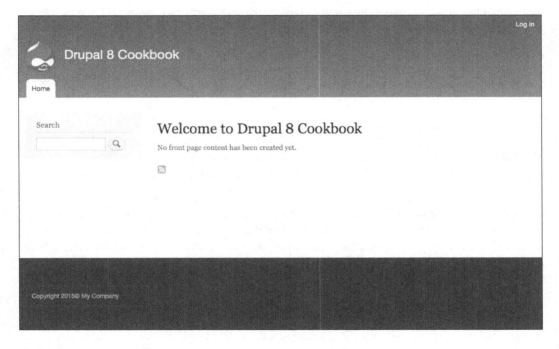

How it works...

The plugin system works through plugin definitions and plugin managers for those definitions. The `\Drupal\Core\Block\BlockManager` class defines the block plugins that need be located in the `Plugin/Block` namespace. It also defines the base interface that needs to be implemented along with the `Annotation` class, which is to be used, when parsing the class's document block.

When Drupal's cache is rebuilt, all available namespaces are scanned to check whether classes exist in the given plugin namespace. The definitions, via annotation, will be processed and the information will be cached.

Blocks are then retrieved from the manager, manipulated, and their methods are invoked. When viewing the `Block` layout page to manage blocks, the `\Drupal\Core\Block\BlockBase` class's `label` method is invoked to display the human-readable name. When a block is displayed on a rendered page, the `build` method is invoked and passed to the theming layer to be output.

There's more...

Altering blocks

Blocks can be altered in two different ways: the plugin definition can be altered, the build array, or the view array out.

A module can implement `hook_block_alter` in its `.module` file and modify the annotation definitions of all the discovered blocks. The will allow a module to change the default `user_login_block` from user login to `Login`:

```
/**
 * Implements hook_block_alter().
 */
function mymodule_block_alter(&$definitions) {
  $definitions['user_login_block']['admin_label'] = t('Login');
}
```

A module can implement `hook_block_build_alter` and modify the build information of a block. The hook is passed the build array and the `\Drupal\Core\Block\BlockPluginInterface` instance for the current block. Module developers can use this to add cache contexts or alter the cache ability of metadata:

```
/**
 * Implements hook_block_build_alter().
 */
function hook_block_build_alter(array &$build, \Drupal\Core\Block\
BlockPluginInterface $block) {
  // Add the 'url' cache the block per URL.
  if ($block->getBaseId() == 'myblock') {
    $build['#contexts'][] = 'url';
  }
}
```

You can test the modification of cache metadata by altering the recipe's block to output a timestamp. With caching enabled, you will see that the value persists on the same URL, but it will be different across each page.

Finally, a module can implement hook_block_view_alter in order to modify the output to be rendered. A module can add content to be rendered or remove content. This can be used to remove the contextual links item, which allows inline editing from the front page of a site:

```
/**
 * Implements hook_block_view_alter().
 */
function hook_block_view_alter(array &$build, \Drupal\Core\Block\
BlockPluginInterface $block) {
  // Remove the contextual links on all blocks that provide them.
  if (isset($build['#contextual_links'])) {
    unset($build['#contextual_links']);
  }
}
```

Block settings forms

Blocks can provide a setting form. This recipe provides the text *My Company* for the copyright text. Instead, this can be defined through a text field in the block's setting form.

Let's revisit the Copyright.php file that contained our block's class. A block can override the default defaultConfiguration method, which returns an array of setting keys and their default values. The blockForm method can then override the \Drupal\Core\Block\ BlockBase empty array implementation to return a Form API array to represent the settings form:

```
/**
 * {@inheritdoc}
 */
public function defaultConfiguration() {
  return [
    'company_name' => '',
  ];
}

/**
 * {@inheritdoc}
 */
public function blockForm($form, \Drupal\Core\Form\
FormStateInterface $form_state) {
```

```
    $form['company_name'] = [
      '#type' => 'textfield',
      '#title' => t('Company name'),
      '#default_value' => $this->configuration['company_name'],
    ];
    return $form;
}
```

The `blockSubmit` method must then be implemented, which updates the block's configuration:

```
/**
 * {@inheritdoc}
 */
public function blockSubmit($form, \Drupal\Core\Form\
FormStateInterface $form_state) {
    $this->configuration['company_name'] = $form_state-
>getValue('company_name');
}
```

Finally, the `build` method can be updated to use the new configuration item:

```
/**
 * {@inheritdoc}
 */
public function build() {
    $date = new \DateTime();
    return [
      '#markup' => t('Copyright @year&copy; @company', [
        '@year' => $date->format('Y'),
        '@company' => $this->configuration['company_name'],
      ]),
    ];
}
```

You can now go back and visit the `Block layout` form, and click on **Configure** in the **Copyright** block. The new setting will be available in the block instance's configuration form.

Defining access to a block

Blocks, by default, are rendered for all users. The default access method can be overridden. This allows a block to only be displayed to authenticated users or based on a specific permission:

```
/**
 * {@inheritdoc}
 */
```

```
protected function blockAccess(AccountInterface $account) {
  $route_name = $this->routeMatch->getRouteName();
  if ($account->isAnonymous() && !in_array($route_name,
    array('user.login', 'user.logout'))) {
    return AccessResult::allowed()
      ->addCacheContexts(['route.name',
        'user.roles:anonymous']);
  }
  return AccessResult::forbidden();
}
```

The preceding code is taken from the user_login_block. It allows access to the block if the user is logged out and is not on the login or logout page. The access is cached based on the current route name and the user's current role being anonymous. If these are not passed, the access returned is forbidden and the block is not built.

Other modules can implement hook_block_access to override the access of a block:

```
/**
 * Implements hook_block_access().
 */
function mymodule_block_access(\Drupal\block\Entity\Block $block,
$operation, \Drupal\Core\Session\AccountInterface $account) {
  // Example code that would prevent displaying the Copyright' block
in
  // a region different than the footer.
  if ($operation == 'view' && $block->getPluginId() == 'copyright') {
    return \Drupal\Core\Access\AccessResult::forbiddenIf($block-
>getRegion() != 'footer');
  }

  // No opinion.
  return \Drupal\Core\Access\AccessResult::neutral();
}
```

A module implementing the preceding hook will deny access to our **Copyright** block if it is not placed in the footer region.

See also

- ▶ Refer to *Creating a custom plugin type* recipe of this chapter
- ▶ **block.api.php** at https://api.drupal.org/api/drupal/
  core%21modules%21block%21block.api.php/8

Creating a custom field type

Fields are powered through the plugin system in Drupal. Field types are defined using the plugin system. Each field type has its own class. A new field type can be defined through a custom class that will provide schema and property information.

In this example, we will create a simple field type called "real name" to store the first and last names.

 Field types just define ways in which data can be stored and handled through the Field API. Field widgets provide means for editing a field type in the user interface. Field formatters provide means for displaying the field data to users. Both are plugins and will be covered in later recipes.

Getting ready

Create a new module like the one existing in the first recipe. We will refer to the module as `mymodule` throughout the recipe. Use your module's appropriate name.

How to do it...

1. We need to create the `src/Plugin/Field/FieldType` directory in the module's base location. The `Field` module discovers field types in the `Plugin\Field\FieldType` namespace.

2. Create a `RealName.php` file in the newly created directory so that we can define the `RealName` class. This will provide our `real name` field for the first and last names:

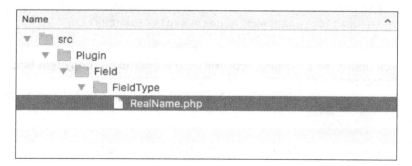

3. The `RealName` class will extend the `\Drupal\Core\Field\FieldItemBase` class:

```php
<?php
/**
 * @file
 * Contains \Drupal\mymodule\Plugin\Field\FieldType\RealName.
 */

namespace Drupal\mymodule\Plugin\Field\FieldType;

use Drupal\Core\Field\FieldItemBase;
use Drupal\Core\Field\FieldStorageDefinitionInterface;
use Drupal\Core\TypedData\DataDefinition;


class RealName extends FieldItemBase {

}
```

The `\Drupal\Core\Field\FieldItemBase` satisfies methods defined by inherited interfaces except for `schema` and `propertyDefinitions`.

4. Field types are annotated plugins. Annotated plugins use documentation blocks to provide details of the plugin. We will provide the field type's identifier, label, description, category, and default widget and formatter:

```php
<?php

/**
 * @file
 * Contains \Drupal\mymodule\Plugin\Field\FieldType\RealName.
 */

namespace Drupal\mymodule\Plugin\Field\FieldType;

use Drupal\Core\Field\FieldItemBase;
use Drupal\Core\Field\FieldStorageDefinitionInterface;
use Drupal\Core\TypedData\DataDefinition;

/**
 * Plugin implementation of the 'realname' field type.
 *
 * @FieldType(
 *   id = "realname",
 *   label = @Translation("Real name"),
```

```
 *     description = @Translation("This field stores a first and
last name."),
 *     category = @Translation("General"),
 *     default_widget = "string_textfield",
 *     default_formatter = "string"
 * )
 */
class RealName extends FieldItemBase {

}
```

The `@FieldType` tells Drupal that this is a `FieldType` plugin. The following properties are defined:

> `Id`: This is the plugin's machine name
>
> `Label`: This is the human-readable name for the field
>
> `description`: This is the human-readable description of the field
>
> `category`: This is the category where the field shows up in the user interface
>
> `default_widget`: This is the default form widget to be used for editing
>
> `default_formatter`: This is the default formatter with which you can display the field

5. The `RealName` class needs to implement the `schema` method defined in the `\Drupal\Core\Field\FieldItemInterface`. This returns an array of the database API schema information:

```
/**
 * {@inheritdoc}
 */
public static function schema(\Drupal\Core\Field\
FieldStorageDefinitionInterface $field_definition) {
  return array(
    'columns' => array(
      'first_name' => array(
        'description' => 'First name.',
        'type' => 'varchar',
        'length' => '255',
        'not null' => TRUE,
        'default' => '',
      ),
      'last_name' => array(
        'description' => 'Last name.',
        'type' => 'varchar',
```

```
            'length' => '255',
            'not null' => TRUE,
            'default' => '',
        ),
      ),
      'indexes' => array(
        'first_name' => array('first_name'),
        'last_name' => array('last_name'),
      ),
    );
  }
```

The `schema` method defines the columns in the field's data table. We will define a column to hold the `first_name` and `last_name` values.

6. We also need to implement the `propertySchema` method to satisfy `\Drupal\Core\TypedData\ComplexDataDefinitionInterface`. This returns a typed definition of the values defined in the `schema` method:

```
  /**
   * {@inheritdoc}
   */
  public static function propertyDefinitions(\Drupal\Core\Field\
FieldStorageDefinitionInterface $field_definition) {
      $properties['first_name'] = \Drupal\Core\TypedData\DataDefinition::create('string')
        ->setLabel(t('First name'));
      $properties['last_name'] = \Drupal\Core\TypedData\DataDefinition::create('string')
        ->setLabel(t('Last name'));

      return $properties;
  }
```

This method returns an array that is keyed with the same column names provided in `schema`. It returns a typed data definition to handle the field type's values.

7. Rebuild Drupal's cache so that the plugin system can discover the new field type.

8. The field will now appear on the field type management screen:

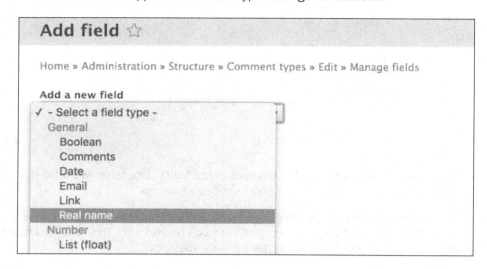

How it works...

Drupal core defines a `plugin.manager.field.field_type` service. By default, this is handled through the `\Drupal\Core\Field\FieldTypePluginManager` class. This plugin manager defines the field type plugins that should be in the `Plugin/Field/FieldType` namespace, and all the classes in this namespace will be loaded and assumed to be field type plugins.

The manager's definition also sets `\Drupal\Core\Field\FieldItemInterface` as the expected interface that all the field type plugins will implement. This is why most field types extend `\Drupal\Core\Field\FieldItemBase` to meet these method requirements.

As field types are annotated plugins, the manager provides `\Drupal\Core\Field\Annotation\FieldType` as the class that fulfills the annotation definition.

When the user interface defines the available fields, the `plugin.manager.field.field_type` service is invoked to retrieve a list of available field types.

There's more...

Altering field types

The `\Drupal\Core\Field\FieldTypePluginManager` class defines the `alter` method as `field_info`. Modules that implement `hook_field_info_alter` in their `.module` files have the ability to modify field type definitions discovered by the manager:

```
/**
 * Implements hook_field_info_alter().
 */
function mymodule_field_info_alter(&$info) {
  $info['email']['label'] = t('E-mail address');
}
```

The preceding `alter` method will change the human-readable label for the `Email` field to the e-mail address.

Defining whether a field is empty

The `\Drupal\Core\TypedDate\ComplexDataInterface` interface provides an `isEmpty` method. This method is used to check whether the field's value is empty, for example, when verifying that the required field has data. The `\Drupal\Core\TypedData\Plugin\DataType\Map` class implements the method. By default, the method ensures that the values are not empty.

Field types can provide their own implementations to provide a more robust verification. For instance, the field can validate that the first name can be entered but not the last name, or the field can require both the first and the last name.

See also

▸ The *Creating blocks using plugins* recipe of this chapter

Creating a custom field widget

Field widgets provide the form interface for editing a field. These integrate with the Form API to define how a field can be edited and the way in which the data can be formatted before it is saved. Field widgets are chosen and customized through the form display interface.

In this recipe, we will create a widget for the field created in the *Creating a custom field type* recipe in this chapter. The field widget will provide two text fields for entering the first and last name items.

Getting ready

Create a new module such as the one existing in the first recipe. We will refer to the module as `mymodule` throughout the recipe. Use your module's appropriate name.

How to do it...

1. We need to create the `src/Plugin/Field/FieldWidget` directory in the module's base location. The `Field` module discovers field widgets in the `Plugin\Field\FieldWidget` namespace.

2. Create a `RealNameDefaultWidget.php` file in the newly created directory so that we can define the `RealNameDefaultWidget` class. This will provide a custom form element to edit the first and last name values of our field:

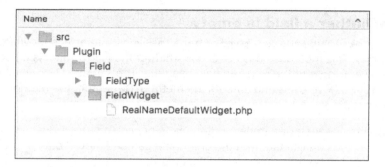

3. The `RealNameDefaultWidget` class will extend the `\Drupal\Core\Field\WidgetBase` class:

```php
<?php

/**
 * @file
 * Contains \Drupal\mymodule\Plugin\Field\FieldWidget\
RealNameDefaultWidget
 */

namespace Drupal\mymodule\Plugin\Field\FieldWidget;

use Drupal\Core\Field\WidgetBase;

class RealNameDefaultWidget extends WidgetBase {

}
```

4. Field widgets are like annotated plugins. Annotated plugins use documentation blocks to provide details of the plugin. We will provide the field widget's identifier, label, and supported field types:

```php
<?php

/**
 * @file
 * Contains \Drupal\mymodule\Plugin\Field\FieldWidget\
RealNameDefaultWidget
 */

namespace Drupal\mymodule\Plugin\Field\FieldWidget;

use Drupal\Core\Field\WidgetBase;
use Drupal\Core\Field\FieldItemListInterface;
use Drupal\Core\Form\FormStateInterface;

/**
 * Plugin implementation of the 'realname_default' widget.
 *
 * @FieldWidget(
 *   id = "realname_default",
 *   label = @Translation("Real name"),
 *   field_types = {
 *     "realname"
 *   }
 * )
 */
class RealNameDefaultWidget extends WidgetBase {

}
```

The `@FieldWidget` tells Drupal that this is a field widget plugin. It defines `id` to represent the machine name, the human-readable name as `label`, and the field types that the widget interacts with.

5. We need to implement the `formElement` method to satisfy the remaining `interface` methods after extending `\Drupal\Core\Field\WidgetBase`:

```php
/**
 * {@inheritdoc}
 */
public function formElement(FieldItemListInterface $items,
$delta, array $element, array &$form, FormStateInterface $form_
state) {
```

```php
      $element['first_name'] = array(
        '#type' => 'textfield',
        '#title' => t('First name'),
        '#default_value' => '',
        '#size' => 25,
        '#required' => $element['#required'],
      );
      $element['last_name'] = array(
        '#type' => 'textfield',
        '#title' => t('Last name'),
        '#default_value' => '',
        '#size' => 25,
        '#required' => $element['#required'],
      );
      return $element;
   }
```

The `formElement` method returns a Form API array that represents the widget to be set, and edits the field data.

6. Next, we need to modify our original `RealName` field type plugin class in order to use the default widget that we created. Update the `default_widget` annotation property as `realname_default`:

```php
/**
 * Plugin implementation of the 'realname' field type.
 *
 * @FieldType(
 *   id = "realname",
 *   label = @Translation("Real name"),
 *   description = @Translation("This field stores a first and
last name."),
 *   category = @Translation("General"),
 *   default_widget = "realname_default",
 *   default_formatter = "string"
 * )
 */
class RealName extends FieldItemBase {
```

7. Rebuild Drupal's cache so that the plugin system can discover the new field widget.

8. Add a `Real name` field and use the new `Real name` widget. For example, add it to a `Comment` type:

How it works...

Drupal core defines a `plugin.manager.field.widget` service. By default, this is handled through the `\Drupal\Core\Field\FieldWidgetPluginManager` class. This plugin manager defines the field widget plugins that should be in the `Plugin/Field/FieldWidget` namespace, and all the classes in this namespace will be loaded and assumed to be field widget plugins.

The manager's definition also sets `\Drupal\Core\Field\FieldWidgetInterface` as the expected interface that all the field widget plugins will implement. This is why most field types extend `\Drupal\Core\Field\WidgetBase` to meet these method requirements.

As field widgets are annotated plugins, the manager provides `\Drupal\Core\Field\Annotation\FieldWidget` as the class that fulfills the annotation definition.

The entity form display system uses the `plugin.manager.field.widget` service to load field definitions and add the field's element, returned from the `formElement` method, to the entity form.

There's more

Field widget settings and summary

The `\Drupal\Core\Field\WidgetInterface` interface defines three methods that can be overridden to provide a settings form and a summary of the current settings:

- `defaultSettings`: This returns an array of the setting keys and default values
- `settingsForm`: This returns a Form API array that is used for the settings form
- `settingsSummary`: This allows an array of strings to be returned and displayed on the manage display form for the field

Widget settings can be used to alter the form presented to the user. A setting can be created that allows the field element to be limited to only enter the first or last name with one text field.

See also

- The *Creating a custom plugin type* recipe of this chapter

Creating a custom field formatter

Field formatters define the way in which a field type will be presented. These formatters return the render array information to be processed by the theming layer. Field formatters are configured on the display mode interfaces.

In this recipe, we will create a formatter for the field created in the *Creating a custom field type* recipe in this chapter. The field formatter will display the first and last names with some settings.

Getting ready

Create a new module like the one existing in the first recipe. We will refer to the module as `mymodule` throughout the recipe. Use your module's appropriate name.

How to do it...

1. We need to create the `src/Plugin/Field/FieldFormatter` directory in the module's base location. The `Field` module discovers field formatters in the `Plugin\Field\ FieldFormatter` namespace.

2. Create a `RealNameFormatter.php` file in the newly created directory so that we can define the `RealNameFormatter` class. This will provide a custom form element to display the field's values:

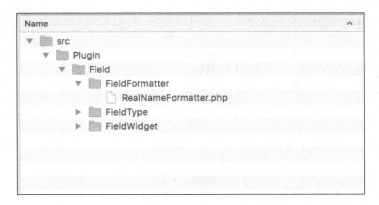

3. The `RealNameFormatter` class will extend the `\Drupal\Core\Field\FormatterBase` class:

```php
<?php

/**
 * @file
 * Contains \Drupal\mymodule\Plugin\Field\FieldFormatter\
RealNameFormatter
 */

namespace Drupal\mymodule\Plugin\Field\FieldFormatter;

use Drupal\Core\Field\FormatterBase;
use Drupal\Core\Field\FieldItemListInterface;

class RealNameFormatter extends FormatterBase {

}
```

4. Field formatters are like annotated plugins. Annotated plugins use documentation blocks to provide details of the plugin. We will provide the field widget's identifier, label, and supported field types:

```php
<?php

/**
 * @file
```

```
 * Contains \Drupal\mymodule\Plugin\Field\FieldFormatter\
RealNameFormatter
 */

namespace Drupal\mymodule\Plugin\Field\FieldFormatter;

use Drupal\Core\Field\FormatterBase;
use Drupal\Core\Field\FieldItemListInterface;

/**
 * Plugin implementation of the 'realname_one_line' formatter.
 *
 * @FieldFormatter(
 *   id = "realname_one_line",
 *   label = @Translation("Real name (one line)"),
 *   field_types = {
 *      "realname"
 *   }
 * )
 */

class RealNameFormatter extends FormatterBase {

}
```

5. We need to implement the `viewElements` method to satisfy the `\Drupal\Core\ Field\FormatterInferface` interface. This is used to render the field data:

```
/**
 * {@inheritdoc}
 */
public function viewElements(FieldItemListInterface $items,
$langcode) {
  $element = [];

  foreach ($items as $delta => $item) {
    $element[$delta] = array(
      '#markup' => $this->t('@first @last', array(
          '@first' => $item->first_name,
          '@last' => $item->last_name,
        )
      ),
    );
  }
  return $element;
}
```

6. Next, we need to modify our original `RealName` field type's `plugin` class in order to use the default formatter that we created. Update the `default_formatter` annotation property as `realname_one_line`:

```
/**
 * Plugin implementation of the 'realname' field type.
 *
 * @FieldType(
 *   id = "realname",
 *   label = @Translation("Real name"),
 *   description = @Translation("This field stores a first and
last name."),
 *   category = @Translation("General"),
 *   default_widget = " string_textfield ",
 *   default_formatter = "realname_one_line"
 * )
 */
```

7. Rebuild Drupal's cache so that the plugin system can discover the new field widget.

8. Update an entity view mode with a `Real name` field to use the **Real name (one line)** formatter:

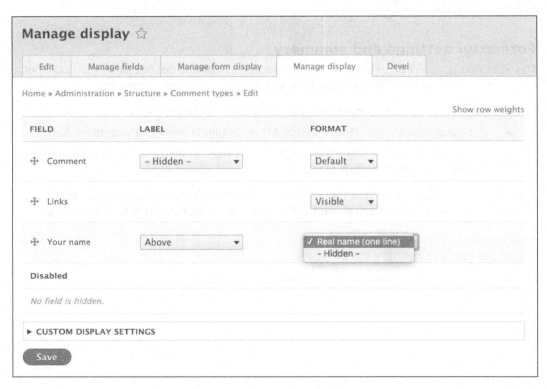

How it works...

Drupal core defines a `plugin.manager.field.formatter` service. By default, this is handled through the `\Drupal\Core\Field\FormatterPluginManager` class. This plugin manager defines the field formatter plugins that should be in the `Plugin/Field/FieldFormatter` namespace, and all the classes in this namespace will be loaded and assumed to be field formatter plugins.

The manager's definition also sets `\Drupal\Core\Field\FormatterInterface` as the expected interface that all field formatter plugins will implement. This is why most field formatters extend `\Drupal\Core\Field\FormatterBase` to meet these method requirements.

As field formatters are annotated plugins, the manager provides `\Drupal\Core\Field\Annotation\FieldFormatter` as the class that fulfills the annotation definition.

The entity view display system uses the `plugin.manager.field.formatter` service to load field definitions and add the field's render array, returned from the `viewElements` method, to the entity view render array.

There's more

Formatter settings and summary

The `\Drupal\Core\Field\FormatterInterface` interface defines three methods that can be overridden to provide a settings form and a summary of the current settings:

▶ `defaultSettings`: This returns an array of the setting keys and default values

▶ `settingsForm`: This returns a Form API array that is used for the settings form

▶ `settingsSummary`: This allows an array of strings to be returned and displayed on the manage display form for the field

Settings can be used to alter how the formatter displays information. For example, these methods can be implemented to provide settings to hide or display the first or last name.

See also

▶ The *Creating a custom plugin type* recipe of this chapter

Creating a custom plugin type

The plugin system provides means to create specialized objects in Drupal that do not require the robust features of the entity system.

In this recipe, we will create a new plugin type called `Unit` that will work with units of measurement and conversions. We will create a plugin manager, default plugin interface, `YAML discovery` method, base class, and plugin definition.

This recipe is based on the work being done to export the `Physical` module to Drupal 8. The `Physical` module provides a way to work with units of volume, weight, and dimensions and attaches them to entities. It discovers unit plugins in the same way that the `Breakpoint` module discovers breakpoint plugins.

Getting ready

Create a new module like the one existing in the first recipe. We will refer to the module as `mymodule` throughout the recipe. Use your module's appropriate name.

How to do it...

1. All plugins need to have a service that acts as a plugin manager. Create a new file in your module's `src` directory called `UnitManager.php`. This will hold the `UnitManager` class.

2. Create the `UnitManager` class by extending the `\Drupal\Core\Plugin\DefaultPluginManager` class:

```php
<?php

/**
 * @file
 * Contains \Drupal\mymodule\UnitManager.
 */

namespace Drupal\mymodule;

use Drupal\Core\Plugin\DefaultPluginManager;
use Drupal\Core\Cache\CacheBackendInterface;
use Drupal\Core\Extension\ModuleHandlerInterface;

class UnitManager extends DefaultPluginManager {

}
```

3. When creating a new plugin type, it is recommended that the plugin manager provides a set of defaults for new plugins, if an item is missing. This is also useful to define the default class a plugin should use:

```php
<?php

/**
 * @file
 * Contains \Drupal\mymodule\UnitManager.
 */

namespace Drupal\mymodule;

use Drupal\Core\Plugin\DefaultPluginManager;
use Drupal\Core\Cache\CacheBackendInterface;
use Drupal\Core\Extension\ModuleHandlerInterface;

class UnitManager extends DefaultPluginManager {
  /**
   * Default values for each unit plugin.
   *
   * @var array
   */
  protected $defaults = [
    'id' => '',
    'label' => '',
    'unit' => '',
    'factor' => 0.00,
    'type' => '',
    'class' => 'Drupal\mymodule\Unit',
  ];

}
```

4. Later, we will create the `Unit` class in our module that unit plugins will be instances of.

5. Next, we need to override the `\Drupal\Core\Plugin|DefaultPluginManager` class constructor to define the module handler and cache backend:

```php
<?php

/**
 * @file
 * Contains \Drupal\mymodule\UnitManager.
 */
```

```php
namespace Drupal\mymodule;

use Drupal\Core\Plugin\DefaultPluginManager;
use Drupal\Core\Cache\CacheBackendInterface;
use Drupal\Core\Extension\ModuleHandlerInterface;

class UnitManager extends DefaultPluginManager {
  /**
   * Default values for each unit plugin.
   *
   * @var array
   */
  protected $defaults = [
    'id' => '',
    'label' => '',
    'unit' => '',
    'factor' => 0.00,
    'type' => '',
    'class' => 'Drupal\physical\Unit',
  ];

  /**
   * Constructs a new \Drupal\mymodule\UnitManager object.
   *
   * @param \Drupal\Core\Cache\CacheBackendInterface $cache_
   backend
   *   Cache backend instance to use.
   * @param \Drupal\Core\Extension\ModuleHandlerInterface $module_
   handler
   *   The module handler to invoke the alter hook with.
   */
  public function __construct(CacheBackendInterface $cache_
  backend, ModuleHandlerInterface $module_handler) {
    $this->moduleHandler = $module_handler;
    $this->setCacheBackend($cache_backend, 'physical_unit_
  plugins');
  }

}
```

6. We override the constructor so that we can specify a specific cache key. This allows plugin definitions to be cached and cleared properly; otherwise, our plugin manager will continuously read the disk to find plugins.

7. We also need to override the `getDiscovery` method. We need to implement a `YAML` discovery method:

```php
<?php

/**
 * @file
 * Contains \Drupal\mymodule\UnitManager.
 */

namespace Drupal\mymodule;

use Drupal\Core\Plugin\DefaultPluginManager;
use Drupal\Core\Cache\CacheBackendInterface;
use Drupal\Core\Extension\ModuleHandlerInterface;

class UnitManager extends DefaultPluginManager {
  /**
   * Default values for each unit plugin.
   *
   * @var array
   */
  protected $defaults = [
    'id' => '',
    'label' => '',
    'unit' => '',
    'factor' => 0.00,
    'type' => '',
    'class' => 'Drupal\mymodule\Unit',
  ];

  /**
   * Constructs a new \Drupal\mymodule\UnitManager object.
   *
   * @param \Drupal\Core\Cache\CacheBackendInterface $cache_
backend
   *   Cache backend instance to use.
   * @param \Drupal\Core\Extension\ModuleHandlerInterface $module_
handler
   *   The module handler to invoke the alter hook with.
   */
  public function __construct(CacheBackendInterface $cache_
backend, ModuleHandlerInterface $module_handler) {
    $this->moduleHandler = $module_handler;
```

```
      $this->setCacheBackend($cache_backend, 'physical_unit_
plugins');
   }

   /**
    * {@inheritdoc}
    */
   protected function getDiscovery() {
      if (!isset($this->discovery)) {
         $this->discovery = new YamlDiscovery('units', $this-
>moduleHandler->getModuleDirectories());
         $this->discovery = new ContainerDerivativeDiscoveryDecorator
($this->discovery);
      }
      return $this->discovery;
   }

}
```

8. The default plugin manager implementation supports an annotated plugin discovery, such as field types, field widgets, and field formatters. By setting the discovery property to `YamlDiscovery`, we are telling Drupal to look for a `*.units.yml` file in all the module directories.

9. The next step is to create a `mymodule.services.yml` in your module's directory. This will describe our plugin manager to Drupal, allowing a plugin discovery:

```
services:
  plugin.manager.unit:
    class: Drupal\mymodule\UnitManager
    arguments: ['@container.namespaces', '@cache.discovery', '@
module_handler']
```

10. Drupal utilizes services and dependency injection. By defining our class as a service, we are telling the application container how to initiate our class. This will allow us to retrieve the manager and access plugins even if another module replaces our defined plugin manager.

11. Next, we will define the plugin interface that we defined in the plugin manager. The plugin manager will validate the `Unit` plugins that implement this interface. Create a `UnitInterface.php` file in your module's `src` directory to hold the interface:

```
<?php

/**
 * @file
 * Contains \Drupal\mymodule\UnitInterface.
```

```php
 */

namespace Drupal\mymodule;

/**
 * Interface UnitInterface.
 */
interface UnitInterface {

  /**
   * Returns the unit's label.
   *
   * @return string
   *    The unit's label.
   */
  public function getLabel();

  /**
   * Returns the unit abbreviation.
   *
   * @return string
   *     The abbreviation.
   */
  public function getUnit();

  /**
   * Returns the factor amount for conversions.
   *
   * @return int|float
   *    The factor amount.
   */
  public function getFactor();

  /**
   * Converts a value to the base unit.
   *
   * @param int|float $value
   *     The amount to convert.
   *
   * @return int|float
   *    The converted amount.
   */
  public function toBase($value);
```

```
/**
 * Converts value from base unit to current unit.
 *
 * @param int|float $value
 *    The amount to convert.
 *
 * @return int|float
 *    The converted amount.
 */
public function fromBase($value);

/**
 * Rounds a value.
 *
 * @param int|float $value
 *    The value to round.
 *
 * @return int|float
 *    The rounded value.
 */
public function round($value);

}
```

12. We provide an interface so that we can guarantee that we have these expected methods when working with a `Unit` plugin and have an output, regardless of the logic behind each method. It pushes for encapsulation when working with plugins.

13. Create a `mymodule.units.yml` file to provide default unit plugin definitions:

```
centimeters:
  label: Centimeters
  unit: cm
  factor: 1E-2
  type: dimensions
meters:
  label: Meters
  unit: m
  factor: 1
  type: dimensions
feet:
  label: Feet
  unit: ft
  factor: 3.048E-1
  type: dimensions
```

```
inches:
  label: Inches
  unit: in
  factor: 2.54E-2
  type: dimensions
```

14. As defined in our plugin's default definition, we need to provide a `Unit` class. Create `Unit.php` in your module's `src` directory. This class will implement our `UnitInterface` interface:

```php
<?php

/**
 * @file
 * Contains \Drupal\mymodule\Unit.
 */

namespace Drupal\mymodule;

use Drupal\Core\Plugin\PluginBase;

/**
 * Class Unit.
 */
class Unit extends PluginBase implements UnitInterface {

  /**
   * {@inheritdoc}
   */
  public function getFactor() {
    return (float) $this->pluginDefinition['factor'];
  }

  /**
   * {@inheritdoc}
   */
  public function getLabel() {
    return $this->t($this->pluginDefinition['label'], array(),
array('context' => 'unit'));
  }

  /**
   * {@inheritdoc}
   */
  public function getUnit() {
```

```
      return $this->pluginDefinition['unit'];
  }

  /**
   * {@inheritdoc}
   */
  public function toBase($value) {
    return $this->round($value * $this->getFactor());
  }

  /**
   * {@inheritdoc}
   */
  public function fromBase($value) {
    return $this->round($value / $this->getFactor());
  }

  /**
   * {@inheritdoc}
   */
  public function round($value) {
    return round($value, 5);
  }

  /**
   * Returns the unit's label.
   *
   * @return string
   *    Unit label.
   */
  public function __toString() {
    return $this->getLabel();
  }
}
```

15. This class implements all the required methods defined in our interface. The `toBase` and `fromBase` methods allow us to convert the unit's value from its defined `factor` value.

16. The `Unit` plugin is now implemented and can be integrated through a custom field type or another custom code.

How it works...

Drupal 8 implements a service container, a concept adopted from the Symfony framework. In order to implement a plugin, there needs to be a manager who can discover and process plugin definitions. This manager is defined as a service in a module's `services.yml` with its required constructor parameters. This allows the service container to initiate the class when it is required.

In our example, the UnitManager plugin manager discovers the `Unit` plugin definitions in YAML files that modules provide. After the first discovery, all the known plugin definitions are then cached under the `physical_unit_plugins` cache key.

Plugin managers also provide a method for returning these definitions or creating an object instance based on an available definition. The instance is created from the `class` key that we defined in our plugin's default definition. This also allows a developer to use a custom class to provide an extended `Unit` plugin as long as it extends the default `Unit` class or implements the `UnitInterface` interface.

An example usage would be to create a custom form that allows users to convert values. The following code can be placed in the `submit` method and will allow us to load our plugin for `feet` and return the value in meters:

```
// Load the manager service.
$unit_manager = \Drupal::service('plugin.manager.unit');

// Create a class instance through the manager.
$feet_instance = $unit_manager->createInstance('feet');

// Convert 12ft into meters.
$meters_value = $feet_instance->toBase(12);
```

There's more

Specifying an alter hook

Plugin managers have the ability to define an alter hook. The following line of code will be added to the `UnitManager` class's constructor to provide `hook_physical_unit_alter`. This is passed to the module handler service for invocations:

```
/**
 * Constructs a new \Drupal\mymodule\UnitManager object.
 *
 * @param \Drupal\Core\Cache\CacheBackendInterface
   $cache_backend
```

```
 *    Cache backend instance to use.
 * @param \Drupal\Core\Extension\ModuleHandlerInterface
   $module_handler
 *    The module handler to invoke the alter hook with.
 */
public function __construct(CacheBackendInterface
  $cache_backend, ModuleHandlerInterface $module_handler) {
  $this->moduleHandler = $module_handler;
  $this->alterInfo('physical_unit');
  $this->setCacheBackend($cache_backend,
    'physical_unit_plugins');
}
```

Modules implementing hook_physical_unit_alter in the .module file have the ability to modify all the discovered plugin definitions. Modules have the ability to remove defined plugin entries or alter any information provided for the annotation definition.

Using a cache backend

Plugins can use a cache backend to improve performance. This can be done by specifying a cache backend with the setCacheBackend method in the manager's constructor. The following line of code will allow the Unit plugins to be cached and only discovered on a cache rebuild.

The $cache_backend variable is passed to the constructor. The second parameter provides the cache key. The cache key will have the current language code added as a suffix.

There is an optional third parameter that takes an array of strings to represent cache tags that will cause the plugin definitions to be cleared. This is an advanced feature and plugin definitions should normally be cleared through the manager's clearCachedDefinitions method. The cache tags allow the plugin definitions to be cleared when a relevant cache is cleared as well.

Accessing plugins through the manager

Plugins are loaded through the manager service, which should always be accessed through the service container. The following line of code will be used in your module's hooks or classes to access the plugin manager:

```
$unit_manager = \Drupal::service('plugin.manager.unit');
```

Plugin managers have various methods to retrieve plugin definitions, which are as follows:

- ▶ getDefinitions: This method will return an array of plugin definitions. It first makes an attempt to retrieve cached definitions, if any, and sets the cache of discovered definitions before returning them.

- ▶ getDefinition: This takes an expected plugin ID and returns its definition.

- ► `createInstance`: This takes an expected plugin ID and returns an initiated class for the plugin.
- ► `getInstance`: This takes an array that acts as a plugin definition and returns an initiated class from the definition.

See also

- ► Services and dependency injection at `https://www.drupal.org/node/2133171`

8

Multilingual and Internationalization

In this chapter, we will cover the following recipes to make that your site is multilingual and internationalized:

- ▶ Translating administrative interfaces
- ▶ Translating configurations
- ▶ Translating content
- ▶ Creating multilingual views

Introduction

This chapter will cover the multilingual and internationalization features of Drupal 8, which have been greatly enhanced since Drupal 7. The previous version of Drupal required many extra modules to provide internationalization efforts, but now the majority is provided by Drupal core.

Drupal core provides the following multilingual modules:

- ▶ **Language**: This provides you with the ability to detect and support multiple languages
- ▶ **Interface translation**: This takes installed languages and translates strings that are presented through the user interface
- ▶ **Configuration translation**: This allows you to translate configuration entities, such as date formats and views
- ▶ **Content translation**: This brings the power of providing content in different languages and displaying it according to the current language of the user

Each module serves a specific purpose in creating the multilingual experience for your Drupal site. Behind the scenes, Drupal supports the language code for all entities and cache contexts. These modules expose the interfaces in order to implement and deliver internationalized experiences.

Translating administrative interfaces

The interface translation module provides a method for translating strings found in the Drupal user interface. Harnessing the Language module, interface translations are automatically downloaded from the Drupal translation server. By default, the interface language is loaded through the language code as a path prefix. With the default `Language` configuration, paths will be prefixed with the default language.

Interface translations are based on strings provided in the code that are passed through the internal translation functions.

In this recipe, we will enable Spanish, import the language files, and review the translated interface strings to provide missing or custom translations.

Getting ready

Drupal 8 provides an automated installation process of translation files. For this to work, your web server must be able to communicate with `https://localize.drupal.org/`. If your web server cannot automatically download the files from the translation server, you can refer to the manual installation instructions, which will be covered in the *There's more* section.

How to do it...

1. Go to **Extend** and install the **Interface Translation** module. It will prompt you to enable the **Language**, **File**, and **Field** modules to be installed as well if they are not.

2. After the module is installed, click on **Configuration**. Go to the **Languages** page under the **Regional and Language** section.

3. Click on **Add language** in the languages overview table:

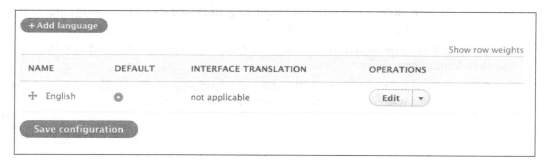

4. The **Add language** page provides a select list of all available languages that the interface can be translated to. Select **Spanish**, and then click on **Add language**.

5. A batch process will run, install the translation language files, and import them.

6. The **INTERFACE TRANSLATION** column specifies the percentage of active translatable interface strings that have a matching translation. Clicking on the link allows you to view the **User interface translation** form:

	NAME	DEFAULT	INTERFACE TRANSLATION	OPERATIONS
				Show row weights
✛	English	◉	not applicable	Edit ▾
✛	Spanish	○	7971/8121 (98.15%)	Edit ▾

Save configuration

7. The **Filter Translatable Strings** form allows you to search for translated strings or untranslated strings. Select **Only untranslated strings** from the **Search in** select list and click on **Filter**.

8. Using the text box on the right-hand side of the screen, a custom translation can be added to **Only untranslated strings**. Type in a translation for the item.

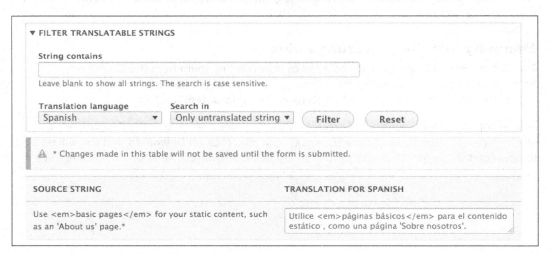

▼ FILTER TRANSLATABLE STRINGS

String contains

Leave blank to show all strings. The search is case sensitive.

Translation language   **Search in**
Spanish ▾   Only untranslated string ▾   Filter   Reset

⚠ * Changes made in this table will not be saved until the form is submitted.

SOURCE STRING	TRANSLATION FOR SPANISH
Use basic pages for your static content, such as an 'About us' page.*	Utilice páginas básicos para el contenido estático , como una página 'Sobre nosotros'.

9. Click on **Save translations** to save the modification.

10. Go to /es/node/add and you will notice that the Basic page content type description will now match your translation.

How it works...

The interface translation module provides `\Drupal\locale\LocaleTranslation`, which implements `\Drupal\Core\StringTranslation\Translator\TranslatorInterface`. This class is registered under the `string_translation` service as an available lookup method.

When the `t` function or the `\Drupal\Core\StringTranslation\` `StringTranslationTrait::t` method is invoked, the `string_translation` service is called to provide a translated string. The `string_translation` service will iterate through the available translators and return a translated string, if possible.

 Developers need to note that this is a key reason to ensure that module strings are passed through translation functions. It allows you to identify strings that need to be translated.

The translator provided in the interface translation will then attempt to resolve the provided string against known translations for the current language. If a translation has been saved, it will be returned.

There's more...

We will explore ways to install other languages, check translation statuses, and many more in the following sections.

Manually installing language files

Translation files can be manually installed by downloading them from the Drupal.org translation server and uploading them through the language interface. You can also use the import interface to upload custom **Gettext Portable Object** (**.po**) files.

Drupal core and most contributed projects have `.po` files available at the Drupal translations site, `https://localize.drupal.org`. On the site, click on **Download** and you will be able to download a `.po` file for Drupal core in all available languages. Additionally, clicking on a language will provide more translations for a specific language across projects.

Spanish overview

Overview Board Translate

Spanish translation team – Grupo de traducción al Español

Nuevo!: Ayuda a probar la nueva versión de localize.drupal.org en Drupal 7!

- Diccionario – Libro de estilo Wiki para crear un glosario de términos, manuales para traductores y libro de estilo en Español.
- Traducción de Drupal core Paquete de archivos .po que componen la traducción de Drupal, y los módulos del Core, al español neutro.
- Interfaz de traducción: Aportar sugerencias de traducción para cadenas de texto pendientes de traducir. Los moderadores validarán las sugerencias y seleccionarán la que será finalmente utilizada por la comunidad. Permite importar nuevas cadenas de texto (actualizaciones de módulos) y exportarlas para ser utilizadas en producción.
- Foro de traducciones: Iniciar y seguir debates sobre palabras o cadenas de texto concretas. Las discusiones sobre palabras establecen una base sólida sobre la que luego construir las sugerencias que serán posteadas en localize.drupal.org
- Glosario de términos: Establece una relación de traducción "automática" para los términos más comunes.
- Directrices para la traducción: Ofrece ideas sobre cómo realizar la traducción al español, de modo que los traductores tengamos un criterio homogéneo. Son ideas abiertas a discusión y por tanto no son realmente un "Libro de Estilo".
- Moderadores de la traducción: Cómo convertirse en moderador y líneas guía para moderar las traducciones.

Top downloads

Drupal core

Project	Version	Downloads	Date created	Up to date as of
Drupal core	5.23	Download (414.14 KB)	2011–Jun–23	2011–Jul–14
Drupal core	6.37	Download (529.03 KB)	2015–Oct–01	2015–Dec–06
Drupal core	7.41	Download (679.04 KB)	2015–Nov–03	2015–Dec–06
Drupal core	8.0.1	Download (1.04 MB)	2015–Dec–04	2015–Dec–06

You can import a `.po` file by going to the `User interface translation` form and selecting the `Import` tab. You need to select the `.po` file and then the appropriate language. You have the ability to treat the uploaded files as custom created translations. This is recommended if you are providing a custom translation file that was not provided by `Drupal.org`. If you are updating Drupal.org translations manually, make sure that you check the box that overwrites existing noncustom translations. The final option allows you to replace customized translations if the `.po` file provides them. This can be useful if you have translated missing strings that might now be provided by the official translation file.

Checking translation status

As you add new modules, the available translations will grow. The `Interface translation` module provides a translation status report that is accessible from the `Reports` page. This will check the default translation server for the project and check whether there is a `.po` available or if it has changed. In the event of a custom module, you can provide a custom translation server, which is covered in *Providing translations for a custom module*.

If an update is available, you will be alerted. You can then import the translation file updates automatically or download and manually import them.

Exporting translations

In the `User interface translation` form, there is an `Export` tab. This form will provide a `Gettext Portable Object` (`.po`) file. You have the ability to export all the available source text that is discovered in your current Drupal site without translations. This will provide a base `.po` for translators to work on.

Additionally, you can download a specific language. Specific language downloads can include noncustomized translations, customized translations, and missing translations. Downloading customized translations can be used to help make contributions to the multilingual and internationalization efforts of the Drupal community!

Interface translation permissions

The interface translation module provides a single permission called **Translate interface text**. This permission grants users the permission to interact with all of the module's capabilities. It is flagged with a security warning as it allows users with this permission to customize all the output text presented to users.

However, it does allow you to provide a role for translators and limits their access to just translation interfaces.

Using interface translation to customize default English strings

The interface translation module is useful beyond its typical multilingual purposes. You can use it to customize strings in the interface that are not available to be modified through typical hook methods, or if you are not a developer!

Firstly, you will need to edit the English language from the **Languages** screen. Check the checkbox for **Enable interface translation for English** and click on **Save language**. You will now have the ability to customize existing interface strings.

 This is only recommended for areas of the interface that cannot already be customized through the normal user interface or provided API mechanisms.

Interface text language detection

The Language module provides detection and selection rules. By default, the module will detect the current language based on the URL, with the language code acting as a prefix to the current path. For example, /es/node will display the node listing page in Spanish:

Interface text language detection

Order of language detection methods for interface text. If a translation of interface text is available in the detected language, it will be displayed.

Show row weights

DETECTION METHOD	DESCRIPTION	ENABLED	OPERATIONS
⊹ Account administration pages	Account administration pages language setting.	☐	
⊹ URL	Language from the URL (Path prefix or domain).	☑	Configure
⊹ Session	Language from a request/session parameter.	☐	Configure
⊹ User	Follow the user's language preference.	☐	
⊹ Browser	Language from the browser's language settings.	☐	Configure
⊹ Selected language	Language based on a selected language.	☑	Configure

You can have multiple detection options enabled at once and use ordering to decide which takes precedence. This can allow you to use the language code in the URL first, but, if missing, a fallback to the language is specified by the user's browser.

Some detection methods have settings. For instance, the URL detection method can be based on the default path prefix or subdomains.

Providing translations for a custom module

Modules can provide custom translations in their directories or point to a remote file. These definitions are added to the module's info.yml file. First, you need to specify the interface translation project key if it differs from the project's machine name.

You need to then specify a server pattern through the interface translation server pattern key. This can be a relative path to Drupal's root, such as modules/custom/mymodule/translation.po, or a remote file URL at http://example.com/files/translations/mymodule/translation.po.

Distributions (or other modules) can implement hook_locale_translation_projects_alter to provide this information on behalf of modules or alter defaults.

The server pattern accepts the following different tokens:

- %core for the version of a course (for example, 8.x)
- %project for the project's name
- %version for the current version string
- %language for the language code

More information on the interface translation keys and variables can be found in the local. api.php document file located in the interface translation module's base folder.

See also

- Refer to the Drupal translation server at https://localize.drupal.org/ translate/drupal8
- You can contribute using the localization server at https://www.drupal.org/ node/302194
- Refer to the locale.api.php documentation at https://api.drupal.org/ api/drupal/core%21modules%21locale%21locale.api.php/8
- Refer to PO and POT files: https://www.drupal.org/node/1814954

Translating configuration

The **Configuration translation** module provides an interface for translating configurations with Interface translation and Language as dependencies. This module allows you to translate configuration entities. The ability to translate configuration entities adds an extra level of internationalization.

Interface translation allows you to translate strings provided in your Drupal site's code base. Configuration translation allows you to translate importable and exportable configuration items that you have created, such as your site title or date formats.

In this recipe, we will translate date format configuration entities. We will provide localized date formats for Danish to provide a more internationalized experience.

Getting ready

Your Drupal site needs to have two languages enabled in order to use **Configuration Translation**. Install **Danish** from the **Languages interface**.

How to do it...

1. Go to the **Extend** and install the **Configuration Translation** module. It will prompt you to enable the **Interface Translation**, **Language**, **File**, and **Field** modules to be installed as well if they are not.

2. After the module is installed, go to the **Configuration**. Go to the **Configuration translation** page under the **Regional and Language** section.

3. Click on the list for the **Date format** option in the configuration entity option table:

4. We will translate the **Default long date format** to represent the **Danish** format. Click on the **Translate for the Default long date format** row.

5. Click on **Add** to create a **Danish** translation:

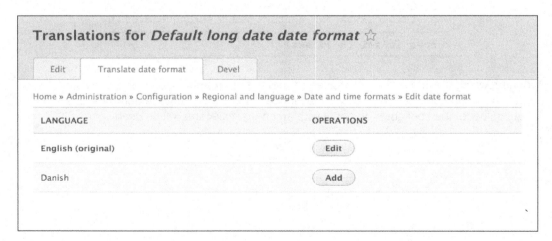

6. For **Danish**, we will provide the following PHP date format: l j. F, Y – H.i. This will display the day of the week, day of the month, the month, full year, and 24 hour notation for time.

7. Click on **Save translation**.

8. Whenever a user is browsing your Drupal site with **Danish** as their language, the date format will now be localized for their experience.

How it works...

The Configuration translation module requires Interface translation; however, it does not work in the same fashion. The module modifies all entity types that extend the `\Drupal\Core\Config\Entity\ConfigEntityInterface` interface. It adds a new handler under the `config_translation_list` key. This is used to build a list of available configuration entities and their bundles.

The module alters the configuration schema in Drupal and updates the default configuration element definitions to use a specified class under `\Drupal\config_translation\Form`. This allows `\Drupal\config_translation\Form\ConfigTranslationFormBase` and its child classes proper saved translated configuration data that can be modified through the configuration translation screens.

When the configuration is saved, it is identified as being part of a collection. The collection is identified as `language.LANGCODE` and all translated configuration entities are saved and loaded by this identifier. Here is an example of how the configuration items are stored in the database:

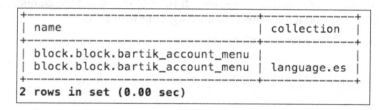

```
+----------------------------------------+----------------+
| name                                   | collection     |
+----------------------------------------+----------------+
| block.block.bartik_account_menu        |                |
| block.block.bartik_account_menu        | language.es    |
+----------------------------------------+----------------+
2 rows in set (0.00 sec)
```

When browsing the site in the es language code, the appropriate `block.block.bartik_account_menu` configuration entity will be loaded. If you are using the default site, or no language code, the configuration entity with an empty collection will be used.

There's more...

Configuration entities and the ability to translate them are a big part of Drupal 8's multilingual capabilities. We'll explore them in detail in the next recipe.

Altering configuration translation info definitions

Modules have the ability to invoke the `hook_config_translation_info_alter` hook to alter discovered configuration mappers. For instance, the `Node` module does this to modify the `node_type` configuration entity:

```
/**
 * Implements hook_config_translation_info_alter().
 */
function node_config_translation_info_alter(&$info) {
  $info['node_type']['class'] = 'Drupal\node\ConfigTranslation\
NodeTypeMapper';
}
```

This updates the `node_type` definition to use the `\Drupal\node\ConfigTranslation\NodeTypeMapper` custom mapper class. This class adds the node type's title as a configurable translation item.

Translating views

Views are configuration entities. When the Configuration translation module is enabled, it is possible to translate Views. This will allow you to translate display titles, exposed form labels, and other items. Refer to the `Creating a multilingual view` recipe in this chapter for more information.

See also

▶ In recipe *Creating a Multilingual View* of *Chapter 8, Multilingual and Internationalization*

Translating content

The content translation module provides a method for translating content entities, such as nodes and blocks. Each content entity needs to have translation enabled, which allows you to granularly decide what properties and fields are translated.

Content translations are duplications of the existing entity but flagged with a proper language code. When a visitor uses a language code, Drupal attempts to load content entities using that language code. If a translation is not present, Drupal will render the default nontranslated entity.

Getting ready

Your Drupal site needs to have two languages enabled in order to use Content translation. Install **Spanish** from the **Languages** interface.

How to do it...

1. Go to **Extend**, and install the **Content translation** module. It will prompt you to enable the **Language** modules to be installed as well if they are not.

2. After the module is installed, go to **Configuration**. Go to the **Content language and translation** page under the **Regional and Language** section.

3. Check the checkbox next to the **Content to expose** settings for the current content types.

4. Enable the content translation for the `Basic` page and keep the provided default settings that enable translation for each field. Click on **Save configuration**:

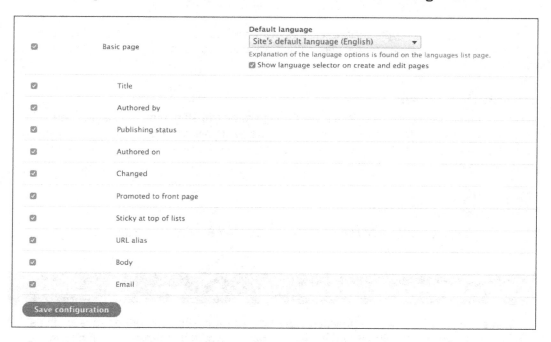

5. First, create a new `Basic` page node. We will create this in the site's default language.

6. When viewing the new node, click on the **Translate** tab. From the **Spanish** language row, click on **Add** to create a translated version of the node:

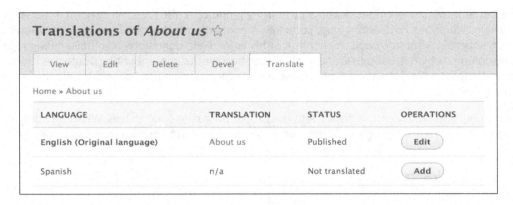

7. The content will be prepopulated with the default language's content. Replace the title and body with the translated text:

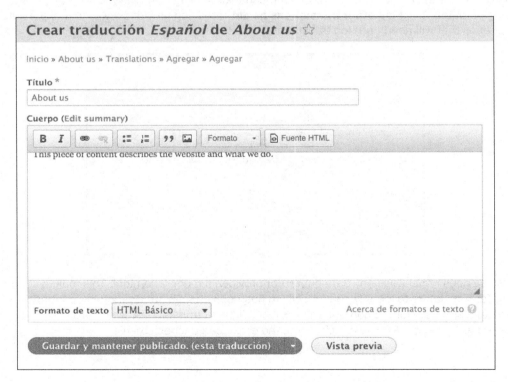

8. Click on **Save and keep published (this translation)** to save the new translation.

How it works

The Content translation module works by utilizing language code flags. All content entities and field definitions have a language code key. A content entity has a language code column, which specifies what language the content entity is for. Field definitions also have a language code column, which is used to identify the translation for the content entity. Content entities can provide handler definitions for handling translations, or else the Content translation module will provide its own.

Each entity and field record is saved with the proper language code to use. When an entity is loaded, the current language code is taken into consideration to ensure that the proper entity is loaded.

There's more

Flagging translations as outdated

The Content translation module provides a mechanism to flag translated entities as possibly being outdated. The **Flag other translations as outdated** flag provides a way to make a note of entities that will need updated translations:

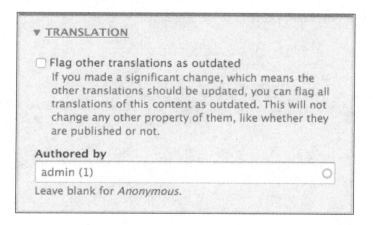

This flag does not change any data but rather provides a moderation tool. This makes it easy for translators to identify content, which has been changed and requires updating. The translation tab for the content entity will highlight all translations, which are still marked as outdated. As they are changed, the editor can uncheck the flag.

Translating content links

Mostly Drupal menus contain links to nodes. Menu links are not translated by default, and the **Custom menu links** option must be enabled under **Content translation**. You will need to translate node links manually from the menu administration interface.

Enabling a menu link from the node create and edit form will not work with translations. If you edit the menu settings from a translation, it will edit the nontranslated menu link.

Defining translation handlers for entities

The Content translation module requires entity definitions to provide information about translation handlers. If this information is missing, it will provide its own defaults. *The Entity API* is covered in *Chapter 10*, but we will quickly discuss how the content translation module interacts with the Entity API.

Content entity definitions can provide a `translation` handler. If not provided, it will default to `\Drupal\content_translation\ContentTranslationHandler`. A node provides this definition and uses it to place the content translation information into the vertical tabs.

The `content_translation_metadata` key defines how to interact with translation metadata information, such as flagging other entities as outdated. The `content_translation_deletion` key provides a form class to handle entity translation deletion.

Currently, as of 8.0.1, no core modules provide implementations that override the default `content_translation_metadata` or `content_translation_deletion`.

See also

▸ *Chapter 10, The Entity API*

Creating multilingual views

Views, being configuration entities, are available for translation. However, the power of multilingual views does not lie just in configuration translation. Views allow you to build filters that react to the current language code. This ensures that the content, which has been translated for the user's language, is displayed.

In this recipe, we will create a multilingual view that provides a block showing recent articles. If there is no content, we will display a translated `no results` message.

Getting ready

Your Drupal site needs to have two languages enabled in order to use **Content Translation**. Install **Spanish** from the **Languages** interface. Enable content translation for **Articles**. You will also need to have some translated content as well.

How to do it...

1. Go to **Views** from **Structure**, and click on **Add new view**.

2. Provide a view name, such as `Recent articles`, and change the type of content to `Article`. Mark that you would like to **Create a block** and then click on **Save** and **edit**.

3. Add a new **Filter criteria**. Search for **Translation language** and add the filter for **Content**. Set the filter to check the **Interface text language selected for page**. This will only display that the content that has been translated or the base language is the current language:

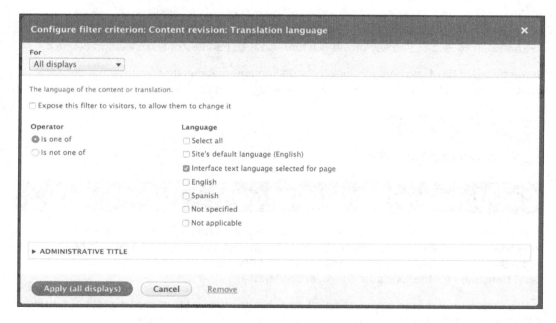

4. Add a `No results behavior` to the `Text area` option. Provide some sample text, such as *Currently no recent articles*.

5. Save the view.

6. Click on the **Translate** tab. Click on **Add** for the **Spanish** row to translate the view for the language.

7. Expand the **Master display settings** and then the **Recent articles** display options fieldsets. Modify the **Display title** option to provided a translated title:

8. Expand **No results behavior** to modify the text on the right-hand side of the screen using the textbox on the left-hand side of the screen as the source for the original text:

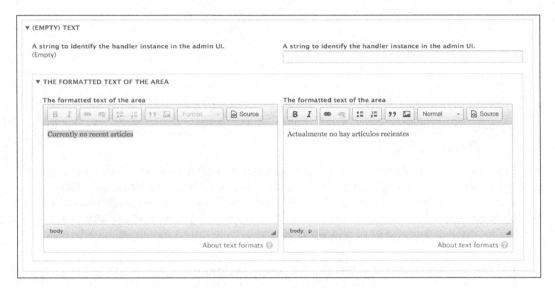

9. Click on **Save translation**.

10. Place the block on your Drupal site. Visit the site through `/es` and notice the translated `Views` block:

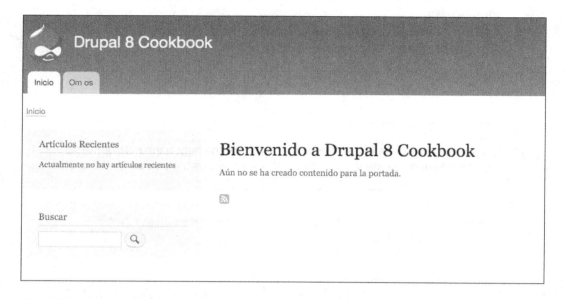

How it works...

Views provide the Translation language filter that builds off of this element. The Views plugin systems provides a mechanism for gathering and displaying all available languages. These will be saved as a token internally and then substituted with the actual language code when the query is executed. If a language code is no longer available, you will see the `Content language for selected` page and Views will fall back to the current language when viewed.

> You will come across this option when editing views provided by Drupal core or contributed modules. While this is not an option in the user interface, it is a default practice to add a language filter defined as *****LANGUAGE_language_content*****, which will force the view to be multilingual.

The filter tells **Views** to query based on the language code of the entity and its fields.

Views are configuration entities. The Configuration translation module allows you to translate views. Views can be translated from the main Configuration translation screens from the `Configuration` area or by editing individual views.

Most translation items will be under the **Master display settings** tab unless overridden in specific displays. Each display type will also have its own specific settings.

There's more...

Translating exposed form items and filters

Each view has the ability to translate the exposed form from the Exposed Form section. This does not translate the labels on the form but the form elements. You have the ability to translate the submit button text, reset button label, sort label, and how ascending or descending should be translated.

You can translate the labels for exposed filters from the Filters section. Each exposed filter will show up as a collapsible fieldset allowing you to configure the administrative label and front facing label.

By default, available translations need to be imported through the global interface translation context.

Translating display and row format items

Some display formats have translatable items. These can be translated in each display mode's section. For example, the following items can be translated with their display format:

- ▸ The Table format allows you to translate the table summary
- ▸ The RSS feed format allows you to translate the feed description
- ▸ The Page format allows you to translate the page's title
- ▸ The Block format allows you to translate the block's title

Translating page display menu items

Custom menu links can be translated through the Content translation module. Views using a page display; however, they do not create custom menu link entities. The `Views` module takes all views with a page display and registers their paths into the routing system directly, as if defined in a module's `routing.yml` file.

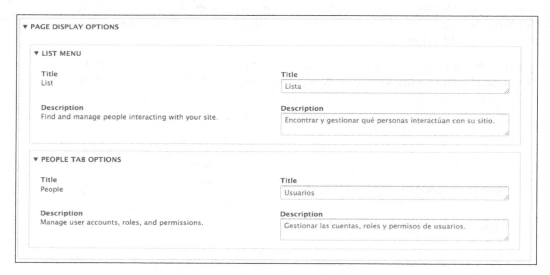

For example, the `People` view that lists all users can be translated to have an updated tab name and link description.

See also

▶ *Chapter 3, Displaying Content through Views*

9
Configuration Management – Deploying in Drupal 8

In this chapter, we will explore the configuration management system and how to deploy configuration changes. Here is a list of the recipes covered in this chapter:

- Importing and exporting configurations
- Synchronizing site configurations
- Using command-line workflow processes
- Using the filesystem for configuration storage

Introduction

Drupal 8 provides a new, unified system for managing configurations. In Drupal 8, all configurations are saved in configuration entities that match a defined configuration schema. This system provides a standard way of deploying the configuration between Drupal site environments and updating the site configuration.

Once the configuration has been created, or imported, it goes into an immutable state. If a module tries to install the configuration that exists, it will throw an exception and be prevented. Outside the typical user interface, the configuration can only be modified through the configuration management system.

The configuration management system can be manipulated through a user interface provided by the `Configuration management` module or through the command-line interface tools. These tools allow you to follow the development paradigm of utilizing a production site and development site where changes are made to the development site and then pushed to production.

 Instead of creating two different Drupal sites for the recipes in this chapter, you can utilize the Drupal multisite functionality. For more information, refer to the *Installing Drupal* recipe of *Chapter 1, Up and Running with Drupal 8*. Note that if you use a multisite, you need to clone your development site's database into the site acting as your production site to replicate a realistic development and production site workflow.

Importing and exporting configurations

Configuration management in Drupal 8 provides a solution to a common problem when working with a website across multiple environments. No matter what the workflow pattern is, at some point the configuration needs to move from one place to another, such as from production to a local environment. When pushing the development work to production, you need to have some way to put the configuration in place.

Drupal 8's user interface provides a way to import and export configuration entities via the YAML format. In this recipe, we will create a content type, export its configuration, and then import it into another Drupal site.

In this recipe, we will export a single configuration entity from a development site. The configuration YAML export will be imported into the production site in order to update its configuration.

Getting ready

You will need a base Drupal site to act as the development site. Another Drupal site, which is a clone of the development site, must be available to act as the production Drupal site.

How to do it...

1. To get started, create a new content type on the development site. Name the content type **Staff Page** and click on **Save and manage fields** to save the content type. We will not be adding any additional fields.

2. Once the content type has been saved, visit **Extend** and install the **Configuration Manager** module if it is not installed:

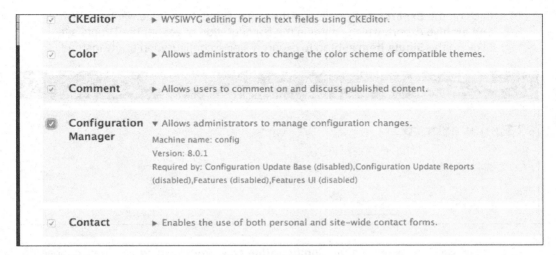

3. From your Drupal site's **Configuration** page, go to **Configuration synchronization** under the **Development** group. This section allows you to import and export configuration:

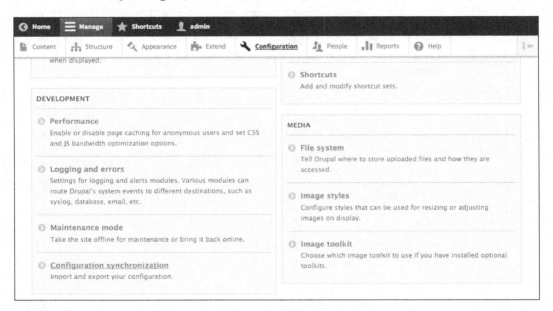

4. Click on the **Export** tab at the top of the page. The default page will be for a **Full archive** export, which contains the configuration of your entire Drupal site. Click on the **Single item** subtab to export a single configuration entity instead:

5. Select **Content type** from the **Configuration type** drop-down menu. Then, choose your content type from the **Configuration name** drop-down menu. Its configuration will populate the configuration textbox:

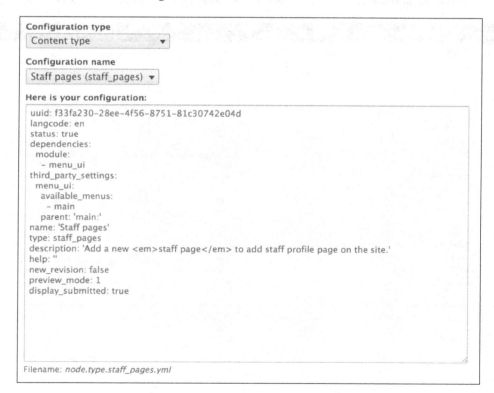

6. Copy the YAML content from the textbox so that you can import it into your other Drupal site.

7. On your production Drupal site, install the Configuration management module just as you did for the development site, if it is not yet installed.

8. Visit the **Configuration synchronization** page and click on the **Import** tab.

9. Click on **Single item** and select **Content type** from the **Configuration type:**

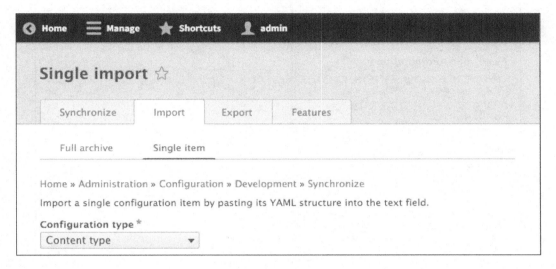

10. Paste your exported configuration YAML into the textbox and click on **Import**:

Full archive   Single item

Home » Administration » Configuration » Development » Synchronize

Import a single configuration item by pasting its YAML structure en el text field.

Configuration type *

Content type ▼

Paste your configuration here *

```
uuid: f33fa230-28ee-4f56-8751-81c30742e04d
langcode: en
status: true
dependencies:
  module:
    - menu_ui
third_party_settings:
  menu_ui:
    available_menus:
      - main
    parent: 'main:'
name: 'Staff pages'
type: staff_pages
description: 'Add a new <em>staff page</em> to add staff profile page on the site.'
help: ''
new_revision: false
preview_mode: 1
display_submitted: true
```

▶ ADVANCED

Import

11. Click on **Confirm** on the confirmation form to finalize your import to the production Drupal site for your custom content type.

12. Visit the **Structure** page and then the **Content Types** page to verify that your content type has been imported.

How it works...

At the most basic level, configurations are just a mapping of keys and values, which can be represented as a PHP array and translated into YAML format.

Configuration management uses schema definitions for configuration entities. The schema definition provides a configuration namespace and the available keys and data types. The schema definition provides a typed data definition for each option that allows validation of the individual values and configuration as a whole.

The export process reads the configuration data and translates it into YAML format. The configuration manager then receives the configuration in the form of YAML and converts it back to a PHP array. The data is then updated in the database.

When importing the configuration, Drupal checks the value of the configuration YAML's `uuid` key, if present, against any current configuration with the same **Universally Unique Identifier (UUID)**. A UUID is a pattern used in software to provide a method of identifying an object across different environments. This allows Drupal to correlate a piece of data from its UUID since the database identifier can differ across environments. If the configuration item has a matching machine name but a mismatching UUID, an error will be thrown.

There's more...

Configuration dependencies

Configuration entities define dependencies when they are exported. The dependency definitions ensure that the configuration entity's schema is available and other module functionality.

When you review the configuration export for `field.storage.node.body.yml`, it defines `node` and `text` as dependencies:

```
dependencies:
  module:
    - node
    - text
```

If the `node` or `text` module is not enabled, the import will fail and throw an error.

Saving to a YAML file for a module's configuration installation

Chapter 6, Creating Forms with the Form API, the providing configuration on install or update, discusses how to use a module to provide configurations on the module's installation. Instead of manually writing configuration YAML files for installation, the Configuration management module can be used to export configurations and save them in your module's config/install directory.

Any item exported through the user interface can be used. The only requirement is that you need to remove the uuid key, as it denotes the site's UUID value and invalidates the configuration when it makes an attempt at installation.

Configuration schemas

The configuration management system in Drupal 8 utilizes the configuration schema to describe configurations that can exist. Why is this important? It allows Drupal to properly implement typed data on stored configuration values and validate them, providing a standardized way of handling configurations for translation and configuration items.

When a module uses the configuration system to store data, it needs to provide a schema for each configuration definition it wishes to store. The schema definition is used to validate and provide typed data definitions for its values.

The following code defines the configuration schema for the navbar_awesome module, which holds two different Boolean configuration values:

```
navbar_awesome.toolbar:
  type: config_object
  label: 'Navbar Awesome toolbar settings'
  mapping:
    cdn:
      type: boolean
      label: 'Use the FontAwesome CDN library'
    roboto:
      type: boolean
      label: 'Include Roboto from Google Fonts CDN'
```

This defines the navbar_awesome.toolbar configuration namespace; it belongs to the navbar_awesome module and has the toolbar configuration. We then need to have two cdn and roboto subvalues that represent typed data values. A configuration YAML for this schema would be named navbar_awesome.toolbar.yml after the namespace, and it contains the following code:

```
cdn: true
roboto: true
```

In turn, this is what the values will look like when represented as a PHP array:

```
[
  'navbar_awesome' => [
    'cdn' => TRUE,
    'roboto' => TRUE,
  ]
]
```

The configuration factory classes then provide an object-based wrapper around these configuration definitions and provide validation of their values against the schema. For instance, if you try to save the `cdn` value as a string, a validation exception will be thrown.

See also

- ▸ *Chapter 4, Extending Drupal*
- ▸ `configuration schema/metadata` in the Drupal.org community handbook at `https://www.drupal.org/node/1905070`

Synchronizing site configurations

A key component to manage a Drupal website is configuration integrity. A key part of maintaining this integrity is ensuring that your configuration changes that are made in development are pushed upstream to your production environments. Maintaining configuration changes by manually exporting and importing through the user interface can be difficult and does not provide a way to track what has or has not been exported or imported. At the same time, manually writing module hooks to manipulate the configuration can be time consuming. Luckily, the configuration management solution provides you with the ability to export and import the entire site's configuration.

A site export can only be imported into another copy of itself. This allows you to export your local development environment's configuration and bring it to staging or production without modifying the content or the database directly.

In this recipe, we will export the development site's complete configuration entities' definitions. We will then take the exported configuration and import it into the production site. This will simulate a typical deployment of a Drupal site with changes created in development that is ready to be released in production.

Getting ready

You will need a base Drupal site to act as the development site. Another Drupal site, which is a clone of the development site, must be available to act as the production Drupal site.

You will need to get the `Configuration management` module enabled.

How to do it...

1. Visit the **Configuration** page and go to **Configuration synchronization**.

2. Navigate to the **Export** tab, and click on the **Export** button to begin the export and download process:

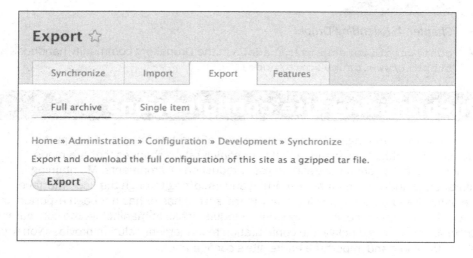

3. Save the `gzipped tarball`; this contains an archive of all the site's configuration as YAML.

4. Visit your other Drupal site and navigate to its **Configuration synchronization** page.

5. Click on the **Import** tab and then on the **Full archive** tab. Use the **Configuration archive** file input, and click on **Choose File** to select the tarball you just downloaded. Click on **Upload** to begin the import process.

6. You will be taken to the **Synchronize** tab to review changes to be imported:

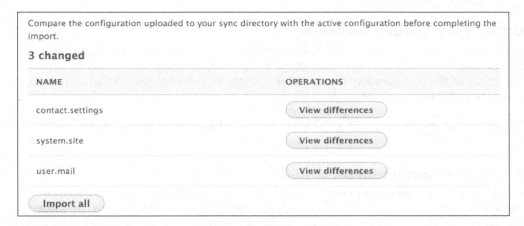

Compare the configuration uploaded to your sync directory with the active configuration before completing the import.

3 changed

NAME	OPERATIONS
contact.settings	View differences
system.site	View differences
user.mail	View differences

Import all

7. Click on **Import all** to update the current site's configuration to the items in the archive.

8. A batch operation will begin with the import process:

Synchronize ☆

Synchronize	Import	Export	Features

Home » Administration » Configuration » Development

✓ The configuration was imported successfully.

How it works...

The **Configuration synchronization** form provides a way to interface with the config database table for your Drupal site. When you visit the **Export** page and create the tarball, Drupal effectively dumps the contents of the config table. Each row represents a configuration entity and will become its own YAML file. The contents of the YAML file represent its database value.

When you import the tarball, Drupal extracts its content. The files are placed in the available CONFIG_SYNC_DIRECTORY directory. The synchronization page parses the configuration entity YAMLs and provides a difference check against the current site's configuration. Each configuration item can be reviewed, and then all the items can be imported. You cannot choose to selectively import individual items.

There's more...

Universally Unique Identifier

When a Drupal site is installed, the UUID is set. This UUID is added to the exported configuration entities and is represented by the `uuid` key. Drupal uses this key to identify the source of the configuration. Drupal will not synchronize configurations that do not have a matching UUID in their YAML definition.

You can review the site's current UUID value by reviewing the `system.site` configuration object.

A synchronization folder

Drupal uses a synchronization folder to hold the configuration YAML files that are to be imported into the current site. This folder is represented by the `CONFIG_SYNC_DIRECTORY` constant. If you have not defined this in the global `$config_directories` variable in your site's `settings.php`, then it will be a randomly named directory in your site's file directory.

> When Drupal 8 entered its beta release cycle, this folder was referenced as a staging folder and referenced by the `CONFIG_STAGING_DIRECTORY`. This is now deprecated; however, the internals of the configuration management system support reading `CONFIG_STAGING_DIRECTORY` as `CONFIG_SYNC_DIRECTORY`. This will be removed in Drupal 9.

The synchronization form will use the configuration management discovery service to look for configuration changes to be imported from this folder.

Installing a configuration from a new site

Drupal's configuration management system will not allow the import of configuration entities that originated at a different Drupal site. When a Drupal site is installed, the `system.site` configuration entity saves a UUID for the current site instance. Only cloned versions of this site's database can accept configuration imports from it.

The configuration installer profile is a custom distribution, which will allow you to import the configuration despite the configuration's site UUID. The profile doesn't actually install itself. When you use the profile, it will provide an interface to upload a configuration export that will then be imported, as shown in the following screenshot:

The distribution can be found at `https://www.drupal.org/project/config_installer`.

Using command-line workflow processes

Drupal 8's configuration systems solve many problems encountered when exporting and deploying configurations in Drupal 7. However, the task of synchronizing the configuration is still a user interface task and requires the manipulation of archive files that contain the configuration exports for a Drupal 8 site.

Configuration management can be done on the command line through Drush without requiring it to be installed. This mitigates any requirement to log in to the production website to import changes. It also opens the ability for more advanced workflows that place the configuration in version control.

In this recipe, we will use Drush to export the development site's configuration to the filesystem. The exported configuration files will then be copied to the production site's configuration directory. Using Drush, the configuration will be imported into production to complete the deployment.

Getting ready...

You will need a base Drupal site to act as the development site. Another Drupal site, which is a clone of the development site, must be available to act as the production Drupal site.

This recipe uses Drush. If you do not have Drush installed, instructions can be found at `http://docs.drush.org/en/master/install/`. Drush needs to be installed at both the locations where your Drupal sites are located.

How to do it...

1. For demonstration purposes, change your development site's name to `Drush Config Sync Demo!`. This way, there is at least one configuration change to be imported to the production Drupal site.

2. Open a command-line terminal and change your directory to the working directory of your development Drupal site.

3. Use the `drush config-export` command to export the configuration to a directory. The command will default to the `sync` configuration directory defined in your Drupal 8 site.

[If you have not explicitly defined a `sync` directory, Drupal automatically creates a protected folder in the current site's uploaded files' directory, with a unique hash suffix on the directory name.]

4. You will receive a message that the configuration has been exported to the directory.

5. Using a method of your choice, copy the contents of the configuration `sync` folder to your other Drupal sites that match the `configuration sync` folder. For example, a default folder generated by Drupal can be `sites/default/files/config_XYZ/sync`.

6. Open a command-line terminal and change your directory to your production Drupal site's working directory.

7. Use the `drush config-import` command to begin the process of importing your configuration.

8. Review the changes made to the configuration entity keys and enter y to confirm the changes:

```
● ● ●                    ▨ www — -bash — 85×19
[Matts-MacBook-Air:www mglaman$ drush config-get system.site
uuid: d847568b-4c6d-4826-9f41-65d40ede72a7
name: Site-Install
mail: admin@example.com
slogan: ''
page:
  403: ''
  404: ''
  front: /node
admin_compact_mode: false
weight_select_max: 100
langcode: en
default_langcode: en

Matts-MacBook-Air:www mglaman$ ▮
```

9. Check whether your configuration changes have been imported.

How it works...

The Drush command-line tool is able to utilize the code found in Drupal to interact with it. The config-export command replicates the functionality provided by the Configuration management module's full site export. However, you do not need to have the Configuration management module enabled for the command to work. The command will extract the available site configuration and write it to a directory, which is unarchived.

The config-import command parses the files in a directory. It will make an attempt to run a difference check against the YAML files like the Configuration management module's synchronize overview form does. It will then import all the changes.

There's more...

Drush config-pull

Drush provides a way of simplifying the transportation of configuration between sites. The config-pull command allows you to specify two Drupal sites and move the export configuration between them. You can either specify a name of a subdirectory under the /sites directory or a Drush alias.

The following command will copy a development site's configuration and import it into the staging server's site:

```
drush config-pull @mysite.local @mysite.staging
```

Additionally, you can specify the `--label` option. This represents a folder key in the `$config_directories` setting. The option defaults to `sync` automatically. Alternatively, you can use the `--destination` parameter to specify an arbitrary folder that is not specified in the setting of `$config_directories`.

Using the Drupal Console

Drush has been part of the Drupal community since Drupal 4.7 and is a custom built command-line tool. The Drupal Console is a Symfony Console-based application used to interact with Drupal. The Drupal Console project provides a means for configuration management over the command line.

 You can learn more about the Drupal Console in *Chapter 13, Drupal CLI* or at `http://www.drupalconsole.com/`.

The workflow is the same, except the naming of the command. The configuration export command is `config:export`, and it is automatically exported to your system's temporary folder until a directory is passed. You can then import the configuration using the `config:import` command.

Editing the configuration from the command line

Both Drush and Drupal Console support the ability to edit the configuration through the command line in YAML format. Both the tools operate in the same fashion and have similar command names:

- Drush: `config-edit [name]`
- Console: `config:edit [name]`

The difference is that Drush will list all the available options to be edited if you do not pass a name, while Console allows you to search.

When you edit a configuration item, your default terminal-based text editor will open. You will be presented with a YAML file that can be edited. Once you save your changes, the configuration is then saved on your Drupal site:

Exporting a single configuration item

Both Drush and Console provide their own mechanisms for exporting a single configuration entity:

- ▶ Drush: `config-get [name]`
- ▶ Console: `config:debug [name]`

Drush will print the configuration's output to the terminal, while Console's default behavior is to write the output to the file disk. For example, the following commands will output the values from `system.site` in YAML format:

```
$ drush config-get system.site
$ drupal config:debug system.site
```

```
● ● ●                     www — -bash — 85×19
[Matts-MacBook-Air:www mglaman$ drush config-get system.site
uuid: d847568b-4c6d-4826-9f41-65d40ede72a7
name: Site-Install
mail: admin@example.com
slogan: ''
page:
  403: ''
  404: ''
  front: /node
admin_compact_mode: false
weight_select_max: 100
langcode: en
default_langcode: en

Matts-MacBook-Air:www mglaman$ █
```

Using version control and command-line workflow

A benefit of having the configuration exportable to YAML files is the fact that the configuration can be kept in version control. The Drupal site's CONFIG_SYNC_DIRECTORY directory can be committed to version control to ensure that it is transported across environments and properly updated. Deployment tools can then use Drush or Console to automatically import changes.

The `config-export` command provided by Drush provides the Git integration:

```
drush config-export --add
```

Appending the `--add` option will run `git add -p` for an interactive staging of the changed configuration files:

```
drush config-export --commit --message="Updating configuration "
```

The `--commit` and optional `--message` options will stage all configuration file changes and commit them with your message:

```
drush config-export --push --message="Updating configuration "
```

Finally, you can also specify `--push` to make a commit and push it to the remote repository.

See also

- ▸ *Chapter 13*, The *Drupal CLI*
- ▸ Drush at `http://docs.drush.org/en/master/`
- ▸ Drupal Console at `http://www.drupalconsole.com/`

Using the filesystem for configuration storage

Originally, Drupal 8 utilized the filesystem for the configuration using the database as a mere cache. During the development cycle, it was changed to keep the configuration in the database and use YAMLs and disks for synchronization. It is possible to enable this setting and have Drupal primarily utilize the disk for configuration storage. This change needs to be defined before you install your Drupal site and existing installations cannot be converted.

In this recipe, we will configure Drupal to write and read its configuration from the filesystem instead of the database. Configuration changes will automatically be imported on the cache rebuild.

Overall, this is an advanced topic. This recipe will explain how to use an alternative storage for the configuration in your Drupal site. For detailed information on Drupal's change from disk to database storage, refer to the issue that committed the change at `https://www.drupal.org/node/2161591`.

How to do it...

1. Create a folder called `config` in the sites/default directory. Create the `active` and `sync` folders in `config`. These will hold the configuration YAMLs for your Drupal site:

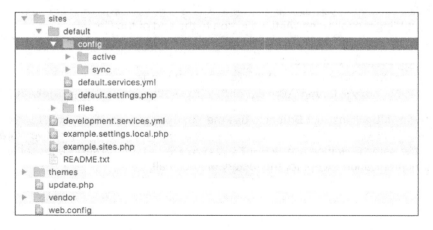

2. Copy the `default.settings.php` file and name it `settings.php`.

3. In the editor of your choice, edit the newly created `settings.php`.

4. Find the empty `$config_directories` array and provide definitions that point to the newly created directories:

```
$config_directories = [
   CONFIG_ACTIVE_DIRECTORY => __DIR__ . 'config/active',
   CONFIG_SYNC_DIRECTORY => __DIR__ . 'config/sync',
];
```

The `CONFIG_ACTIVE_DIRECTORY` constant represents `active` and will be deprecated in Drupal 9, since this is an alternative workflow. `CONFIG_SYNC_DIRECTORY` represents the synchronization folder for the confirmation. The `__DIR__` PHP magic constant will represent the file's current working directory, providing an absolute path to the configuration folders.

5. Find the section for **Active configuration settings**. At the time of writing, the document block for the setting is at line 584.

6. Remove the # to uncomment `$settings['bootstrap_config_storage']`. This will override the default configuration storage backend to use the file storage:

```
$settings['bootstrap_config_storage'] = array('Drupal\Core\Config\
BootstrapConfigStorageFactory', 'getFileStorage');
```

The `\Drupal\Core\Config\BootstrapConfigStorageFactory` class method's `getFileStorage` will return an initiated class that provides a storage backend for the configuration. We are telling it to return a file storage service.

7. Save your `settings.php` file.

8. Copy the `default.services.yml` file and name it `services.yml` in `sites/default` to provide a mechanism for overriding the default service definitions provided by the Drupal core.

9. Edit `services.yml` to alter the default `config.storage.active` implementation by adding the following YAML definition to the end of the file:

```
services:
   config.storage.active:
      class: Drupal\Core\Config\FileStorage
      factory: Drupal\Core\Config\FileStorageFactory::getActive
```

This YAML will instruct Drupal to use the `\Drupal\Core\Config\FileStorage` class and `\Drupal\Core\Config\FileStorageFactory` for active storage. This is the same definition as the `config.storage.staging` service for configuration synchronization except for the factory method call.

10. Install your Drupal site and the active configuration will be in `sites/default/config/active`. Your configuration will go live on the disk but will be cached in the database.

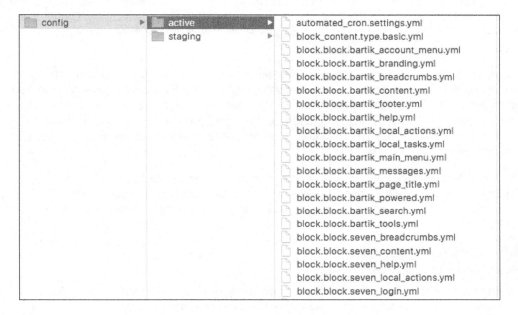

11. Edit the `block.block.bartik_search.yml` file to modify the block's configuration. Change the region from `sidebar_first` to `sidebar_second`.

12. Rebuild Drupal's cache and the configuration changes will be imported from the disk and displayed on your Drupal site:

How it works...

Drupal provides a constant that identifies the active and synchronization configuration folders, `CONFIG_ACTIVE_DIRECTORY` and `CONFIG_SYNC_DIRECTORY`, respectively. Drupal uses, and expects, the `$config_directories` global variable to be an array of configuration folder names and their destinations.

The `bootstrap_config_storage` setting allows you to override the default database storage backend for the configuration. The value needs to be a factory-based static method, which returns a class implementing `\Drupal\Core\Config\StorageInterface`. The example provided in `settings.php` uses the `\Drupal\Core\Config\FileStorage` class. The `\Drupal\Core\DrupalKernel` then caches this storage backend and uses it to retrieve configuration values.

The container's service for `config.storage.active` also needs to be overridden to point to the appropriate class. This way, when modules or internal processes invoke `\Drupal::service('config.storage.active')` they receive the proper storage backend.

There's more...

Although deprecated, filesystem storage for the configuration explores how to provide alternative storage backends. We will explore this in more detail.

Deprecated for Drupal 9

The concepts of an active configuration directory are deprecated and set to be removed by Drupal 9. This is due to the change in the methodology of how the configuration management works. However, just because it is deprecated in the Drupal core does not mean that it will go away. The implementation can very easily be imported into a contributed or custom project.

The `\Drupal\Core\Config\FileStorage` class, which interacts with the configuration as YAML files, will persist for synchronization purposes. To continue using filesystem-based storage, you will need to just write your own file storage factory that the service calls instead of the deprecated class provided by the core:

```php
<?php

/**
 * @file
 * Contains \Drupal\mymodule\MyCustomFileStorageFactory.
 */

namespace Drupal\mymodule;
```

```
/**
 * Provides a factory for creating config file storage objects.
 */
class MyCustomFileStorageFactory {

  /**
   * Returns a FileStorage object working with the active config
directory.
   *
   * @return \Drupal\Core\Config\FileStorage FileStorage
   * no longer creates an active directory.
   */
  static function getActive() {
    return new FileStorage(config_get_config_directory(CONFIG_ACTIVE_
DIRECTORY));
  }

}
```

This class can represent a service factory replacement. The getActive method instructs the file storage backend to discover YAML files in the defined CONFIG_ACTIVE_DIRECTORY location.

See also

- ▶ The change default active config from file storage to DB storage issue at https://www.drupal.org/node/2161591

- ▶ The default active config changed from file storage to DB storage change record at https://www.drupal.org/node/2241059

10
The Entity API

In this chapter, we will explore the Entity API to create custom entities and see how they are handled:

- ▶ Creating a configuration entity type
- ▶ Creating a content entity type
- ▶ Creating a bundle for a content entity type
- ▶ Implementing custom access control for an entity
- ▶ Providing a custom storage handler
- ▶ Creating a route provider

Introduction

In Drupal, entities are a representation of data that have a specific structure. There are specific entity types, which have different bundles and fields attached to those bundles. Bundles are implementations of entities that can have fields attached to themselves. In terms of programming, you can consider an entity that supports bundles an abstract class and each bundle a class that extends that abstract class. Fields are added to bundles. This is part of the reasoning for the term, as an entity type can contain a *bundle* of fields.

An entity is an instance of an entity type defined in Drupal. Drupal 8 provides two entity types: **configuration** and **content**. Configuration entities are not fieldable and represent a configuration within a site. Content entities are fieldable and can have bundles. Bundles are controlled through configuration entities.

In Drupal 8, the **Entity** module lives on, even though most of its functionalities from Drupal 7 are now in core. The goal of the module is to develop improvements for the developer experience around entities by merging more functionalities into core during each minor release cycle (8.1.x, 8.2.x, and so on). Each recipe will provide a *There's more* section that relates to how the Entity module can simplify the recipe.

Creating a configuration entity type

Drupal 8 harnesses the entity API for configuration to provide configuration validation and extended functionality. Using the underlying entity structure, the configuration has a proper **Create, Read, Update, Delete** (**CRUD**) process that can be managed. Configuration entities are not fieldable. All the attributes of a configuration entity are defined in its configuration schema definition.

Most common configuration entities interact with Drupal core's `config_object` type, as discussed in *Chapter 4, Extending Drupal,* and *Chapter 9, Configuration Management – Deploying in Drupal 8,* to store and manage a site's configuration. There are other uses of configuration entities, such as menus, view displays, form displays, contact forms, tours, and many more, which are all configuration entities.

In this recipe, we will create a new configuration entity type called `SiteAnnouncement`. This will provide a simple configuration entity that allows you to create, edit, and delete simple messages that can be displayed on the site for important announcements.

Getting ready

You will need a custom module to place code into in order to implement a configuration entity type. Create an `src` directory for your classes.

How to do it...

1. In your module's base directory, create a `config` directory with a `schema` subdirectory. In the subdirectory, make a file named `mymodule.schema.yml` that will hold our configuration entity's schema:

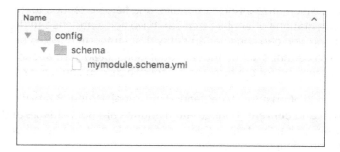

2. In your `mymodule.schema.yml`, add a definition to `mymodule.announcement.*` to provide our label and message storage:

```yaml
# Schema for the configuration files of the Site Announcement.

mymodule.announcement.*:
  type: config_entity
  label: 'Site announcement'
  mapping:
    id:
      type: string
      label: 'ID'
    label:
      type: label
      label: 'Label'
    message:
      type: text
      label: 'Text'
```

We define the configuration entity's namespace as an announcement, which we will provide to Drupal in the entity's annotation block. We tell Drupal that this is a `config_entity` and provide a label for the schema.

Using the mapping array, we provide the attributes that make up our entity and the data that will be stored.

3. Create an `Entity` directory in your module's `src` folder. First, we will create an interface for our entity by making a `SiteAnnouncementInterface.php` file. The `SiteAnnouncementInterface` will extend the `\Drupal\Core\Config\Entity\ConfigEntityInterface`:

```php
<?php

/**
 * @file Contains \Drupal\mymodule\Entity\
 * SiteAnnouncementInterface.
 */

namespace Drupal\mymodule\Entity;

use Drupal\Core\Config\Entity\ConfigEntityInterface;

interface SiteAnnouncementInterface  extends ConfigEntityInterface
{

  /**
   * Gets the message value.
```

```
   *
   * @return string
   */
  public function getMessage();

}
```

This will be implemented by our entity and will be provided the method requirements. It is best practice to provide an interface for entities. This allows you to provide the required methods if another developer extends your entity or if you are doing advanced testing and need to mock an object. We also provide a method for returning our custom attribute.

4. Create SiteAnnouncement.php in your Entity directory in src. This file will contain the SiteAnnouncement class, which extends \Drupal\Core\Config\ Entity\ConfigEntityBase and implements our entity's interface:

```php
<?php

/**
 * @file Contains \Drupal\mymodule\Entity\SiteAnnouncement
 */

namespace Drupal\mymodule\Entity;

use Drupal\Core\Config\Entity\ConfigEntityBase;

class SiteAnnouncement extends ConfigEntityBase implements
SiteAnnouncementInterface {

  /**
   * The announcement's message.
   *
   * @var string
   */
  protected $message;

  /**
   * {@inheritdoc|}
   */
  public function getMessage() {
    return $this->message;
  }

}
```

We added the `message` property defined in our schema as a class property. Our method defined in the entity's interface is used to return that value and interact with our configuration entity.

5. Entities use annotation documentation blocks. We will start our annotation block by providing the entity's ID, label, configuration prefix, and configuration export key names:

```php
<?php

/**
 * @file Contains \Drupal\mymodule\Entity\SiteAnnouncement
 */

namespace Drupal\mymodule\Entity;

use Drupal\Core\Config\Entity\ConfigEntityBase;

/**
 * @ConfigEntityType(
 *   id ="announcement",
 *   label = @Translation("Site Announcement"),
 *   config_prefix = "announcement",
 *   entity_keys = {
 *     "id" = "id",
 *     "label" = "label"
 *   },
 *   config_export = {
 *     "id",
 *     "label",
 *     "message",
 *   }
 * )
 */
class SiteAnnouncement extends ConfigEntityBase implements
SiteAnnouncementInterface {

  /**
   * The announcement's message.
   *
   * @var string
   */
  protected $message;
```

```
/**
 * {@inheritdoc}
 */
public function getMessage() {
  return $this->message;
}

}
```

The annotation document block tells Drupal that this is an instance of the `ConfigEntityType` plugin. The `id` is the internal machine name identifier for the entity type and the `label` is the human-readable version. The `config_prefix` matches with how we defined our schema with `mymodule.announcement`. The entity keys definition tells Drupal which attributes represent our identifiers and labels.

When specifying `config_export`, we are telling the configuration management system what properties are to be exportable when exporting our entity.

6. Next, we will add `handlers` to our entity. We will define the class that will display the available entity entries and the forms to work with our entity:

```
/**
 * @ConfigEntityType(
 *   id ="announcement",
 *   label = @Translation("Site Announcement"),
 *   handlers = {
 *     "list_builder" = "Drupal\mymodule\
SiteAnnouncementListBuilder",
 *     "form" = {
 *       "default" = "Drupal\mymodule\SiteAnnouncementForm",
 *       "add" = "Drupal\mymodule\SiteAnnouncementForm",
 *       "edit" = "Drupal\mymodule\SiteAnnouncementForm",
 *       "delete" = "Drupal\Core\Entity\EntityDeleteForm"
 *     }
 *   },
 *   config_prefix = "announcement",
 *   entity_keys = {
 *     "id" = "id",
 *     "label" = "label"
 *   },
 *   config_export = {
 *     "id",
 *     "label",
 *     "message",
 *   }
 * )
 */
```

The `handlers` array specifies classes that provide the interaction functionality with our entity. The `list_builder` class will be created to show you a table of our entities. The form array provides classes for forms to be used when creating, editing, or deleting our configuration entity.

7. Lastly, for our annotation, we need to define routes for our `delete`, `edit`, and `collection` (list) pages. Drupal will automatically build the routes based on our annotation:

```
/**
 * @ConfigEntityType(
 *   id ="announcement",
 *   label = @Translation("Site Announcement"),
 *   handlers = {
 *     "list_builder" = "Drupal\mymodule\
SiteAnnouncementListBuilder",
 *     "form" = {
 *       "default" = "Drupal\mymodule\SiteAnnouncementForm",
 *       "add" = "Drupal\mymodule\SiteAnnouncementForm",
 *       "edit" = "Drupal\mymodule\SiteAnnouncementForm",
 *       "delete" = "Drupal\Core\Entity\EntityDeleteForm"
 *     }
 *   },
 *   config_prefix = "announcement",
 *   entity_keys = {
 *     "id" = "id",
 *     "label" = "label"
 *   },
 *   links = {
 *     "delete-form" = "/admin/config/system/site-announcements/
manage/{announcement}/delete",
 *     "edit-form" = "/admin/config/system/site-announcements/
manage/{announcement}",
 *     "collection" = "/admin/config/system/site-announcements",
 *   },
 *   config_export = {
 *     "id",
 *     "label",
 *     "message",
 *   }
 * )
 */
```

There is a routing service for entities that will automatically provide Drupal a route with the proper controllers based on this annotation. The add form route is not yet supported and needs to be manually added.

8. Create a `mymodule.routing.yml` in your module's root directory to manually provide a route to add a `Site-announcement` entity:

```yaml
entity.announcement.add_form:
  path: '/admin/config/system/site-announcements/add'
  defaults:
    _entity_form: 'announcement.add'
    _title: 'Add announcement'
  requirements:
    _permission: 'administer content'
```

9. We can use the `_entity_form` property to tell Drupal to look up the class defined in our handlers.

10. Before we implement our `list_builder` handler, we also need to add the route in `mymodule.routing.yml` for our collection link definition, as this is not auto generated by route providers:

```yaml
entity.announcement.collection:
  path: '/admin/config/system/site-announcements'
  defaults:
    _entity_list: 'announcement'
    _title: 'Site Announcements'
  requirements:
    _permission: 'administer content
```

11. The `_entity_list` key will tell the route to use our `list_builder` handler to build the page. We will reuse the `administer content` permission provided by the Node module.

12. Create the `SiteAnnouncementListBuilder` class defined in our `list_builder` handler by making a `SiteAnnouncementListBuilder.php` and extending the `\Drupal\Core\Config\Entity\ConfigEntityListBuilder`:

```php
<?php

/**
 * @file
 * Contains \Drupal\mymodule\SiteAnnouncementListBuilder.
 */

namespace Drupal\mymodule;

use Drupal\Core\Config\Entity\ConfigEntityListBuilder;
use Drupal\mymodule\Entity\SiteAnnouncementInterface;

class SiteAnnouncementListBuilder extends ConfigEntityListBuilder
{
```

```
/**
 * {@inheritdoc}
 */
public function buildHeader() {
  $header['label'] = t('Label');
  return $header + parent::buildHeader();
}

/**
 * {@inheritdoc}
 */
public function buildRow(SiteAnnouncementInterface $entity) {
  $row['label'] = $entity->label();
  return $row + parent::buildRow($entity);
}
}
```

13. In our list builder handler, we override the `buildHeader` and `builderRow` methods so that we can add our configuration entity's properties to the table.

14. Now we need to create an entity form, as defined in our form handler array, to handle our add and edit functionalities. Create `SiteAnnouncementForm.php` in the `src` directory to provide the `SiteAnnouncementForm` class that extends the `\Drupal\Core\Entity\EntityForm` class:

```
<?php

namespace Drupal\mymodule;

use Drupal\Component\Utility\Unicode;
use Drupal\Core\Entity\EntityForm;
use Drupal\Core\Form\FormStateInterface;
use Drupal\Core\Language\LanguageInterface;

class SiteAnnouncementForm extends EntityForm {
  /**
   * {@inheritdoc}
   */
  public function form(array $form, FormStateInterface $form_
state) {
    $form = parent::form($form, $form_state);

    /** @var \Drupal\mymodule\Entity\SiteAnnouncementInterface
$entity */
    $entity = $this->entity;
```

```
      $form['label'] = [
        '#type' => 'textfield',
        '#title' => t('Label'),
        '#required' => TRUE,
        '#default_value' => $entity->label(),
      ];
      $form['message'] = [
        '#type' => 'textarea',
        '#title' => t('Message'),
        '#required' => TRUE,
        '#default_value' => $entity->getMessage(),
      ];

      return $form;
  }

  /**
   * {@inheritdoc}
   */
  public function save(array $form, FormStateInterface $form_
state) {
      $entity = $this->entity;
      $is_new = !$entity->getOriginalId();

      if ($is_new) {
        // Configuration entities need an ID manually set.
        $machine_name = \Drupal::transliteration()
           ->transliterate($entity->label(),
LanguageInterface::LANGCODE_DEFAULT, '_');
        $entity->set('id', Unicode::strtolower($machine_name));

        drupal_set_message(t('The %label announcement has been
created.', array('%label' => $entity->label())));
      }
      else {
        drupal_set_message(t('Updated the %label announcement.',
array('%label' => $entity->label())));
      }

      $entity->save();

      // Redirect to edit form so we can populate colors.
      $form_state->setRedirectUrl($this->entity-
>toUrl('collection'));
  }
}
```

15. We override the `form` method to add Form API elements to our `label` and `message` properties. We also override the `save` method to provide user messages about the changes that are made. We utilize the entity's `toUrl` method to provide a redirect back to the `collection` (list) page. We use the transliteration service to generate a machine name based on the label for our entity's identifier.

16. Next, we will provide a `mymodule.links.action.yml` file in your module's directory. This will allow us to define action links on a route. We will be adding an `Add announcement` link to our entity's add form on its collection route:

```
announcement.add:
  route_name: entity.announcement.add_form
  title: 'Add announcement'
  appears_on:
    - entity.announcement.collection
```

17. This will instruct Drupal to render the `entity.announcement.add_form` link on the specified routes in the `appears_on` value.

18. Your module structure should look like the following screenshot:

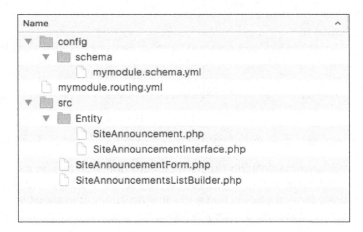

19. Install your module and review the **Configuration** page. You can now manage the `Site Announcement` entries from the **Site Announcement** link.

How it works

When creating a configuration schema definition, one of the first properties used for the configuration namespace is `type`. This value can be `config_object` or `config_entity`. When the type is `config_entity`, the definition will be used to create a database table rather than structure the serialized data for the `config` table.

Entities are powered by the plugin system in Drupal, which means there is a plugin manager. The default `\Drupal\Core\Entity\EntityTypeManager` provides discovery and handling of entities. The `ConfigEntityType` class for the entity type's plugin class will force the setting of the `uuid` and `langcode` in the `entity_keys` definition. The storage handler for configuration entities defaults to `\Drupal\Core\Config\Entity\ConfigEntityStorage`. The `ConfigEntityStorage` class interacts with the configuration management system to load, save, and delete custom configuration entities.

There's more...

Drupal 8 introduces a typed data system that configuration entities, and fields use.

Available data types for schema definitions

Drupal core provides its own configuration information. There is a `core.data_types.schema.yml` file located at `core/config/schema`. These are the base types of data that core provides and can be used when making configuration schema. The file contains YAML definitions of data types and the class which represents them:

```
boolean:
  label: 'Boolean'
  class: '\Drupal\Core\TypedData\Plugin\DataType\BooleanData'
email:
  label: 'Email'
  class: '\Drupal\Core\TypedData\Plugin\DataType\Email'
string:
  label: 'String'
  class: '\Drupal\Core\TypedData\Plugin\DataType\StringData'
```

When a configuration schema definition specifies an attribute that has an e-mail for its type, that value is then handled by the `\Drupal\Core\TypedData\Plugin\DataType\Email` class. Data types are a form of plugins and each plugin's annotation specifies constraints for validation. This is built around the Symfony Validator component.

See also

- *Chapter 6, Creating Forms with the Form API*
- *Chapter 4, Extending Drupal*
- *Chapter 9, Confiuration Management – Deploying in Drupal 8*
- Refer to configuration schema/metadata at `https://www.drupal.org/node/1905070`

Creating a content entity type

Content entities provide base field definitions and also configurable fields through the Field module. There is also support for revisions and translations with content entities. Display modes, both form and view, are available for content entities to control how the fields are edited and displayed. When an entity does not specify bundles, there is automatically one bundle instance with the same name as the entity.

In this recipe, we will create a custom content entity that does not specify a bundle. We will create a `Message` entity that can serve as a content entity for generic messages.

Getting ready

You will need a custom module to place code into in order to implement a configuration entity type. Create an `src` directory for your classes.

How to do it...

1. Create an `Entity` directory in your module's `src` folder. First, we will create an interface for our entity by making a `MessageInterface.php` file:

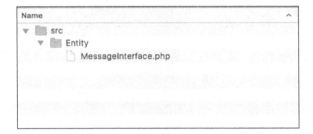

2. The `MessageInterface` will extend `\Drupal\Core\Entity\ContentEntityInterface`:

```php
<?php

/**
 * @file Contains \Drupal\mymodule\Entity\MessageInterface.
 */

namespace Drupal\mymodule\Entity;

use Drupal\Core\Entity\ContentEntityInterface;
```

```
interface MessageInterface extends ContentEntityInterface {

    /**
     * Gets the message value.
     *
     * @return string
     */
    public function getMessage();

}
```

This will be implemented by our entity and provide the method requirements. It is best practice to provide an interface for entities. This allows you to provide required methods if another developer extends your entity or if you are doing advanced testing and need to mock an object. We also provide a method to return our main base field definition (to be defined).

3. Create `Message.php` in your `Entity` directory in `src`. This file will contain the `Message` class, which extends `\Drupal\Core\Entity\ContentEntityBase` and implements our entity's interface:

```
<?php

/**
 * @file Contains \Drupal\mymodule\Entity\Message
 */

namespace Drupal\mymodule\Entity;

use Drupal\Core\Entity\ContentEntityBase;

class Message extends ContentEntityBase implements
MessageInterface {

}
```

4. We need to create an annotation document block to provide information about our entity, such as its `ID`, `label`, `entity` keys, and so on:

```
<?php

/**
 * @file Contains \Drupal\mymodule\Entity\Message
 */

namespace Drupal\mymodule\Entity;
```

```
use Drupal\Core\Entity\ContentEntityBase;

/**
 * Defines the message entity class.
 *
 * @ContentEntityType(
 *   id = "message",
 *   label = @Translation("Message"),
 *   base_table = "message",
 *   fieldable = TRUE,
 *   entity_keys = {
 *     "id" = "message_id",
 *     "label" = "title",
 *     "langcode" = "langcode",
 *     "uuid" = "uuid"
 *   },
 * )
 */
class Message extends ContentEntityBase implements
MessageInterface {

}
```

The `id` is the internal machine name identifier for the entity type and the label is the human-readable version. The entity keys definition tells Drupal which attributes represent our identifier and label.

`base_table` defines the database table in which the entity will be stored and `fieldable` allows custom fields to be configured through the Field UI module.

5. Next, we will add `handlers` to our entity. We will use the default handlers provided by Drupal:

```
/**
 * Defines the profile entity class.
 *
 * @ContentEntityType(
 *   id = "message",
 *   label = @Translation("Message"),
 *   handlers = {
 *     "list_builder" = "Drupal\mymodule\MessageListBuilder",
 *     "form" = {
 *       "default" = "Drupal\Core\Entity\ContentEntityForm",
 *       "add" = "Drupal\Core\Entity\ContentEntityForm",
 *       "edit" = "Drupal\Core\Entity\ContentEntityForm",
 *       "delete" = "Drupal\Core\Entity\ContentEntityDeleteForm",
```

```
 *      },
 *      },
 *    base_table = "message",
 *    fieldable = TRUE,
 *    entity_keys = {
 *      "id" = "message_id",
 *      "label" = "title",
 *      "langcode" = "langcode",
 *      "uuid" = "uuid"
 *    },
 *  )
 */
```

The `handlers` array specifies classes that provide the interaction functionality with our entity. The list builder class will be created to show you a table of our entities. The form array provides classes for forms to be used when creating, editing, or deleting our content entity.

6. An additional `handler` can be added, the `route_provider`, to dynamically generate our canonical (view), edit, and delete routes:

```
/**
 * Defines the profile entity class.
 *
 * @ContentEntityType(
 *    id = "message",
 *    label = @Translation("Message"),
 *    handlers = {
 *      "list_builder" = "Drupal\mymodule\MessageListBuilder",
 *      "form" = {
 *        "default" = "Drupal\Core\Entity\ContentEntityForm",
 *        "add" = "Drupal\Core\Entity\ContentEntityForm",
 *        "edit" = "Drupal\Core\Entity\ContentEntityForm",
 *        "delete" = "Drupal\Core\Entity\ContentEntityDeleteForm",
 *      },
 *      "route_provider" = {
 *        "html" = "Drupal\Core\Entity\Routing\
DefaultHtmlRouteProvider",
 *      },
 *    },
 *    base_table = "message",
 *    fieldable = TRUE,
 *    entity_keys = {
 *      "id" = "message_id",
 *      "label" = "title",
 *      "langcode" = "langcode",
```

```
 *    "uuid" = "uuid"
 *    },
 *  links = {
 *    "canonical" = "/messages/{message}",
 *    "edit-form" = "/messages/{message}/edit",
 *    "delete-form" = "/messages/{message}/delete",
 *    "collection" = "/admin/content/messages"
 *    },
 * )
 */
```

There is a routing service for entities that will automatically provide Drupal a route with the proper controllers based on this annotation. The add form route is not yet supported and needs to be manually added.

7. We need to implement `baseFieldDefinitions` to satisfy the `FieldableEntityInterface` interface, which will provide our field definitions to the entity's base table:

```
/**
 * {@inheritdoc}
 */
public static function baseFieldDefinitions(EntityTypeInterface $entity_type) {
  $fields['message_id'] = BaseFieldDefinition::create('integer')
    ->setLabel(t('Message ID'))
    ->setDescription(t('The message ID.'))
    ->setReadOnly(TRUE)
    ->setSetting('unsigned', TRUE);
  $fields['langcode'] = BaseFieldDefinition::create('language')
    ->setLabel(t('Language code'))
    ->setDescription(t('The message language code.'))
    ->setRevisionable(TRUE);
  $fields['uuid'] = BaseFieldDefinition::create('uuid')
    ->setLabel(t('UUID'))
    ->setDescription(t('The message UUID.'))
    ->setReadOnly(TRUE);

  $fields['title'] = BaseFieldDefinition::create('string')
    ->setLabel(t('Title'))
    ->setRequired(TRUE)
    ->setTranslatable(TRUE)
    ->setRevisionable(TRUE)
    ->setSetting('max_length', 255)
    ->setDisplayOptions('view', array(
      'label' => 'hidden',
```

```
        'type' => 'string',
        'weight' => -5,
      ))
      ->setDisplayOptions('form', array(
        'type' => 'string_textfield',
        'weight' => -5,
      ))
      ->setDisplayConfigurable('form', TRUE);

    $fields['content'] = BaseFieldDefinition::create('text_long')
      ->setLabel(t('Content'))
      ->setDescription(t('Content of the message'))
      ->setTranslatable(TRUE)
      ->setDisplayOptions('view', array(
        'label' => 'hidden',
        'type' => 'text_default',
        'weight' => 0,
      ))
      ->setDisplayConfigurable('view', TRUE)
      ->setDisplayOptions('form', array(
        'type' => 'text_textfield',
        'weight' => 0,
      ))
      ->setDisplayConfigurable('form', TRUE);

    return $fields;
  }
```

8. The `FieldableEntityInterface` is implemented by the `ContentEntityBase` class through the `ContentEntityInterface`. The method needs to return an array of `BaseFieldDefinitions` for typed data definitions. This includes the keys provided in the `entity_keys` value in our entity's annotation along with any specific fields for our implementation.

9. The `content` base field definition will hold the actual text for the message.

10. Next, we will implement the `getMessage` method to satisfy our interface and provide a means to retrieve our message's text value:

```
/**
 * {@inheritdoc}
 */
public function getMessage() {
  return $this->get('content')->value;
}
```

11. This method provides a wrapper around the defined base field's value and returns it.

12. Create a `mymodule.routing.yml` to manually provide a route to add a `message` entity:

```
entity.message.add_form:
  path: '/messages/add'
  defaults:
    _entity_form: 'message.add'
    _title: 'Add message'
  requirements:
    _entity_create_access: 'message'
```

13. We can use the `_entity_form` property to tell Drupal to look up the class defined in our handlers.

14. Before we implement our `list_builder` handler, we also need to add the route to `routing.yml` for our collection link definition, as this is not auto generated by route providers:

```
entity.message.collection:
  path: '/admin/content/messages'
  defaults:
    _entity_list: 'message'
    _title: 'Messages'
  requirements:
    _permission: 'administer messages'
```

15. The `_entity_list` key will tell the route to use our `list_builder` handler to build the page.

16. Create the `MessageListBuilder` class defined in our `list_builder` handler by making a `MessageListBuilder.php` file and extend `\Drupal\Core\Entity\EntityListBuilder`. We need to override the default implementation to display our base field definitions:

```php
<?php

/**
 * @file Contains \Drupal\mymodule\MessageListBuilder
 */

namespace Drupal\mymodule;

use Drupal\Core\Entity\EntityInterface;
use Drupal\Core\Entity\EntityListBuilder;

class MessageListBuilder extends EntityListBuilder {
  public function buildHeader() {
```

```
        $header['title'] = t('Title');
        return $header + parent::buildHeader();
    }

    public function buildRow(EntityInterface $entity) {
        $row['title'] = $entity->label();
        return $row + parent::buildRow($entity);
    }

}
```

17. In our list builder handler, we override the `buildHeader` and `builderRow` methods so that we can add our configuration entity's properties to the table.

18. Your module's structure should resemble the following screenshot:

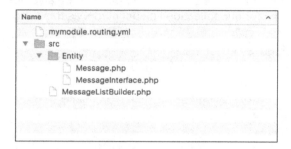

19. Install your module. Visit `/messages/add` to create your first custom content entity entry and then view it on `/admin/content/messages`:

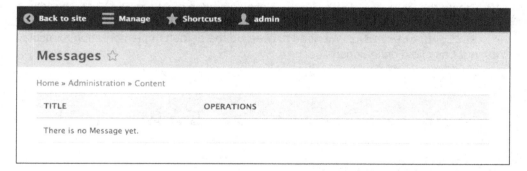

How it works...

Content entities are a version of the `EntityType` plugin. When you define a content entity type, the annotation block begins with `@ContentEntityType`. This declaration, and the properties in it, represents the definition to initiate an instance of the `\Drupal\Core\Entity\ContentEntityType` class just like all other plugin annotations. The `ContentEntityType` plugin class implements a constructor to provide default `storage` and `view_builder` handlers, forcing us to implement the `list_builder` and `form` handler arrays.

The plugin manager for entity types lives under the `entity_type.manager` service name and is provided through `\Drupal\Core\Entity\EntityTypeManager` by default. However, while the annotation defines the plugin information, our `Message` class that extends `ContentEntityBase` provides a means for manipulating the data it represents.

There's more...

We will discuss how to add additional functionality to your entity, and use the Entity module to simplify the developer expedience.

Using the AdminHtmlRouteProvider provider

Our `Message` entity type implementes the `DefaultHtmlRouteProvider` class. There is also the `\Drupal\Core\Entity\Routing\AdminHtmlRouteProvider` class. This overrides the `getEditFormRoute` and `getDeleteFormRoute` and marks them with `_admin_route`. This will cause those forms to be rendered in the administration theme.

Simplifying base field definitions using the Entity module

Content entities need to define field definitions for each field listed in the `entity_keys` array. This often results in a lot of boilerplate code to make identifier, language code, UUID, and bundle entity reference fields. The `Entity` module provides the `\Drupal\entity\EntityKeysFieldsTrait` trait. A content entity type class can use this trait to provide field definitions for the possible `entity_key` values.

The `Message` content entity class can be reduced to the following code using this trait:

```
class Message extends ContentEntityBase implements MessageInterface {
  use EntityKeysFieldsTrait;

  /**
   * {@inheritdoc}
   */
  public function getMessage() {
    return $this->get('content')->value;
  }
```

```
/**
 * {@inheritdoc}
 */
public static function baseFieldDefinitions(EntityTypeInterface
$entity_type) {
    $fields = self::entityKeysBaseFieldDefinitions($entity_type);

    $fields['content'] = BaseFieldDefinition::create('text_long')
      ->setLabel(t('Content'))
      ->setDescription(t('Content of the message'))
      ->setTranslatable(TRUE)
      ->setDisplayOptions('view', array(
        'label' => 'hidden',
        'type' => 'text_default',
        'weight' => 0,
      ))
      ->setDisplayConfigurable('view', TRUE)
      ->setDisplayOptions('form', array(
        'type' => 'text_textfield',
        'weight' => 0,
      ))
      ->setDisplayConfigurable('form', TRUE);
    return $fields;
  }
}
```

The `entityKeysBaseFieldDefinitions` method provided by the trait will check whether the possible `entity_key` values have been provided and adds a default base definition for them. Now, we only need to worry about implementing base fields that are unique to our entity types.

The entity type's admin permission

The entity access handler provided by core will check whether entities implement an `admin_permission` option. If it is provided, it will be used as the basis for most access checks unless a custom access handler is implemented. This can be done by providing the following code snippet into an entity type's annotation:

```
 *   admin_permission = "administer messages",
```

The `\Drupal\Core\Entity\EntityAccessControlHandler` class will check whether users have this permission when validating create access or any other access operation.

Making the collection route a local task tab

In this recipe, we specified the message collection route as `/admin/content/messages`. Without implementing this route as a local task under the `/admin/content` route, it will not show up as a tab. This can be done by creating a `links.task.yml` file for the module.

In `mymodule.links.task.yml`, add the following YAML content:

```
entity.message.collection_tab:
  route_name: entity.message.collection
  base_route: system.admin_content
  title: 'Messages'
```

This instructs Drupal to use the `entity.messages.collection` route, defined in our `routing.yml` file, to be based under the `system.admin_content` route:

See also

▶   *Chapter 6, Extending Drupal*

Creating a bundle for a content entity type

Bundles allow you to have different variations of a content entity. All bundles share the same base field definitions but not configured fields. This allows each bundle to have its own custom fields. Display modes are also dependent on a specific bundle. This allows each bundle to have its own configuration for the form mode and view mode.

Using the custom entity from the previous recipe, we will add a configuration entity to act as the bundle. This will allow you to have different message types for multiple custom field configurations.

Getting ready

You will need a custom module to place the code into in order to implement a configuration entity type. Create an `src` directory for your classes. We need a custom content entity type to be implemented, such as the one in the *Creating a content entity type* recipe.

How to do it...

1. Since content entity bundles are configuration entities, we need to define our configuration entity schema. Create a `config/schema` directory and a `mymodule.schema.yml` file that will contain the configuration entity's schema:

```
mymodule.message_type.*:
  type: config_entity
  label: 'Message type settings'
  mapping:
    id:
      type: string
      label: 'Machine-readable name'
    uuid:
      type: string
      label: 'UUID'
    label:
      type: label
      label: 'Label'
    langcode:
      type: string
      label: 'Default language'
```

2. We define the configuration entity's config prefix as `message_type`, which we will provide to Drupal in the entity's annotation block. We tell Drupal that this is a `config_entity` and provide a label for the schema.

3. With the mapping array, we provide the attributes that make up our entity and the data that will be stored.

4. In your module's `src/Entity` directory, create an interface for our bundle by making a `MessageTypeInterface.php` file. The `MessageTypeInterface` will extend the `\Drupal\Core\Config\Entity\ConfigEntityInterface`:

```php
<?php

/**
 * @file Contains \Drupal\mymodule\Entity\MessageTypeInterface.
 */
```

```
namespace Drupal\mymodule\Entity;

use Drupal\Core\Config\Entity\ConfigEntityInterface;

interface MessageTypeInterface extends ConfigEntityInterface {
  // Empty for future enhancements.
}
```

5. This will be implemented by our entity and provide the method requirements. It is best practice to provide an interface for entities. This allows you to provide required methods if another developer extends your entity or if you are doing advanced testing and need to mock an object.

6. We will be implementing a very basic bundle. It is still wise to provide an interface in the event of future enhancements and mocking ability in tests.

7. Create a `MessageType.php` file in `src/Entity`. This will hold the `MessageType` class, which will extend `\Drupal\Core\Config\Entity\ConfigEntityBundleBase` and implement our bundle's interface:

```php
<?php

/**
 * @file Contains \Drupal\mymodule\Entity\MessageType.
 */

namespace Drupal\mymodule\Entity;

use Drupal\Core\Config\Entity\ConfigEntityBundleBase;

class MessageType extends ConfigEntityBundleBase implements
MessageTypeInterface {

}
```

8. In most use cases, the bundle entity class can be an empty class that does not provide any properties or methods. If a bundle provides additional attributes in its schema definition, they would also be provided here, like any other configuration entity.

9. Entities need to be annotated. Create a base annotation for the ID, label, entity keys, and `configuration export` keys:

```php
<?php

/**
 * @file Contains \Drupal\mymodule\Entity\MessageType.
 */
```

```
namespace Drupal\mymodule\Entity;

use Drupal\Core\Config\Entity\ConfigEntityBundleBase;

/**
 * Defines the profile type entity class.
 *
 * @ConfigEntityType(
 *   id = "message_type",
 *   label = @Translation("Message type"),
 *   config_prefix = "message_type",
 *   bundle_of = "message",
 *   entity_keys = {
 *     "id" = "id",
 *     "label" = "label",
 *     "uuid" = "uuid",
 *     "langcode" = "langcode"
 *   },
 *   config_export = {
 *     "id",
 *     "label",
 *   }
 * )
 */
class MessageType extends ConfigEntityBundleBase implements
MessageTypeInterface {

}
```

10. The annotation document block tells Drupal that this is an instance of the
    `ConfigEntityType` plugin. The `id` is the internal machine name identifier for the
    entity type and the `label` is the human-readable version. The `config_prefix`
    matches with how we defined our schema with `mymodule.message_type`. The
    entity keys definition tells Drupal which attributes represent our identifiers and labels.

11. When specifying `config_export`, we are telling the configuration management
    system what properties are to be exported when exporting our entity.

12. We will then add handlers, which will interact with our entity:

```
/**
 * Defines the profile type entity class.
 *
 * @ConfigEntityType(
 *   id = "message_type",
 *   label = @Translation("Message type"),
 *   handlers = {
```

```
 *       "list_builder" = "Drupal\mymodule\MessageTypeListBuilder",
 *       "form" = {
 *         "default" = "Drupal\Core\Entity\EntityForm",
 *         "add" = "Drupal\Core\Entity\EntityForm",
 *         "edit" = "Drupal\Core\Entity\EntityForm",
 *         "delete" = "Drupal\Core\Entity\EntityDeleteForm"
 *       },
 *     },
 *   config_prefix = "message_type",
 *   bundle_of = "message",
 *   entity_keys = {
 *     "id" = "id",
 *     "label" = "label",
 *     "uuid" = "uuid",
 *     "langcode" = "langcode"
 *   },
 *   config_export = {
 *     "id",
 *     "label",
 *   },
 * )
 */
```

13. The `handlers` array specifies classes that provide the interaction functionality with our entity. The list builder class will be created to show you a table of our entities. The form array provides classes for forms to be used when creating, editing, or deleting our configuration entity.

14. An additional handler can be added, the `route_provider`, to dynamically generate our canonical (view), edit, and delete routes:

```
/**
 * Defines the profile type entity class.
 *
 * @ConfigEntityType(
 *   id = "message_type",
 *   label = @Translation("Message type"),
 *   handlers = {
 *     "list_builder" = "Drupal\profile\MessageTypeListBuilder",
 *     "form" = {
 *       "default" = "Drupal\Core\Entity\EntityForm",
 *       "add" = "Drupal\Core\Entity\EntityForm",
 *       "edit" = "Drupal\Core\Entity\EntityForm",
 *       "delete" = "Drupal\Core\Entity\EntityDeleteForm"
 *     },
```

```
 *        "route_provider" = {
 *          "html" = "Drupal\Core\Entity\Routing\
DefaultHtmlRouteProvider",
 *        },
 *      },
 *      config_prefix = "message_type",
 *      bundle_of = "message",
 *      entity_keys = {
 *        "id" = "id",
 *        "label" = "label"
 *      },
 *      config_export = {
 *        "id",
 *        "label",
 *      },
 *      links = {
 *        "delete-form" = "/admin/structure/message-types/{message_
type}/delete",
 *        "edit-form" = "/admin/structure/message-types/{message_
type}",
 *        "admin-form" = "/admin/structure/message-types/{message_
type}",
 *        "collection" = "/admin/structure/message-types"
 *      }
 * )
 */
```

15. There is a routing service for entities that will automatically provide Drupal a route with the proper controllers based on this annotation. The add form route is not yet supported and needs to be manually added.

16. We need to modify our content entity to use the bundle configuration entity that we defined:

```
/**
 * Defines the profile entity class.
 *
 * @ContentEntityType(
 *   id = "message",
 *   label = @Translation("Message"),
 *   handlers = {...},
 *   base_table = "message",
 *   fieldable = TRUE,
 *   bundle_entity_type = "message_type",
 *   field_ui_base_route = "entity.message_type.edit_form",
 *   entity_keys = {
```

```
 *      "id" = "message_id",
 *      "label" = "title",
 *      "langcode" = "langcode",
 *      "bundle" = "type",
 *      "uuid" = "uuid"
 *    },
 *  links = {...},
 *  )
 */
```

17. The `bundle_entity_type` key specifies the entity type used as the bundle. The plugin validates this as an actual entity type and marks it for configuration dependencies. With the `field_ui_base_route` key pointed to the bundle's main edit form, it will generate the `Manage Fields`, `Manage Form Display`, and `Manage Display` tabs on the bundles. Finally, the `bundle` entity key instructs Drupal which field definition to use in order to identify the entity's bundle, which is created in the next step.

18. A new field definition needs to be added to provide the `type` field that we defined to represent the `bundle` entity key:

```
$fields['type'] = BaseFieldDefinition::create('entity_
reference')
    ->setLabel(t('Message type'))
    ->setDescription(t('The message type.'))
    ->setSetting('target_type', 'message_type')
    ->setSetting('max_length', EntityTypeInterface::BUNDLE_MAX_
LENGTH);
```

19. The field that identifies the bundle will be typed as an entity reference. This allows the value to act as a foreign key to the bundle's base table.

20. In your `mymodule.routing.yml`, provide a route for adding a `Message Type` entity:

```
entity.message_type.add_form:
  path: '/admin/structure/message-types/add'
  defaults:
    _entity_form: 'message_type.add'
    _title: 'Add message type'
  requirements:
    _entity_create_access: 'message_type'
```

21. We can use the `_entity_form` property to tell Drupal to look up the class defined in our handlers.

22. Before we implement our `list_builder` handler, we also need to add the route to `routing.yml` for our collection link definition, as this is not auto generated by route providers:

```
entity.message_type.collection:
  path: '/admin/structure/message-types'
  defaults:
    _entity_list: 'message_type'
    _title: 'Message types'
  requirements:
    _permission: 'administer message types'
```

23. The `_entity_list` key will tell the route to use our `list_builder` handler to build the page.

24. Create the `MessageTypeListBuilder` class defined in our `list_builder` handler in a `MessageTypeListBuilder.php` file and extend `\Drupal\Core\Config\Entity\ConfigEntityListBuilder`. We need to override the default implementation to display our configuration entity properties:

```php
<?php

/**
 * @file Contains \Drupal\mymodule\MessageListBuilder
 */

namespace Drupal\mymodule;

use Drupal\Core\Entity\EntityInterface;
use Drupal\Core\Config\Entity\ConfigEntityListBuilder;

class MessageTypeListBuilder extends EntityListBuilder {
  public function buildHeader() {
    $header['label'] = t('Label');
    return $header + parent::buildHeader();
  }

  public function buildRow(EntityInterface $entity) {
    $row['label'] = $entity->label();
    return $row + parent::buildRow($entity);
  }

}
```

25. In our list builder handler, we override the `buildHeader` and `builderRow` methods so that we can add our configuration entity's properties to the table:

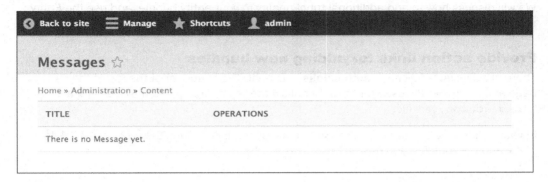

26. Your module's structure should resemble the following screenshot:

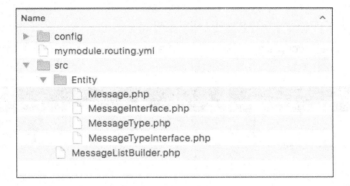

How it works...

Bundles are most utilized in the configured field levels via the `Field` and `Field UI` modules. When you create a new field, it has a base storage item for its global settings. Once a field is added to a bundle, there is a new field configuration that is created and assigned to the bundle. Fields can then have their own settings for a specific bundle along with form and view display configurations.

Content entity bundles work just like any other configuration entity implementation, but they extend the usability of the Field API for your content entity types.

We will discuss how to add additional functionality to your entity bundle, and use the Entity module to simplify the developer expedience.

Provide action links for adding new bundles

There are special links called **action links** in Drupal. These appear at the top of the page and are generally used for links that allow the creation of an item by creating a `links.action.yml` file.

In your `mymodule.links.action.yml`, each action link defines the route it will link to, titles, and the routes it appears on:

```
message_type_add:
  route_name: entity.message_type.add_form
  title: 'Add message type'
  appears_on:
    - entity.message_type.collection
```

The `appears_on` key accepts multiple values that will allow this route link to appear on multiple pages:

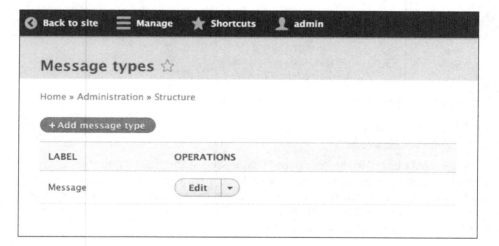

 ▶ *Chapter 4, Extending Drupal*

 ▶ *Chapter 9, Configuration Management*

 ▶ Recipe *Creating a Confiuration Entity Type* in *Chapter 10, The Entity API*

Implementing custom access control for an entity

All entities have a set of handlers that control specific pieces of functionalities. One handler in particular handles access control. When the access handler is not specified, the base \ Drupal\Core\Entity\EntityType module will implement \Drupal\Core\Entity\ EntityAccessControlHandler as the access handler. By default, this will check whether any modules have implemented hook_entity_create_access or hook_entity_type_ create_access and use their opinions. Otherwise, it defaults to the admin permission for the entity type, if implemented.

In this recipe, we will provide an admin permission for our entity along with create, update, view, and delete permissions for each of the entity's bundles. We will base this on an entity called **Message**.

Getting ready

You will need a custom module to place the code into in order to implement a configuration entity type. Create an src directory for your PSR-4 style classes. We need to implement a custom content entity type, such as the one in the *Creating a content entity type* recipe.

How to do it...

1. First, we need to define an administration permission for the entity. This is done by adding the admin_permission key to the entity's annotation document block:

```
/**
 * Defines the profile entity class.
 *
 * @ContentEntityType(
 *   id = "message",
 *   label = @Translation("Message"),
 *   handlers = {...},
 *   base_table = "message",
 *   fieldable = TRUE,
 *   admin_permission = "administer messages",
 *   entity_keys = {
 *     "id" = "message_id",
 *     "label" = "title",
 *     "langcode" = "langcode",
 *     "uuid" = "uuid"
 *   },
 *   links = {...},
 * )
 */
```

2. The entity access handler provided by core will check whether entities implement this option. If it is provided, it will be used as the basis for most access checks unless a custom access handler is implemented.

3. Create a `mymodule.permissions.yml` to provide the administrative permission to Drupal. We will be defining a permission callback as well to support dynamic permissions based on current bundles:

```yaml
administer messages:
  title: 'Administer messages'
  restrict access: true
permission_callbacks:
  - \Drupal\mymodule\MessagePermissions::messageTypePermissions
```

4. Along with defining specific permissions, we need to specify the `class` and `static` methods to return dynamic permissions. Refer to the *Defining permissions* recipe in *Chapter 4, Extending Drupal,* for more information.

5. Create the `MessagePermissions` class in the `src` directory. This will contain the `profileTypePermissions` method that returns an array of permissions. Our class will add `create`, `view`, `update`, and `delete` permissions to our entities:

```php
<?php

/**
 * @file
 * Contains \Drupal\mymodule\MessagePermissions.
 */

namespace Drupal\mymodule;

use Drupal\Core\StringTranslation\StringTranslationTrait;
use Drupal\mymodule\Entity\MessageType;

/**
 * Defines a class containing permission callbacks.
 */
class MessagePermissions {
  use StringTranslationTrait;

  /**
   * Returns an array of message type permissions.
   *
   * @return array
   *     Returns an array of permissions.
   */
```

```php
  public function messageTypePermissions() {
    $perms = [];
    // Generate message permissions for all message types.
    foreach (MessageType::loadMultiple() as $type) {
      $perms += $this->buildPermissions($type);
    }
    return $perms;
  }


  /**
   * Builds a standard list of permissions for a given profile
type.
   *
   * @param \Drupal\mymodule\Entity\MessageType $message_type
   *   The machine name of the message type.
   *
   * @return array
   *   An array of permission names and descriptions.
   */
  protected function buildPermissions(MessageType $message_type) {
    $type_id = $message_type->id();
    $type_params = ['%type' => $message_type->label()];

    return [
      "add $type_id message" => [
        'title' => $this->t('%type: Add message', $type_params),
      ],
      "view $type_id message" => [
        'title' => $this->t('%type: View message', $type_params),
      ],
      "edit $type_id message" => [
        'title' => $this->t('%type: Edit message', $type_params),
      ],
      "delete $type_id message" => [
        'title' => $this->t('%type: Delete message', $type_
params),
      ],
    ];
  }
}
```

6. In our permission callback, `messageTypePermissions`, we invoke the
   `MessageType::loadMultiple` method with no parameters. This will return
   all the available entities for `message_type`. We then pass this entity to another
   method, which defines create, read, update, and delete permissions.

7. To utilize the dynamic permissions, we will extend the default
   `\Drupal\Core\Entity\EntityAccessControlHandler`.
   Create a `MessageAccessControlHandler` class for your module:

```php
<?php

/**
 * @file Contains \Drupal\mymodule\MessageAccessControlHandler.
 */

namespace Drupal\mymodule;

use Drupal\Core\Entity\EntityAccessControlHandler;

/**
 * Defines the access control handler for the message entity type.
 */
class MessageAccessControlHandler extends
EntityAccessControlHandler {

}
```

8. We will override the `checkAccess` method. The default implementation notes in the documentation state that this method is supposed to be overridden by entities using custom access checking:

```php
<?php

/**
 * @file Contains \Drupal\mymodule\MessageAccessControlHandler.
 */

namespace Drupal\mymodule;

use Drupal\Core\Access\AccessResult;
use Drupal\Core\Entity\EntityAccessControlHandler;
use Drupal\Core\Entity\EntityInterface;
use Drupal\Core\Session\AccountInterface;

/**
 * Defines the access control handler for the message entity type.
 */
class MessageAccessControlHandler extends
EntityAccessControlHandler {
```

```
/**
 * {@inheritdoc}
 */
protected function checkAccess(EntityInterface $entity,
$operation, AccountInterface $account) {
    // Re-use admin permission check.
    $result = parent::checkAccess($entity, $operation, $account);

    if ($result->isNeutral()) {
        // Check if user has permission: ex, "add message message".
        $result = AccessResult::allowedIfHasPermission($account,
"$operation {$entity->bundle()} message");
    }

    return $result;
}

}
```

9. In our overridden method, we check the parent class result. This handles our admin permission check and the basic *you cannot delete a new, non-saved entity* logic. If the parent class comes back neutral, we can check it based on our dynamic permissions and return that.

10. We need to follow the same pattern for the parent `checkCreateAccess` method, which is called on create. It specifies that it should be overridden if you are implementing custom access checks:

```
/**
 * {@inheritdoc}
 */
protected function checkCreateAccess(AccountInterface $account,
array $context, $entity_bundle = NULL) {
    // Re-use admin permission check.
    $result = parent::checkCreateAccess($account, $context,
$entity_bundle);

    if ($result->isNeutral()) {
        $result = AccessResult::allowedIfHasPermission($account,
"add $entity_bundle message");
    }

    return $result;
}
```

11. For this method, we follow the same pattern and reuse the parent's check for the admin permission.

12. After the access handler is created, we need to add it to the list of our entities' handlers:

```
*    handlers = {
*        "list_builder" = "Drupal\mymodule\ProfileTypeListBuilder",
*        "access" = "Drupal\mymodule\MessageAccessControlHandler",
*        "form" = {
*          "default" = "Drupal\Core\Entity\EntityForm",
*          "add" = "Drupal\Core\Entity\EntityForm",
*          "edit" = "Drupal\Core\Entity\EntityForm",
*          "delete" = "Drupal\Core\Entity\EntityDeleteForm"
*        },
*        "route_provider" = {
*          "html" = "Drupal\Core\Entity\Routing\
DefaultHtmlRouteProvider",
*        },
*    },
```

13. Rebuild Drupal's caches.

14. Verify that the permissions are available on the permission's overview page:

PERMISSION	ANONYMOUS USER	AUTHENTICATED USER	ADMINISTRATOR
My Module			
Administer messages *Warning: Give to trusted roles only; this permission has security implications.*	☐	☐	☑
Message: Add message	☐	☐	☑
Message: Delete message	☐	☐	☑
Message: Edit message	☐	☐	☑
Message: View message	☐	☐	☑

How it works...

Entities are powered by the plugin system in Drupal, which means that there is a plugin manager. The default `\Drupal\Core\Entity\EntityTypeManager` provides the discovery and handling of entities. Both the `ContentEntityType` and `ConfigEntityType` entity types and classes extend the base `\Drupal\Core\Entity\EntityType` class.

The `EntityType` class constructor provides a default `access` handler if it is not provided, through the `\Drupal\Core\Entity\EntityAccessControlHandler` class. There are several methods provided by the class, but the notable ones are `checkAccess`, `checkCreateAccess`, and `checkFieldAccess`. These are designed to be overridden by entity implementations that need their own access checking.

Every core module that provides an entity type implements this to override at least `checkAccess` and `checkCreateAccess`.

`\Drupal\Core\Access\AccessibleInterface` defines an `access` method and all the entities inherit this interface. The default implementation in `\Drupal\Core\Entity\Entity` will invoke `checkCreateAccess` if the operation is `create`; otherwise, it invokes the generic `access` method of the access controller, which will invoke entity access hooks and the class' own `checkAccess` method.

There's more...

We will discuss how to implement custom access control for an entity, and use the Entity to simplify the controlling access.

Controlling access to entity fields

The `checkFieldAccess` method can be overridden to control access to specific entity fields when modifying an entity. Without being overridden by a child class, the `\Drupal\Core\Entity\EntityAccessControlHandler::checkFieldAccess` will always return an allowed access result. The method receives the following parameters:

▸ The view and edit operations

▸ The current field's definition

▸ The user session to check access against

▸ And a possible list of field item values

Entity types can implement their own access control handlers and override this method to provide granular control over the modification of their base fields. A good example would be the `User` module and its `\Drupal\user\UserAccessControlHandler`.

User entities have a `pass` field that is used for the user's current password. There is also a `created` field that records when the user was added to the site.

For the `pass` field, it returns `denied` if the operation is `view`, but allows access if the operation is `edit`:

```
case 'pass':
  // Allow editing the password, but not viewing it.
  return ($operation == 'edit') ? AccessResult::allowed() :
AccessResult::forbidden();
```

The `created` field uses the opposite logic. When a user became part of the site can be viewed, but should not be able to be edited:

```
case 'created':
  // Allow viewing the created date, but not editing it.
  return ($operation == 'view') ? AccessResult::allowed() :
AccessResult::forbidden();
```

See also

▸   *Chapter 4, Extending Drupal*

Providing a custom storage handler

Storage handlers control the loading, saving, and deleting of an entity. `\Drupal\Core\Entity\ContentEntityType` provides the base entity type definition for all content entity types. If it is not specified, then the default storage handler is `\Drupal\Core\Entity\Sql\SqlContentEntityStorage`. This class can be extended to implement alternative `load` methods or adjustments on save.

In this recipe, we will implement a method that supports loading an entity by a specific property instead of having to write a specific `loadByProperties` method call.

Getting ready

You will need a custom module to place the code into in order to implement a configuration entity type. Create an `src` directory for your PSR-4 style classes. A custom content entity type needs to be implemented, such as the one in the *Creating a content entity type* recipe.

How to do it...

1. Create a `MessageStorage` class in the module's `src` directory. This class will extend the default `\Drupal\Core\Entity\Sql\SqlContentEntityStorage` class:

```php
<?php

/**
 * @file Contains \Drupal\mymodule\MessageStorage.
 */

namespace Drupal\mymodule;

use Drupal\Core\Entity\Sql\SqlContentEntityStorage;

/**
 * Defines the entity storage for messages.
 */
class MessageStorage extends SqlContentEntityStorage {

}
```

2. By extending the default storage class for our entity type, we can simply add new methods that are relevant to our requirements rather that implementing the extra business logic.

3. Create a `loadMultipleByType` method and we will use this method to provide a simple way of loading all profiles of a specific bundle:

```php
/**
 * Load multiple messages by bundle type.
 *
 * @param string $message_type
 *    The message type.
 *
 * @return array|\Drupal\Core\Entity\EntityInterface[]
 *    An array of loaded message entities.
 */
public function loadMultipleByType($message_type) {
  return $this->loadByProperties([
    'type' => $message_type,
  ]);
}
```

4. We pass the `type` property so that we can query it based on the message bundle and return all matching message entities.

5. Update the entity's annotation block to have the new storage handler defined:

```
*    handlers = {
*       "list_builder" = "Drupal\mymodule\MessageListBuilder",
*       "storage" = "Drupal\mymodule\MessageStorage",
*       "form" = {
*         "default" = "Drupal\Core\Entity\EntityForm",
*         "add" = "Drupal\Core\Entity\EntityForm",
*         "edit" = "Drupal\Core\Entity\EntityForm",
*         "delete" = "Drupal\Core\Entity\EntityDeleteForm"
*       },
*       "route_provider" = {
*         "html" = "Drupal\Core\Entity\Routing\
DefaultHtmlRouteProvider",
*       },
*    },
```

6. You can now programmatically interact with your profile entities using the following code:

```
// Get the entity type manager from the container.
\Drupal::entityTypeManager()

// Access the storage handler.
->getStorage('message')

// Invoke the new method on custom storage class.
->loadMultipleByType('message');
```

How it works...

When defining a content entity type, the annotation block begins with @ContentEntityType. This declaration, and the properties in it, represents the definition to initiate an instance of the \Drupal\Core\Entity\ContentEntityType class just like all other plugin annotations.

In the class constructor, there is a merge to provide default handlers for the storage handler if it is not provided. This will always default to \Drupal\Core\Entity\Sql\ SqlContentEntityStorage as it provides methods and logic to help its parent class, ContentEntityStorageBase, interact with the SQL-based storage.

Configuration entities can have their default `\Drupal\Core\Config\Entity\ConfigEntityStorage` as well. However, for configuration entities, the configuration management utilizes the `\Drupal\Core\Config\StorageInterface` implementations for storage rather than classes, which extend `ConfigEntityStorage`. This logic resides in the configuration factory service.

Extending `SqlContentEntityStorage` reuses methods required for default Drupal implementations and provides an easy method to create custom methods to interact with loading, saving, and so on.

There's more...

We will discuss about the custom storage handler and utilizing of different storage backend.

Utilizing a different storage backend for an entity

Drupal provides mechanisms for supporting different database storage backends that are not provided by Drupal core, such as MongoDB. While it is not stable for Drupal 8 at the time of writing this book, there is a MongoDB module that provides storage interaction.

The module provides `\Drupal\mongodb\Entity\ContentEntityStorage`, which extends `\Drupal\Core\Entity\ContentEntityStorageBase`. This class overrides the methods used to create, save, and delete, to write them to a MongoDB collection.

While there are many more steps to provide a custom storage backend for content entities and their fields, this serves as an example for how you can choose to place a custom entity in a different storage backend.

See also

- ▶ *Chapter 4, Extending Drupal*
- ▶ *Chapter 7, Plug and Play with Plugins*

Creating a route provider

Entities can implement a route provider that will create the route definitions for the entity's canonical (view), edit, and delete routes. As of Drupal 8.0.1, the add path for an entity is not handled through the default route provider.

In this recipe, we will extend the default `\Drupal\Core\Entity\Routing\DefaultHtmlRouteProvider` and provide the add routes for our entity.

Getting ready

You will need a custom module to place the code into in order to implement a configuration entity type. Create an `src` directory for your classes. A custom content entity type needs to be implemented, such as the one in the *Creating a content entity type* recipe.

How to do it...

1. Create a `MessageHtmlRouteProvider` class in the `src` directory that extends `\Drupal\Core\Entity\Routing\DefaultHtmlRouteProvider`:

```php
<?php

/**
 * @file Contains \Drupal\mymodule\MessageHtmlRouteProvider.
 */

namespace Drupal\mymodule;

use Drupal\Core\Entity\Routing\DefaultHtmlRouteProvider;

/**
 * Provides HTML routes for the message entity type.
 */
class MessageHtmlRouteProvider extends DefaultHtmlRouteProvider {

}
```

2. Override the provided `getRoutes` method and collect the parent class's collection of routes returned:

```php
<?php

/**
 * @file Contains \Drupal\mymodule\MessageHtmlRouteProvider.
 */

namespace Drupal\mymodule;

use Drupal\Core\Entity\EntityTypeInterface;
use Drupal\Core\Entity\Routing\DefaultHtmlRouteProvider;

/**
 * Provides HTML routes for the message entity type.
 */
```

```
class MessageHtmlRouteProvider extends DefaultHtmlRouteProvider {

  /**
   * {@inheritdoc}
   */
  public function getRoutes(EntityTypeInterface $entity_type) {
    $collection = parent::getRoutes($entity_type);

    return $collection;
  }
}
```

3. The parent method for `getRoutes` invokes other methods that check whether the entity has defined edit, canonical, or delete route links in its annotation definition. If the entity has, it will return those as a `\Symfony\Component\Routing\RouteCollection` containing the available routes.

4. Add a new route to the `collection` that represents the message entity's add route. This will allow us to remove the `mymodule.routing.yml` file:

```
  /**
   * {@inheritdoc}
   */
  public function getRoutes(EntityTypeInterface $entity_type) {
    $collection = parent::getRoutes($entity_type);

    $route = (new Route('/messages/add'))
      ->addDefaults([
        '_entity_form' => 'message.add',
        '_title' => 'Add message',
      ])
      ->setRequirement('_entity_create_access', 'message');
    $collection->add('entity.message.add_form', $route);

    return $collection;
  }
```

5. This section of the code defines the route programmatically. The definition created in the `routing.yml` is implemented in the `\Symfony\Component\Routing\Route` instance:

Delete the `mymodule.routing.yml` file!

6. Now, we will add routes based on each bundle, iterate through each message bundle, and add a new route that will provide a route to add a message based on the type specified in the route:

```
/**
 * {@inheritdoc}
 */
public function getRoutes(EntityTypeInterface $entity_type) {
  $collection = parent::getRoutes($entity_type);

  $route = (new Route('/messages/add'))
    ->addDefaults([
      '_entity_form' => 'message.add',
      '_title' => 'Add message',
    ])
    ->setRequirement('_entity_create_access', 'message');
  $collection->add('entity.message.add_form', $route);

  /** @var \Drupal\mymodule\Entity\MessageTypeInterface
$message_type */
  foreach (MessageType::loadMultiple() as $message_type) {
    $route = (new Route('/messages/add/{message_type}'))
      ->addDefaults([
        '_entity_form' => 'message.add',
        '_title' => "Add {$message_type->label()} message",
      ])
      ->setRequirement('_entity_create_access', 'message');
    $collection->add("entity.message.{$message_type->id()}.add_
form", $route);
  }

  return $collection;
}
```

7. This new code loads all the message type entities and adds a new route to each. A route will be created at /messages/add/{message_type} that will predefine the type of message being created.

How it works...

Entities are powered by the plugin system in Drupal, which means that there is a plugin manager. The default \Drupal\Core\Entity\EntityTypeManager provides discovery and handling of entities. The \Drupal\Core\Entity\EntityTypeManagerInterface specifies a getRouteProviders method that is expected to return an array of strings that provide the fully qualified class name of an implementation of the \Drupal\Core\Entity\Routing\EntityRouteProviderInterface interface.

There is an event subscriber defined in `core.services.yml` called the `entity_route_subscriber`. This service subscribes to the dynamic route event. When this happens, it uses the entity type manager to retrieve all entity type implementations, which provide route subscribers. It then aggregates all the `\Symfony\Component\Routing\RouteCollection` instances received and merges them into the main route collection for the system.

There's more...

Drupal 8 introduces a router types and provide the add routes for our entity.

The Entity API module provides add generation

In Drupal 8, the **Entity** module lives on, even though most of its functionalities from Drupal 7 are now in core. The goal of the module is to develop improvements for the developer experience around entities. One of these is the generation of the *add* form and its routes.

The Entity module provides two new route provider aimed specifically for *add* routes, the `\Drupal\entity\Routing\CreateHtmlRouteProvider` and `\Drupal\entity\Routing\AdminCreateHtmlRouteProvider`. The latter option forces the add form to be presented in the administrative theme.

With the Entity module installed, you can add a `create` entry for the `router_providers` array pointing to the new route provider:

```
*      "route_provider" = {
*        "html" = "Drupal\Core\Entity\Routing\
DefaultHtmlRouteProvider",
*        "create" = "Drupal\entity\Routing\CreateHtmlRouteProvider",
*      },
```

Then, you just need to define the `add-form` entry in your entity's `links` definition, if not already present:

```
*    links = {
*      "add-form" = "/admin/structure/message-types/add",
*      "delete-form" = "/admin/structure/message-types/{message_type}/
delete",
*      "edit-form" = "/admin/structure/message-types/{profile_type}",
*      "admin-form" = "/admin/structure/message-types/{profile_type}",
*      "collection" = "/admin/structure/message-types"
*    }
```

This reduces the amount of boilerplate code required to implement an `Entity`.

Providing a collection route

In the previous recipe, we also needed to define a `collection` route manually. The route provider can be used to provide this `collection` route:

```
$route = (new Route('/admin/content/messages'))
    ->addDefaults([
        '_entity_list' => 'message',
        '_title' => 'Messages',
    ])
    ->setRequirement('permission', $entity_type-
>getAdminPermission());
    $collection->add('entity.message.collection', $route);
```

This route definition will replace the one in `routing.yml`. Route generation items should exist in their own handlers, even if only for a specific item. The `collection` route generation will go into a `CollectionHtmlRouteProvider` class and can be added as a new route handler. The reasoning is that for `ease` of deprecation in the event such a functionality is added to Drupal core.

See also

> ▸ *Chapter 4, Extending Drupal*

> ▸ Refer to the Routing system in Drupal 8 at `https://www.drupal.org/developing/api/8/routing`

11

Off the Drupalicon Island

In this chapter, we will see how to use third-party libraries, such as JavaScript, CSS, and PHP in detail:

- ▶ Implementing and using a third-party JavaScript library
- ▶ Implementing and using a third-party CSS library
- ▶ Implementing and using a third-party PHP library
- ▶ Using Composer manager

Introduction

Drupal 8 comes with a *Proudly Built Elsewhere* attitude. There has been an effort made to use more components created by the PHP community at large and other communities. Drupal 8 is built with Symfony. It includes Twig as its templating system, the provided WYSIWYG editor as its CKEditor, and uses PHPUnit for testing.

How does Drupal 8 promote using libraries made elsewhere? The new asset management system in Drupal 8 makes it easier to use frontend libraries. Drupal implements PSR-0 and PSR-4 from the **PHP Framework Interoperability Group** (**PHP-FIG**) and **PHP Standards Recommendations** (**PSRs**) are suggested standards used to increase interoperability between PHP applications. This has streamlined integrating third-party PHP libraries.

Both areas will be constantly improved with each minor release of Drupal 8. These areas will be mentioned throughout the chapter.

Implementing and using a third-party JavaScript library

In the past, Drupal has only shipped with jQuery and a few jQuery plugins used by Drupal core for the JavaScript API. This has changed with Drupal 8. `Underscore.js` and `Backbone.js` are now included in Drupal, bringing two popular JavaScript frameworks to its developers.

However, there are many JavaScript frameworks that can be used. In *Chapter 5, Frontend for the Win,* you learned about the asset management system and libraries. In this recipe, we will create a module that provides `Angular.js` as a library and a custom Angular application; the demo is available on the AngularJS home page.

Getting ready

In this example, we will use Bower to manage our third-party `angular.js` library components. If you are not familiar with Bower, it is simply a package manager for frontend components. Instead of using Bower, you can just manually download and place the required files.

If you do not have Bower, you can follow the instructions to install it from `bower.io` at `http://bower.io/#install-bower`. If you do not want to install Bower, we will provide links to manually download libraries.

Having a background of AngularJS is not required but is beneficial. This recipe implements the example from the home page of the library.

How to do it...

1. Create a custom module named `mymodule` that will serve the AngularJS library and its implementation:

   ```
   name: My Module!
   type: module
   description: Provides an AngularJS app.
   core: 8.x
   ```

2. Run the bower `init` to create a bower project in your module. We will use most of the default values for the prompted questions:

   ```
   $ bower init
   ? name mymodule
   ? description Example module with AngularJS
   ? main file
   ? what types of modules does this package expose?
   ? keywords
   ```

```
? authors Matt Glaman <nmd.matt@gmail.com>

? license GPL

? homepage

? set currently installed components as dependencies? Yes

? would you like to mark this package as private which prevents it
from being accidentally published to the registry? No

{
  name: 'mymodule',
  authors: [
    'Matt Glaman <nmd.matt@gmail.com>'
  ],
  description: 'Example module with AngularJS',
  main: '',
  moduleType: [],
  license: 'GPL',
  homepage: '',
  ignore: [
    '**/.*',
    'node_modules',
    'bower_components',
    'test',
    'tests'
  ]
}


? Looks good? Yes
```

3. Next, we will install the AngularJS library using bower install:

```
$ bower install --save angular
bower angular#*                    cached git://github.com/angular/
bower-angular.git#1.5.0
bower angular#*                    validate 1.5.0 against git://github.
com/angular/bower-angular.git#*
bower angular#^1.5.0               install angular#1.5.0
angular#1.5.0 bower_components/angular
```

The `--save` option will ensure that the package's dependency is saved in the
created `bower.json`. If you do not have Bower, you can download AngularJS from
`https://angularjs.org/` and place it in a `bower_components` folder.

4. Create `mymodule.libraries.yml`. We will define AngularJS as its own library entry:

```
angular:
  js:
    bower_components/angular/angular.js: {}
  css:
    component:
      'bower_components/angular/angular-csp.css': {}
```

5. When the `angular` library is attached, it will add the AngularJS library file and attach the CSS stylesheet.

6. Next, create a `mymodule.module` file. We will use the theme layer's preprocess functions to add a `ng-app` attribute to the root HTML element:

```php
<?php

/**
 * Implements hook_preprocess_html().
 */
function mymodule_preprocess_html(&$variables) {
    $variables['html_attributes']['ng-app'] = '';
}
```

7. AngularJS uses the `ng-app` attribute as a directive for bootstrapping an AngularJS application. It marks the root of the application.

8. We will use a custom block to implement the HTML required for the AngularJS example. Make a `src/Plugin/Block` directory and make an `AngularBlock.php` file.

9. Extend the `BlockBase` class and implement the build method to return our Angular app's HTML:

```php
<?php

/**
 * @file
 * Contains \Drupal\mymmodule\Plugin\Block\AngularBlock.
 */

namespace Drupal\mymodule\Plugin\Block;

use Drupal\Core\Block\BlockBase;
```

```php
/**
 * Provides a block for AngularJS example.
 *
 * @Block(
 *   id = "mymodule_angular_block",
 *   admin_label = @Translation("AngularJS Block")
 * )
 */
class AngularBlock extends BlockBase {

  public function build() {
    return [
      'input' => [
        '#type' => 'textfield',
        '#title' => $this->t('Name'),
        '#placeholder' => $this->t('Enter a name here'),
        '#attributes' => [
          'ng-model' => 'yourName',
        ],
      ],
      'name' => [
        '#markup' => '<hr><h1>Hello {{yourName}}!</h1>',
      ],
      '#attached' => [
        'library' => [
          'mymodule/angular',
        ],
      ],
    ];
  }

}
```

10. We return a render array that contains the input, name, and our library attachments. The input array returns the Form API render information for a text field. The name returns a regular markup that will bind Angular's changes to the yourName scope variable.

11. Install your custom module.

12. Visit the block layout form from the **Structure** page and place your block.

13. View your Drupal site and interact with your block, which is powered by AngularJS:

How it works...

The simplicity of integrating with a JavaScript framework is provided by the new asset management system in Drupal 8. The usage of **Bower** is optional, but it is usually a preferred method used to manage frontend dependencies. Using Bower, we can place bower_components in an ignore file that can be used to keep third-party libraries out of version control.

See also

- ▸ Refer to the core issue to add Backbone.js and Underscore.js at https://www.drupal.org/node/1149866

- ▸ The recipe *Using the new asset management system*, in *Chapter 5, Frontend for the Win*

- ▸ *Chapter 4, Extending Drupal*, in recipe *Creating a Module*

Implementing and using a third-party CSS library

Drupal provides many things. However, one thing that it does not provide is any kind of CSS component library. In the recipe *Using the new asset management system*, in *Chapter 5, Frontend for the Win*, we added `FontAwesome` as a library. CSS frameworks implement robust user interface design components and they can be quite large if using a compiled version with everything bundled. The asset management system can be used to define each component as its own library to only deliver the exact files required for a strong frontend performance.

In this recipe, we will implement the Semantic UI framework, using the CSS only distribution, which provides each individual component's CSS file. We will register the `form`, `button`, `label`, and `input` components as libraries. Our custom theme will then alter the Drupal elements for `buttons`, `labels`, and `inputs` to have the Semantic UI classes and load the proper library.

Getting ready

In this example, we will use Bower to manage our third-party components. If you are not familiar with Bower, it is simply a package manager used for frontend components. Instead of using Bower, you can just manually download and place the required files.

How to do it...

1. For this recipe, create a new custom theme named `mytheme` using Classy as a base theme. This way, we can reuse some existing styling. If you are unfamiliar with creating a base theme, refer to the recipe *Creating a custom theme based on Classy*, in *Chapter 5, Frontend for the Win*.

2. Using your terminal, navigate to your theme's directory. Run bower `init` to create a `bower` project:

```
$ bower init
? name mytheme
? description Example theme with Semantic UI
? main file
? what types of modules does this package expose?
? keywords
? authors Matt Glaman <nmd.matt@gmail.com>
? license GPL
? homepage
```

```
? set currently installed components as dependencies? Yes
? would you like to mark this package as private which prevents it
from being accidentally published to the registry? No
{
  name: 'mytheme',
  authors: [
    'Matt Glaman <nmd.matt@gmail.com>'
  ],
  description: 'Example theme with Semantic UI,
  main: '',
  moduleType: [],
  license: 'GPL',
  homepage: '',
  ignore: [
    '**/.*',
    'node_modules',
    'bower_components',
    'test',
    'tests'
  ]
}


? Looks good? Yes
```

3. Next, user `bower install` to save the Semantic UI library:

```
$ bower install --save semantic-ui
bower semantic-ui#*         not-cached git://github.com/Semantic-
Org/Semantic-UI.git#*
bower semantic-ui#*            resolve git://github.com/Semantic-
Org/Semantic-UI.git#*
bower semantic-ui#*           download https://github.com/
Semantic-Org/Semantic-UI/archive/2.1.8.tar.gz
bower semantic-ui#*            extract archive.tar.gz
bower semantic-ui#*           resolved git://github.com/Semantic-
Org/Semantic-UI.git#2.1.8
bower jquery#>=1.8         not-cached git://github.com/jquery/
jquery-dist.git#>=1.8
```

```
bower jquery#>=1.8          resolve git://github.com/jquery/
jquery-dist.git#>=1.8

bower jquery#>=1.8          download https://github.com/jquery/
jquery-dist/archive/2.2.0.tar.gz

bower jquery#>=1.8          extract archive.tar.gz

bower jquery#>=1.8          resolved git://github.com/jquery/
jquery-dist.git#2.2.0

bower semantic#^2.1.8       install semantic#2.1.8

bower jquery#>=1.8          install jquery#2.2.0
```

The `--save` option will ensure that the package's dependency is saved in the created `bower.json`. If you do not have Bower, you can download Semantic UI from `https://github.com/semantic-org/semantic-ui/` and place it in a `bower_components` folder.

4. Create `mytheme.libraries.yml` in your theme's base directory. This will hold our main Semantic UI definition along with specific component library definitions.

5. First, we will add a new library to the `form` component:

```
semantic_ui.form:
  js:
    bower_components/semantic/dist/components/form.js: {}
  css:
    component:
      bower_components/semantic/dist/components/form.css: {}
```

The `form` component for Semantic UI has a stylesheet and JavaScript file. Our library ensures that both are loaded when the library is attached.

6. The `button`, `input`, and `label` components do not have any JavaScript files. Add a library for each component:

```
semantic_ui.button:
  css:
    component:
      bower_components/semantic/dist/components/button.css: {}
semantic_ui.input:
  css:
    component:
      bower_components/semantic/dist/components/input.css: {}
semantic_ui.label:
  css:
    component:
      bower_components/semantic/dist/components/label.css: {}
```

7. Now that the libraries are defined, we can use the `attach_library` Twig function to add our libraries to the appropriate templates when we add the Semantic UI classes.

8. Copy the `form.html.twig` file from the Classy theme's `templates` folder and paste it into your theme' templates folder. We will attach `mytheme/semantic_ui.form` and add the `ui` and `form` classes:

```
{{ attach_library('mytheme/semantic_ui.form') }}
<form{{ attributes.addClass(['ui', 'form']) }}>
  {{ children }}
</form>
```

The `attach_library` function will attach the specified library. Use the `addClass` method from Twig to add the `ui` and form classes. Semantic UI requires all elements to have the matching `ui` class.

9. Next, copy the `input.html.twig` file from the Classy theme and paste it into your theme's template folder. We will attach `mytheme/semantic_ui.input` and add the `ui` and `input` classes:

```
{{ attach_library('mytheme/semantic_ui.input') }}
<input{{ attributes.addClass(['ui', 'input']) }} />{{ children }}
```

10. Copy the `input.html.twig` file that we just created and use it to make `input-submit.html.twig`. This template file will be used for `submit` and other buttons:

```
{{ attach_library('mytheme/semantic_ui.button') }}
<input{{ attributes.addClass(['ui', 'button', 'primary']) }} />{{
children }}
```

11. Finally, copy the `form-element-label.html.twig` file from Classy to your theme. We will add the label library and appropriate class, along with the defaults that Classy has defined:

```
{{ attach_library('mytheme/semantic_ui.label') }}

{%
  set classes = [
    title_display == 'after' ? 'option',
    title_display == 'invisible' ? 'visually-hidden',
    required ? 'js-form-required',
    required ? 'form-required',
    'ui',
    'label',
  ]
%}
{% if title is not empty or required -%}
  <label{{ attributes.addClass(classes) }}>{{ title }}</label>
{%- endif %}
```

12. View a form and check whether it has been styled by the Semantic UI CSS framework:

Site information

▼ Site details

Site name *

My Drupal Site

Slogan

How this is used depends on your site's theme.

Email address *

admin@example.com

The *From* address in automated emails sent during registration and new password requests, and other notifications.

▶ Front page

▶ Error pages

Save configuration

How it works...

The simplicity of integrating with a CSS framework is provided by the new template system, Twig, and the asset management system in Drupal 8. The usage of Bower is optional, but it is usually a preferred method for managing frontend dependencies and can be used to keep third-party libraries out of version control.

While it may be a task to add each component as its own library and attach when specifically needed, it ensures optimal asset delivery. With CSS and JavaScript aggregation enabled, each page will only have the minimal resources that are needed. This is an advantage when the entire Semantic UI minified is still 524 kb.

See also

- ▶ Refer to Semantic UI at `http://semantic-ui.com/`
- ▶ In the recipe *Creating a custom theme based on Classy*, in *Chapter 5*, *Frontend for the Win*
- ▶ In the recipe *Using the new asset management system*, in *Chapter 5*, *Frontend for the Win*
- ▶ In the recipe *Twig templating*, in *Chapter 5*, *Frontend for the Win*

Implementing and using a third-party PHP library

Drupal 8 uses Composer for package dependencies and `autoloading` classes based on PSR standards. This allows us to use any available PHP library much more easily than in previous versions of Drupal.

In this recipe, we will add the `Stack/Cors` library to add CORS support to Drupal 8. `Stack/Cors` is a stack middleware that adds support to the **Access-Control-Allow-Origin** header used in web applications. Without specification, AJAX requests across different domains may fail.

> In order to test CORS, you will need to make a cross-domain asynchronous JavaScript request. The **Access-Control-Allow-Origin** header defines domains that are allowed to perform these requests.

Getting ready

You need to have Composer installed in order to use the Composer manager workflow. You can follow the *Getting Started* documentation at `https://getcomposer.org/doc/00-intro.md`. We will add the `asm89/stack-cors` library as a dependency to our Drupal installation.

How to do it...

1. Using your terminal, navigate to your Drupal site's root directory.

2. Use the `require` command from Composer to add the library:

    `composer require asm89/stack-cors`

3. Composer will then add the library to the `composer.json` file and install the library along with any dependencies. Its namespace will now be registered.

4. Now, we need to implement a module that registers the `Stack/Cors` library as a middleware service. We'll call the module `asm_stack_cors`. Add the following code to the `asm_stack_cors.info.yml` file:

    ```
    name: Stack/Cors
    type: module
    description: Adds CORS support to Drupal via the asm89/stack-cors
    library
    core: 8.x
    ```

5. Create `asm_stack_cors.services.yml`. This will register the library with Drupal's service container:

```yaml
parameters:
  cors:
    enabled: true
    allowedHeaders: []
    allowedMethods: ['GET']
    allowedOrigins: ['*']
    exposedHeaders: []
    maxAge: false
    supportsCredentials: false

services:
  asm_stack_cors.cors:
    class: Asm89\Stack\Cors
    arguments: ['%cors%']
    tags:
      - { name: http_middleware }
```

6. Next, we will need to implement a compiler pass injection. This will allow us to inject our service into the container when it is compiled. Create a `src/Compiler` directory and make `CorsPass.php`.

7. The `CorsPass.php` will provide the `CorsPass` class, which implements `\Symfony\Component\DependencyInjection\Compiler\CompilerPassInterface`:

```php
<?php

/**
 * @file
 * Contains \Drupal\webprofiler\Compiler\StoragePass.
 */

namespace Drupal\asm_stack_cors\Compiler;

use Symfony\Component\DependencyInjection\ContainerBuilder;
use Symfony\Component\DependencyInjection\Compiler\
CompilerPassInterface;

/**
 * Class CorsPass
 */
class CorsPass implements CompilerPassInterface {

  /**
```

```
 *   {@inheritdoc}
 */
public function process(ContainerBuilder $container) {
   if (FALSE === $container->hasDefinition('asm_stack_cors.
cors')) {
      return;
   }

   $cors_config = $container->getParameter('cors');

   if (!$cors_config['enabled']) {
      $container->removeDefinition('asm_stack_cors.cors');
   }
 }

}
```

8. Enable the new `Stack/Cors` module. The stack middleware service will be registered and now support CORS requests. To test this, modify the `allowedOrigins` to only accept your Drupal 8 site's domain:

```
parameters:
  cors:
    enabled: true
    allowedHeaders: []
    allowedMethods: ['GET']
    allowedOrigins: ['http://drupal-8-cookbook.platform']
    exposedHeaders: []
    maxAge: false
    supportsCredentials: false
```

9. Make a request to your website and pass an **Origin** header for a different website, such as `http://example.com`. The request should return a `403 Forbidden` since it is not an allowed domain:

```
$ curl -I 'http://drupal-8-cookbook.platform/' --header 'origin:
http://example.com'

HTTP/1.1 403 Forbidden
Server: nginx/1.9.6
Date: Sat, 13 Feb 2016 05:04:45 GMT
Content-Type: text/html; charset=UTF-8
Connection: keep-alive
X-Powered-By: PHP/5.6.8
Cache-Control: no-cache
```

How it works...

Drupal 8 utilizes Symfony components. One of them is the service container and the services it has registered. During the building of the container, there is a compiler pass process that allows alterations of the container's services.

First, we need to register the service in the module's `services.yml` file. The `\Drupal\Core\DependencyInjection\Compiler\StackedKernelPass` class provided by the core will automatically load all the services tagged with `http_middleware`, such as our `asm_stack_cors.cors` service.

Our `arguments` definition loads items defined in the `parameters.cores` that are used for the class's constructor.

With our provided `CorePass` class, we are also tapping into the container's compile cycle. We check the parameter values for the `cors` section to see whether they are enabled. If the enabled setting is set to false, we remove our service from the container.

See also

- Refer to the Cross-Origin Resource Sharing specification at `http://www.w3.org/TR/cors/`
- Refer to the Symfony Service Container documentation at `http://symfony.com/doc/current/book/service_container.html`
- Refer to the Symfony Dependency Injection component documentation at `http://symfony.com/doc/current/components/dependency_injection/introduction.html`

Using Composer manager

Drupal 8 has an interesting predicament. It utilizes third-party PHP libraries *Proudly Built Elsewhere* that are managed through Composer. However, the packages managed by Composer are committed into version control and Composer is (as of 8.0.x) not part of the Drupal build or installation process.

The Composer manager module provides a way to fully support a Composer-based workflow when working with Drupal. Drupal Commerce requires a Composer-based workflow because it uses third-party PHP libraries. In this recipe, we will examine the Drupal Commerce `composer.json` file and install the module.

 Ideally, future versions of Drupal, such as 8.1.x or 8.2.x, will remove the need for the Composer manager and the previous recipe can use a `composer.json` in the module itself to define the external library dependency.

Getting ready

You need to have Composer installed in order to use the Composer manager workflow. You can follow the *Getting Started* documentation at `https://getcomposer.org/doc/00-intro.md`.

How to do it...

1. Download the latest version of Composer manager, and place it in your Drupal site's modules folder:

Other releases		
Version	**Download**	**Date**
8.x-1.0-rc1	tar.gz (16.95 KB) | zip (25.14 KB)	2015-Oct-18
Development releases		
Version	**Download**	**Date**
8.x-1.x-dev	tar.gz (16.96 KB) | zip (25.15 KB)	2015-Oct-18

2. The Drupal 8 version will most likely remain as an **Other release**, as the goal is to improve Drupal core's Composer integration and remove the need for this module.

3. Download the Drupal Commerce module and place it in your Drupal site's `modules` folder. Do not install the module.

4. The Drupal Commerce module contains a `composer.json` that requires three external PHP libraries:

```
{
    "name": "drupal/commerce",
    "type": "drupal-module",
    "description": "Drupal Commerce is a flexible eCommerce
solution.",
    "homepage": "http://drupal.org/project/commerce",
    "license": "GPL-2.0+",
    "require": {
        "commerceguys/intl": "dev-master",
        "commerceguys/pricing": "dev-master",
        "commerceguys/tax": "dev-master"
    },
    "minimum-stability": "dev"
}
```

5. In order to allow Composer to download our dependencies, we need to run a script provided by Composer manager that will patch Drupal core's `composer.json`. Run this command from the root of your Drupal site's directory:

    ```
    php modules/composer_manager/scripts/init.php
    ```

6. Now, Drupal core's `composer.json` will be aware of any module requirements. The next command will download all the required dependencies:

    ```
    composer drupal-update
    ```

7. The `commerceguys/intl`, `commerceguys/pricing`, and `commerceguys/tax` libraries will now be in the root `vendor` folder of your Drupal site.

8. You can now successfully install Drupal Commerce and its submodules:

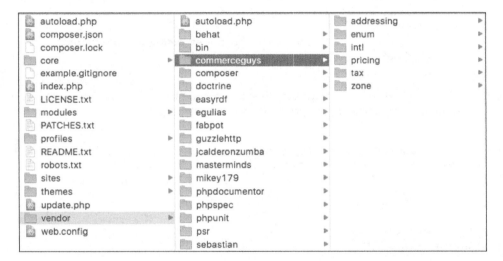

How it works...

The `composer.json` in the root Drupal 8 directory actually acts as a meta configuration. It defines a requirement for the Wikimedia library that merges the `composer.json` files. The Composer manager module adds the discovered `composer.json` files used for extensions to the list of files to be merged.

When you run the `init.php` script, it updates the root `composer.json` file to manually add a namespace to the module's Composer script and two custom commands: `drupal-rebuild` and `drupal-update`:

```
"autoload": {
    "psr-4": {
        "Drupal\\Core\\Composer\\": "core/lib/Drupal/Core/
Composer",
```

```
            "Drupal\\composer_manager\\Composer\\": "modules/contrib/
composer_manager/src/Composer"
        }
    },
    "scripts": {
        "pre-autoload-dump": "Drupal\\Core\\Composer\\
Composer::preAutoloadDump",
        "post-autoload-dump": "Drupal\\Core\\Composer\\
Composer::ensureHtaccess",
        "post-package-install": "Drupal\\Core\\Composer\\Composer::ven
dorTestCodeCleanup",
        "post-package-update": "Drupal\\Core\\Composer\\Composer::vend
orTestCodeCleanup",
        "drupal-rebuild": "Drupal\\composer_manager\\Composer\\
Command::rebuild",
        "drupal-update": "Drupal\\composer_manager\\Composer\\
Command::update"
    },
```

The `drupal-rebuild` command updates the files that are to be merged. Then, the `drupal-update` command will download or update the required dependencies.

 Currently, the discovery of the extension `composer.json` files is the major functionality provided by the module. You can follow the issue to provide automatic discovery at `https://www.drupal.org/node/2609568`.

There's more...

Soon Drupal core will support Composer in custom and contributed modules. We will cover how to simplify the previous *Implementing and using a third-party PHP library* recipe using a `composer.json` file in your module.

Updating the Stack/Cors recipe

The *Implementing and using a third-party PHP library* recipe manually adds the `asm89/stack-cors` library to the root `composer.json` as a dependency. A problem with this is that any Drupal core upgrade will remove this modification, this being one reason we require Composer manager.

This can be mitigated by adding a `composer.json` in your module's base directory file that contains the following code:

```
{
  "name": "drupal/asm_stack-cors",
```

```
"type": "drupal-module",
"description": "Implements stack middleware Stack/Cors",
"license": "GPL-2.0+",
"require": {
  "asm89/stack-cors": "^0.2.1"
},
"minimum-stability": "dev"
}
```

Drupal 8 has the Wikimedia `composer-merge-plugin` as a dependency. This package allows you to merge multiple `composer.json` files into one, such as a `composer.json` that is provided by modules. Composer manager provides the missing steps that allow the module's `composer.json` be merged into the root `composer.json` and download the PHP library.

See also

- ▸ Refer to the Composer documentation for *replace* at
  `https://getcomposer.org/doc/04-schema.md#replace`

- ▸ Refer to the `wikimedia/composer-merge-plugin` library at
  `https://github.com/wikimedia/composer-merge-plugin`

- ▸ Refer to `wikimedia/composer-merge-plugin manage contrib`
  dependencies at `https://www.drupal.org/node/2609568`

12

Web Services

Drupal 8 ships with the RESTful functionality, to implement web services to interact with your application. This chapter shows you how to enable these features and build your own API:

- ▶ Enabling RESTful interfaces
- ▶ Using GET to retrieve data
- ▶ Using POST to create data
- ▶ Using PATCH to update data
- ▶ Using Views to provide custom data sources
- ▶ Authentication

Introduction

There are several modules provided by Drupal 8 that enable the ability to turn it into a web services provider. The Serialization module provides a means of serializing data to, or deserializing from formats such as JSON and XML. The RESTful Web Services module then exposes entities and other APIs through web APIs.

The HAL module serializes entities using **Hypertext Application Language** format. (**HAL**) is an Internet Draft standard convention used to hyperlink between resources in an API. HAL JSON is required when working with POST and PATCH methods. For authentication, the HTTP Basic Authentication module provides a simplistic authentication via HTTP headers.

This chapter covers how to work with the RESTful Web Services module and the supporting modules around developing a RESTful API powered by Drupal 8. We will cover how to use the GET, POST, and PATCH HTTP methods to manipulate content on the website. Additionally, we will cover how to use Views to provide custom content that lists endpoints. And finally, we will cover how to handle custom authentication for your API.

In an article, Putting off PUT, the team behind the web services initiative chose to not implement PUT and only support PATCH. For more information, refer to the original article at https:// groups.drupal.org/node/284948. However, the API is open for contributed modules to add the PUT support for core resources or their own.

Enabling RESTful interfaces

The RESTful Web Services module provides routes that expose endpoints for your RESTful API. It utilizes the Serialization module to handle the normalization to a response and denormalization of data from requests. Endpoints support specific formats and authentication providers.

There is one caveat: RESTful Web Services does not provide a user interface and relies on a single configuration object to enable RESTful endpoints for content entities. Individual endpoints are not their own configuration entities.

When the RESTful Web Services module is first installed, it will enable GET, POST, PATCH, and DELETE methods for the node entity. Each method will support the hal_json format and basic_auth for its support authentication methods. This ends up with a highly coupled relationship between the HAL and HTTP Basic Authentication modules.

In this recipe, we will install RESTful Web Services and enable the proper permissions to allow the retrieval of nodes via REST to receive our formatted JSON.

We will cover using GET, POST, PATCH, and DELETE in other recipes. This recipe covers the installation and configuration of the base modules to enable web services.

Getting ready

There is a configuration change that might be required if you are running PHP 5.6, the always_populate_raw_post_data setting. If you try to enable the RESTful Web Services module without changing the default setting, you will see the following error message on installation:

```
The always_populate_raw_post_data PHP setting should be set to -1 in
PHP version 5.6. Please check the PHP manual for information on how
to correct this. (Currently using always_populate_raw_post_data PHP
setting version Not set to -1.)
```

You will need to modify your PHP's configuration to set always_populate_raw_post_data to -1.

How to do it...

1. Visit **Extend** from the administrative toolbar and install the **Web Services** modules: **Serialization**, **RESTful Web Services**, and **HAL**:

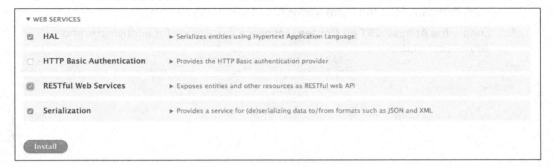

2. The RESTful Web Services module provides the default installation configuration in its `config/install/rest.settings.yml` file. This enables the `entity:node` endpoint, allowing it to be manipulated over a RESTful interface:

```
resources:
  entity:node:
    GET:
      supported_formats:
        - hal_json
      supported_auth:
        - basic_auth
    POST:
      supported_formats:
        - hal_json
      supported_auth:
        - basic_auth
    PATCH:
      supported_formats:
        - hal_json
      supported_auth:
        - basic_auth
    DELETE:
      supported_formats:
        - hal_json
      supported_auth:
        - basic_auth
```

3. In the `rest.settings` configuration namespace, there is a resources section. Each enabled RESTful interface resides under an `entity:ENTITY_TYPE` format with each HTTP method it supports. This `YAML` settings enables `GET`, `POST`, `PATCH`, and `DELETE` using HAL JSON and Basic Auth.

4. The RESTful Web Services module exposes each `HTTP` method as a permission for each endpoint. Visit the Permissions form from the People page.

5. Enable the **Access GET on Content resource** permission for anonymous and authenticated users:

RESTful Web Services			
Access DELETE on *Content* resource	☐	☐	☑
Access GET on *Content* resource	☑	☑	☑
Access PATCH on *Content* resource	☐	☐	☑
Access POST on *Content* resource	☐	☐	☑

6. Additionally, you can enable `DELETE`, `PATCH`, and `POST` on other roles, such as authenticated users.

7. Save the permissions form. Node entities are now available in REST endpoints.

How it works...

The `RESTful Web Services` module works by implementing an event subscriber service, `rest.resource_routes`, that adds routes to Drupal based on implementations of its `RestResource` plugin. Each plugin returns the available routes based on HTTP methods that are enabled for the resource.

When routes are built, the `\Drupal\rest\Routing\ResourceRoutes` class uses the `RestResource` plugin manager to retrieve all the available definitions. The `rest.settings` configuration object is loaded and inspected. If the resource plugin provides an HTTP method that is enabled in the `rest.settings.resources` definitions, it begins to build a new route. Verification is done against the defined supported formats and supported `auth` definitions. If the basic validation passes, the new route is added to the `RouteCollection` and returned.

If you provide a `supported_formats` or `supported_auth` value that is not available, the endpoint will still be created. There will be an error, however, if you attempt to use the route with the invalid plugin. For example, routes need to define an authentication provider key, whether it is a disabled provider or an empty YAML array.

There's more...

The RESTful Web Services module provides a robust API that has some additional items to make a note of. We will explore these in the next recipe.

Soft dependency on the HAL module

For all intents and purposes, the HAL module is not technically a dependency when you install the RESTful Web Services module. The issue, however, resides in the fact that the default installation configuration sets the allowed format to `hal_json`. In the event that the HAL module is not enabled, an error will be thrown using the default node endpoint configuration.

There is work being done in the Drupal core issue queue to resolve the high coupling of the web services modules.

RestResource plugin to expose data through RESTful Web Services

The RESTful Web Services module defines a `RestResource` plugin. This plugin is used to define resource endpoints. They are discovered in a module's `Plugin/rest/resource` namespace and need to implement the `\Drupal\rest\Plugin\ResourceInterface` interface.

Drupal 8 provides two implementations of the `RestResource` plugin. The first is the `EntityResource` class that is provided by the RESTful Web Services module. It implements a `driver` class that allows it to represent each entity type. The second is the Database Logging module that provides its own RestResource plugin as well. It allows you to retrieve logged messages by IDs.

The `\Drupal\rest\Plugin\ResourceBase` class provides an abstract base class that can be extended for `RestResource` plugin implementations. If the `child` class provides a method that matches the available `HTTP` methods, it will support them. For example, if a class has only a `get` method, you can only interact with that endpoint through `HTTP GET` requests. On the other hand, you can provide a `trace` method that allows an endpoint to support `HTTP TRACE` requests.

The REST UI module

As stated in the recipe's introduction, the RESTful Web Services module does not have a user interface to enable, disable, or configure REST endpoints. The REST UI module provides an interface to configure the available REST endpoints. While the interface is rudimentary, it provides a way to enable and disable content entity endpoints. You can then edit the endpoints and enable or disable the specific HTTP methods and their supported formats.

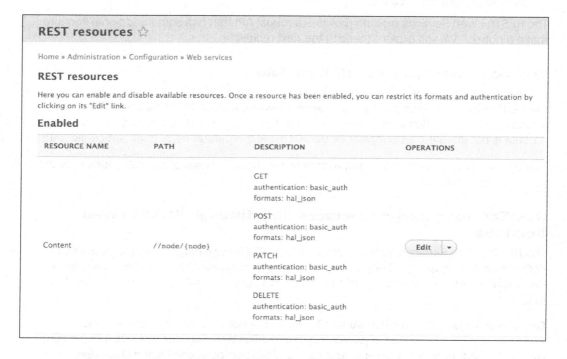

The REST UI module can be downloaded from Drupal.org at `https://www.drupal.org/project/restui`.

Rate limiting your API

Many APIs implement a rate limit to prevent abuse of public APIs. When you have publicly exposed APIs, you need to control the amount of traffic hitting the service and prevent abusers from slowing down or stopping your service.

The **Rate Limiter** module implements multiple ways to control access to your public APIs. There is an option to control the rate limit on specific requests, IP address-based limiting, and IP whitelisting.

You can download the Rate Limiter module from `https://www.drupal.org/project/rate_limiter`.

See also

- ▶ Refer to the Drupal.org documentation for the RESTful Web Services module at `https://www.drupal.org/documentation/modules/rest`

- ▶ Change record: Accept header based routing got replaced by a query parameter, `https://www.drupal.org/node/2501221`

- ▶ *Chapter 7, Plug and Play with Plugins*

- ▶ Refer to the Rate Limiter module at `https://www.drupal.org/project/rate_limiter`

- ▶ Refer to the REST UI module at `https://www.drupal.org/project/restui`

Using GET to retrieve data

The RESTful Web Services module's entity resource plugin implements a `get` method that is called when an HTTP GET request is made on an appropriate route. The entity is processed and then returned in the appropriate format requested.

In this recipe, we will enable the REST endpoint for taxonomy term entities through `GET` through both the JSON and HAL JSON formats. Since there is no user interface provided by the Drupal core to edit the RESTful Web Services settings, we will use a command-line tool to modify the values.

 Since both Drush and Console, as discussed in *Chapter 9, Configuration Management – Deploying in Drupal 8*, in the recipe *Using command-line workflow processes*, support manipulating configuration objects, this recipe will provide commands for both.

Getting ready

We will be modifying the `rest.settings` configuration object using command-line tools. You need to have either Drush or Drupal Console installed with the ability to manipulate your Drupal site.

If you are using Mac OS X and Vim is the default editor on the command line, you may experience difficulties. Vim does not always report its exit code as expected, and the command-line tool may not recognize that you have finished editing your code. Each command-line tool provides a method used to specify an editor (such as Nano).

We need to have a taxonomy vocabulary created with some terms so that there is data to be retrieved.

How to do it...

1. Visit **Extend** from the administrative toolbar and install the **Web Services** modules: `Serialization`, `RESTful Web Services`, and `HAL`.

2. Once the modules are installed, open a terminal and navigate to your Drupal site's directory.

3. Edit the `rest.settings` configuration by running the appropriate configuration edit command:

    ```
    # For Drush
    drush config-edit rest.settings


    # For Console
    drupal config:edit rest.settings
    ```

4. Once the editor is loaded, we need to add an `entity:taxonomy_term` section with a GET definition:

    ```
    resources:
      'entity:taxonomy_term':
        GET:
          support_formats:
            - json
            - hal_json
          supported_auth:
            - cookie
    ```

5. The `entity:taxnomy_term` points to the entity resource plugin's derivative for the taxonomy term entity. The definitions under `GET` provide the supported formats, which can be returned, and supported authentications.

6. Commit the changes in your editor so that they can be imported into your Drupal site.

7. We need to rebuild Drupal's routes for our endpoints to be activated, since the definition only lives in a configuration object:

    ```
    # For Drush
    drush cache-rebuild


    # For Console
    drupal router:rebuild
    ```

8. Console provides a way to rebuild the routing system, whereas with Drush you need to rebuild all caches.

9. Visit the **Permissions** form from the **People** page. Enable the **Access GET on Taxonomy term resource** permission for anonymous and authenticated users.

10. Access a taxonomy term by visiting your Drupal site with the `/taxonomy/term/1?_format=json` path. You will see the following response in your browser:

```
{"message":"Not acceptable"}
```

11. In order to retrieve data through the endpoint, you need to pass the appropriate `Accept` header. You can use `curl` to simulate a request that passes this header:

```
curl --request GET \
   --url 'http://example.com/taxonomy/term/1?_format=json' \
   --header 'accept: application/json'
```

12. The command will return the formatted JSON with your taxonomy term's information.

How it works...

The RESTful Web Services module compiles routes based on the `rest.settings.resources` values. When we implement a content entity endpoint, it actually adds a variation to the canonical URL. It allows us to specify a request format on the same path and have the data returned in that format.

The default routes provided by the `\Drupal\rest\Plugin\ResourceBase` class, the base class for resource plugins, return `\Drupal\rest\RequestHandler::handle` for the controller. This method checks the passed _format parameter against the configured plugin. If the format is valid, the data is passed to the appropriate serializer.

The serialized data is then returned in the request with appropriate content headers.

There's more...

There are details that involve the way in which a request is formulated to a Drupal web service resource. We will explore these now.

Using _format instead of the Accept header

Early in the Drupal 8 life cycle, up until 8.0.0-beta12, Drupal supported the use of the `Accept` header instead of using the `_format` parameter. Unfortunately, there were issues with external caches since HTML and other formats are served on the same path, only having different `Accept` headers. The only solution to prevent cache poisoning on these external caches, such as Varnish, was to ensure the implementation of the `Vary: Accept` header. There were, however, too many issues regarding CDNs and variance of implementation, so the `_format` parameter was introduced instead of appending extensions (`.json`, `.xml`) to paths.

A detail of the problem can be found on these core issues:

- Refer to external caches mix up response formats on URLs where content negotiation is in use at `https://www.drupal.org/node/2364011`
- Check how to implement query parameter-based content negotiation as an alternative to extensions at `https://www.drupal.org/node/2481453`

See also

- Refer to Change record: `Accept` header-based routing got replaced by a query parameter at `https://www.drupal.org/node/2501221`
- *Chapter 9, Configuration Management – Deploying in Drupal 8*, in the recipe *Using command-line workflow processes*

Using POST to create data

When working with RESTful Web Services, the HTTP POST method is used to create new entities. We will use the `Basic HTTP Authentication` to authenticate a user and create a new node.

In this recipe, we will use the exposed node endpoint to create a new piece of article content through the RESTful Web Services module. It is a requirement to use HAL JSON when making POST requests, which is provided as the default format for the node endpoint.

Getting ready

We will be using the `Article` content type provided by the standard installation.

How to do it...

1. Visit **Extend** from the administrative toolbar and install the `Web Services` modules: `Serialization`, `RESTful Web Services`, and `HAL`
2. We also need to install the **HTTP Basic Authentication** module. This will allow us to authenticate our requests, and it is the default method for the node endpoint.
3. Enable the **Access POST on Content resource** permission for authenticated users.
4. First, we will start constructing the pieces of our JSON payload. We need to provide a `_links` entry that contains objects defining relationship links, which is part of the **Hypertext Application Language** definition implemented by Drupal:

```
{
  "_links": {
    "type": {
```

```
        "href": "http://example.com/rest/type/node/page"
      }
    }
}
```

5. The _links is a collection of href values that link to /rest/some/path.

6. We can now provide the title and body values after our _links definition:

```
{
  "_links": {
    "type": {
      "href": "http://example.com/rest/type/node/page"
    }
  },
  "title": [
    { "value" : "Article via POST!" }
  ],
  "body": [
    { "value" : "We created this over the RESTful API!" }
  ]
}
```

7. Before we send our JSON payload, we need to retrieve a CSRF token. We do this by performing a GET request against /rest/session/token:

```
curl --request GET \
  --url http://example.com/rest/session/token \
  --header 'accept: text/plain'
```

8. We can send send the request containing our body payload to the /entity/node?_format=hal_json path through an HTTP POST to create our node:

```
curl --verbose --request POST \
  --url 'http://example.com/entity/node?_format=hal_json' \
  --user admin:admin \
  --header 'accept: application/hal+json' \
  --header 'content-type: application/hal+json' \
  --data '{"_links":{"type":{"href":"http://example.com/
rest/type/node/page"}},"title":[{"value":"Article via
POST!"}],"body":[{"value":"We created this over the RESTful
API!"}]}'
```

9. We have to append ?_format=hal_json to ensure that our response comes back in a non-HTML format.

10. A successful request will return an empty message with a 201 header code.

11. View your Drupal site and verify that the node was created.

How it works...

When working with content entities and the POST method, the endpoint is different to the one used for GET requests. The `\Drupal\rest\Plugin\rest\resource\EntityResource` class extends the `\Drupal\rest\Plugin\ResourceBase` base class, which provides a route method. If a resource plugin provides an `https://www.drupal.org/link-relations/ create` link template, then that path will be used for the POST path.

 The link template is hardcoded to `https://www.drupal.org` and does not relate to your host name. I tried to research why the creation link uses the drupal.org domain. The information can be found at `https://www. drupal.org/node/2019123` and can be resolved by navigating to `https://www.drupal.org/node/2113345`.

The `EntityResource` class defines `/entity/{entity_type}` as the create link template. It then overrides the `getBaseRoute` method to ensure that the `entity_type` parameter is properly populated from the definition.

The `EntityResource` class will run a set of conditions for the request. First, it will validate the POST request by checking whether the entity is null. Then the current user is authorized to create the entity type, if the current user also has access to edit all fields provided, and finally it checks that an identifier was not passed. The last condition is important as updates are only to be made through a PATCH request.

If the entity is validated, it will be saved. On a successful save, an empty **HTTP 201** response will be returned.

 There is currently an issue in the Drupal core issue queue to support JSON for POST and PATCH requests (https://www.drupal.org/node/1964034).

There's more...

Working with POST requests requires some specific formatting to be covered in the recipe. We'll explain them in the next recipe.

Understanding available _links requirements

As stated previously, Drupal requires the use of HAL JSON for the format of requests using the POST method. This is done to ensure that the entity is properly created with any relationships it requires, such as the entity type for a content entities bundle. Another example would be to create a comment over a RESTful interface. You would need to provide a _links entry for the user owning the comment.

The rest.link_manager service uses the rest.link_manager.type and rest.link_manager.relation and is responsible for returning the URIs for types and relations. By default, a bundle will have a path that resembles /rest/type/{entity_type}/{bundle} and relations will resemble /rest/relation/{entity_type}/{bundle}/{field_name}.

Taking a user reference as an example; we would have to populate a uid field, as follows:

```
{
  "_links": {
    "type": {
      "href": "http://master-rpusmp4jcny2c.us.platform.sh/rest/type/
node/page"
    },
    "http://example.com/rest/relation/node/article/uid": [
      {
        "href": "http://example.com/user/1?_format=hal_json",
        "lang": "en"
      }
    ]
  }
}
```

Unfortunately, the documentation is sparse, and the best way to learn what _links are required is to perform a GET request and study the returned _links from the HAL JSON.

Working with images

Most RESTful APIs utilize base64 encoding of files to support POST operations for uploading an image. Unfortunately, this is not supported in the Drupal core. While there is a `serializer.normalizer.file_entity.hal` service that serializes file entities into HAL JSON, it does not currently work as of 8.0.x and does not appear to be part of 8.1.x.

The `\Drupal\hal\Normalizer\FileEntityNormalizer` class supports denormalization; however, it does not handle base64 and expects binary data.

There is a Drupal core issue for this problem, which is available at `https://www.drupal.org/node/1927648`.

Using Cross-Site Request Forgery tokens

When working with a POST request, you will need to pass a Cross-Site Request Forgery token if you are authenticating with a session cookie. The **X-CSRF-Token** header is required when using a session cookie to prevent accidental API requests.

If you are using the cookie provider for authentication, you will need to request a CSRF token from the `/rest/session/token` route:

```
curl --request GET \
  --url http://example.com/rest/session/token
```

Take the token string returned in the response and use it as the value for the **X-CSRF-Token** header in your POST request:

```
curl --request POST \
  --url 'http://example.com/entity/node/?_format=hal_json' \
  --header 'content-type: application/hal+json' \
  --header 'x-csrf-token: tmd1RcICiED9D4GCt0_npMWlIOI4MkgW_2lnYKfjlMc'
```

See also

- ▶ Refer to the Drupal core issue to support POST with `json` at `https://www.drupal.org/node/1964034`
- ▶ Refer to how to serialize file content (base64) to support REST GET/POST/PATCH on file entity at `https://www.drupal.org/node/1927648`

Using PATCH to update data

When working with RESTful Web Services, the HTTP PATCH method is used to update entities. We will use the `Basic HTTP Authentication` to authenticate a user and update a node.

In this recipe, we will use the exposed node endpoint to create a new piece of article content through the RESTful Web Services module. It is a requirement to use HAL JSON when making PATCH requests, which is provided as the default format for the node endpoint.

Getting ready

We will be using the `Article` content type provided by the standard installation.

How to do it...

1. Visit **Extend** from the administrative toolbar and install the `Web Services` modules: `Serialization`, `RESTful Web Services`, and `HAL`

2. We need to also install the `HTTP Basic Authentication` module. This will allow us to authenticate our requests, and it is the default method for the node endpoint.

3. Enable the **Access PATCH on Content resource** permission for authenticated users.

4. Create a sample article node on your Drupal site that we will modify using the REST endpoint:

5. First, we will start building our JSON payload. We need to provide a `_links` entry that contains objects that define relationship links, which is part of the Hypertext Application Language definition implemented by Drupal:

```
{
  "_links": {
    "type": {
      "href": "http://master-rpusmp4jcny2c.us.platform.sh/rest/
type/node/page"
    }
  }
}
```

6. The `_links` is a collection of href values that link to `/rest/some/path`.

7. We will change the node's title by adding a `title` attribute:

```
{
  "_links": {
    "type": {
      "href": "http://master-rpusmp4jcny2c.us.platform.sh/rest/
type/node/page"
    }
  },
  "title": [
    { "value" : "Node updated via REST!" }
  ]
}
```

8. Before we send our JSON payload, we need to retrieve a CSRF token. We do this by performing a GET request against `/rest/session/token`:

```
curl --request GET \
  --url http://example.com/rest/session/token \
  --header 'accept: text/plain'
```

9. We can send the request containing our body payload to the `/node/NODE_ID?_format=hal_json` path through an HTTP POST to create our node. Replace NODE_ID with the appropriate identifier for the node on your Drupal site:

```
curl --verbose --request PATCH \
  --url 'http://example.com/node/52?_format=hal_json' \
  --user admin:admin \
  --header 'accept: application/hal+json' \
  --header 'content-type: application/hal+json' \
  --data '{"_links":{"type":{"href":"http://example.com/rest/type/
node/page"}},"title":[{"value":"Node updated via REST!"}]}'
```

10. If it is successful, you will receive a 204 HTTP code with no content.

11. View your Drupal site and verify that the node was updated:

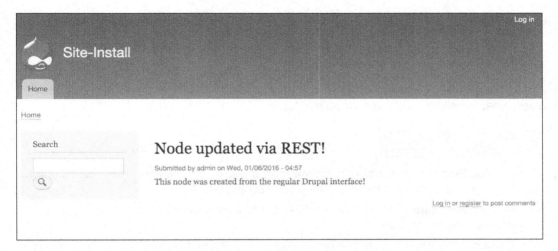

How it works...

When working with content entities and the PATCH method, the endpoint is the same as the GET method path. The only validation is the matching of the content type in the headers, which needs to be application/hal+json. The current user's access is checked to see whether they have the permission to update the entity type and each of the submitted fields provided in the request body.

Each field provided will be updated on the entity and then validated. If the entity is validated, it will be saved. On a successful save, an empty HTTP 204 response will be returned.

 There is currently an issue in the Drupal core issue queue to support JSON for POST and PATCH requests (https://www.drupal.org/node/1964034).

See also

▶ Refer to the Drupal core issue to support POST with json at https://www.drupal.org/node/1964034

Using Views to provide custom data sources

The RESTful Web Services module provides Views plugins that allow you to expose data over Views for your RESTful API. This allows you to create a view that has a path and outputs data using a serializer plugin. You can use this to output entities, such as JSON, HAL JSON, or XML, and it can be sent with appropriate headers.

In this recipe, we will create a view that outputs the users of the Drupal site, providing their username, e-mail, and picture if provided.

How to do it...

1. Visit **Extend** from the administrative toolbar and install the `Web Services` modules: `Serialization`, `RESTful Web Services`, and `HAL`.

2. Visit **Structure** and then **Views**. Click on **Add new view**. Name the view `API Users` and have it show Users.

3. Check the **Provide a REST export** checkbox, and use the `api/users` path. This is where requests will be made:

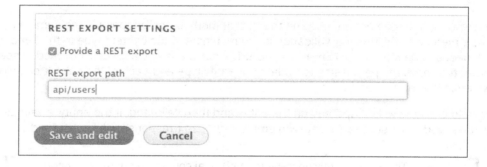

4. Click on **Save and edit**.

5. Change the format of the row plugin from `Entity to Fields` instead so that we can control the specific output.

6. Ensure that your view has the following user entity fields: `Name`, `Email`, and `Picture`.

7. Change the **User: Name** field to the Plain text formatter and do not link it to the user, so the response does not contain any HTML.

8. Save your view.

9. Access your view by visiting /api/users and you will receive a JSON response containing the user information:

```
[
  {
    "name": "houotrara",
    "mail": "houotrara@example.com",
    "user_picture": "  <img src=\"http://example.com/sites/
default/files/pictures/2016-01/generateImage_a7JEUp.jpeg\"
width=\"89\" height=\"87\" alt=\"Abdo bene blandit comis esse
eum lobortis minim qui.\" title=\"Abdo aptent bene saepius si
vulputate.\" typeof=\"foaf:Image\" />\n\n"
  },
  {
    "name": "cragedrelohi",
    "mail": "cragedrelohi@example.com",
    "user_picture": "  <img src=\"http://example.com/sites/
default/files/pictures/2016-01/generateImage_pQDdBa.jpeg\"
width=\"94\" height=\"98\" alt=\"Aliquip decet eu iaceo jus obruo
praesent premo.\" title=\"Exerci turpis wisi. Commodo gravis
scisco venio.\" typeof=\"foaf:Image\" />\n\n"
  }
]
```

How it works...

The RESTful Web Services module provides a display, row, and format plugin that allows you to export content entities to a serialized format. The REST Export display plugin is what allows you to specify a path to access the RESTful endpoint, and properly assigns the Content-Type header for the requested format.

The Serializer style is provided as the only supported style plugin for the REST Export display. This style plugin only supports row plugins that identify themselves as data display types. It expects data from the row plugin to be raw so that it can be passed to the appropriate serializer.

You then have the option of using the Data entity or Data field row plugins. Instead of returning a render array from their render method, they return raw data that will be serialized into the proper format.

With the row plugins returning raw format data and the data then serialized by the style plugin, the display plugin will then return the response, converted into the proper format via the Serialization module.

There's more...

Views provide a way to deliver specific RESTful endpoints. We will explore some additional features in the next recipe.

Controlling the key name in JSON output

The `Data fields` row plugin allows you to configure field aliases. When the data is returned through the view, it will have Drupal's machine names. This means that custom fields will look something like `field_my_field`, which may not make sense to the consumer. By clicking on **Settings** next to Fields you can set aliases in the modal form:

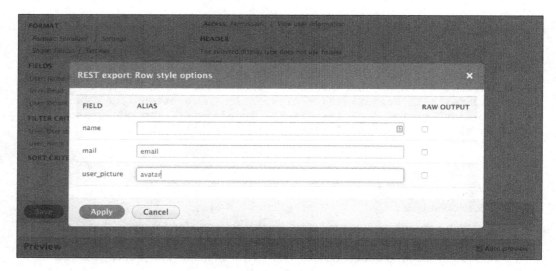

When you provide an alias, the fields will match. For example, `user_picture` can be changed to avatar and the `mail` key can be changed to e-mail:

```
[{
  "name": "houotrara",
  "mail": "houotrara@example.com",
  "avatar": "
}]
```

Controlling access of RESTful Views

When you create a RESTful endpoint with Views, you are not using the same permissions created by the RESTful Web Services module. You need to define the route permissions within the view, allowing you to specify specific roles or permissions for the request.

The default GET method provided by the `EntityResource` plugin does not provide a way to list entities, and allows any entity to be retrieved by an ID. Using Views, you can provide a list of entities, limiting them to specific bundles and many more.

Using Views, you can even provide a new endpoint to retrieve a specific entity. Using `Contextual filters`, you can add route parameters and filters to limit and validate entity IDs. For example, you may want to expose the article content over the API, but not pages.

Add a URL formatter for the image field

As you may have noticed, our `user_picture` field returned the complete HTML for the image and not a URL for the image directly. In fact, currently, there is no option, as of 8.0.x, to return the URL or endpoint resource for the image file. There is, however, an item in the issue queue to resolve this, which is available at `https://www.drupal.org/node/2517030`, slated for 8.1.x.

You have the option of implementing your own field formatter or applying the patch in your build to get the formatter. Or, you can use the Backports module. At the time of writing this book, the URL field formatter is the only patch provided by the module. However, the purpose of the module is to implement a functionality that is not provided by Drupal but will be provided in the near future. You can get the Backports module at `https://www.drupal.org/project/backports`.

See also

▸   Refer to the Backports module at `https://www.drupal.org/project/backports`

Authentication

Using the RESTful Web Services module, we define specific supported authentication providers for an endpoint. The Drupal core provides a `cookie` provider, which authenticates through a valid cookie, such as your regular login experience. Then, there is the `HTTP Basic Authentication` module to support HTTP authentication headers.

There are alternatives that provide more robust authentication methods. With cookie-based authentication, you need to use CSRF tokens to prevent unrequested page loads by an unauthorized party. When you use the HTTP authentication, you are sending a password for each request in the request header.

A popular, and open, authorization framework is OAuth. OAuth is a proper authentication method that uses tokens and not passwords. In this recipe, we will implement the `Simple OAuth` module to provide OAuth 2.0 authentication for GET and POST requests.

Getting ready

If you are not familiar with OAuth or OAuth 2.0, it is a standard for authorization. The implementation of OAuth revolves around the usage of tokens sent in HTTP headers. Refer to the OAuth home page for more information at `http://oauth.net/`.

How to do it...

1. Download the `Simple OAuth` module and place it in your Drupal site's modules directory.

2. Visit **Extend** from the administrative toolbar and install the `Web Services` modules: `Serialization`, `RESTful Web Services`, `HAL`, and `Simple OAuth`.

3. Edit the `rest.settings` configuration by running the appropriate configuration edit command:

```
# For Drush
drush config-edit rest.settings


# For Console
drupal config:edit rest.settings
Modify the entity:node resource and replace basic_auth for the GET
and POST method with token_bearer.
resources:
  'entity:node':
    GET:
      supported_formats:
        - hal_json
      supported_auth:
        - token_bearer
    POST:
      supported_formats:
        - hal_json
      supported_auth:
        - token_bearer
```

4. Commit the changes in your editor so that they can be imported into your Drupal site.

5. We need to rebuild Drupal's routes for our endpoint to be activated, since the definition only lives in a configuration object:

```
# For Drush
drush cache-rebuild


# For Console
drupal router:rebuild
```

6. Enable the `Access GET` on `Content` resource and `Access POST` on `Content` resource permissions for authenticated users.

7. View your user profile, and click on the **OAuth 2 Tokens** tab.

8. Click on the **Add Access Token** button to create an `OAuth token`. Then, save the following form:

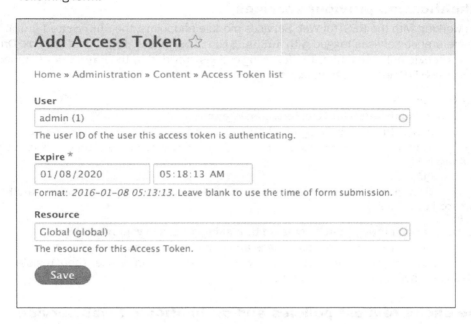

9. Copy the generated token; this will allow you to authenticate requests.

10. Rest a node over REST with the Authorization: Bearer [token] header:

```
curl --request GET \
    --url 'http://example.com/node/1?_format=hal_json' \
    --header 'accept: application/json' \
    --header 'authorization: Bearer JT9zgBgMEDlk2QIF0ecpZEOcsYC7-
x649Bovo83HXQM'
How it works
```

In a typical authentication request, there is an `authentication` manager that uses the `authentication_collector` service to collect all the tagged authentication provider servers. Based on the provider's set priority, each service is invoked to check whether it applies to the current request. Each applied authentication provider then gets invoked to see whether the authentication is invalid.

For the RESTful Web Services module, the process is more explicit. The providers identified in the `supported_auth` definition for the endpoint are the only services that run through the applies and authenticates process.

There's more...

We will explore more information on working with authentication providers and the RESTful Web Services module.

Authentication provider services

When working with the RESTful Web Services module endpoints, the `supported_auth` values reference services tagged with `authentication_provider`. Out of the box, Drupal supports cookie authentication. The following code is provided by the `basic_auth` module to support the HTTP header authentication:

```
services:
  basic_auth.authentication.basic_auth:
    class: Drupal\basic_auth\Authentication\Provider\BasicAuth
    arguments: ['@config.factory', '@user.auth', '@flood', '@entity.
manager']
    tags:
      - { name: authentication_provider, provider_id: 'basic_auth',
priority: 100 }
```

An authentication provider can be created by making a class in your module's `Authentication\Provider` namespace and implementing the `\Drupal\Core\Authentication\AuthenticationProviderInterface` interface. Then, register the class as a service in your module's `services.yml`.

Page cache request policies and authenticated web service requests

When working with data that expects authenticated users, the authentication service provider needs to also provide a page cache service handler. Services that are tagged with `page_cache_request_policy` have the ability to check whether the content is cached or not.

The following code is taken from the `basic_auth` module:

```
basic_auth.page_cache_request_policy.disallow_basic_auth_requests:
    class: Drupal\basic_auth\PageCache\DisallowBasicAuthRequests
    public: false
    tags:
      - { name: page_cache_request_policy }
```

The `\Drupal\basic_auth\PageCache\DisallowBasicAuthRequests` class implements the `\Drupal\Core\PageCache\RequestPolicyInterface` interface. The `check` method allows the page cache policy to explicitly deny or remain neutral on a page's ability to be cached. The `basic_auth` module checks whether the default authentication headers are present. For the `simple_oauth` module, it checks whether a valid token is present.

This is an important security measure if you are implementing your own authentication services.

A page cache policy service can be implemented by making a class in your module's `PageCache` namespace and implementing the `\Drupal\Core\PageCache\ResponsePolicyInterface` interface. Then, we need to register the class as a service in your module's `services.yml`.

IP Authentication Provider

Some APIs that implement server-to-server communication will authenticate using IP address whitelists. For this use case, we have the `IP Consumer Auth` module. Whitelisted IP addresses are controlled by a form that saves a configuration value. If an IP address is whitelisted, the user is authenticated as an anonymous user. While this may not be recommended for POST, PATCH, and DELETE requests, it can provide a simple way to control specific GET endpoints in a private network.

You can download `IP Consumer Auth` from its project page at `https://www.drupal.org/project/ip_consumer_auth`.

See also

- ▸ Refer to the OAuth Community Site at `http://oauth.net/`
- ▸ Refer to the OAuth module for OAuth 1.0 support at `https://www.drupal.org/project/oauth`
- ▸ Refer to the simple OAuth module for OAuth 2.0 support at `https://www.drupal.org/project/simple_oauth`
- ▸ Refer to the IP Consumer Auth module at `https://www.drupal.org/project/ip_consumer_auth`

13

The Drupal CLI

There are two command-line tools for Drupal 8: **Console** and **Drush**. In this chapter, we will discuss how they make working with Drupal easier by covering the following recipes:

- ▶ Rebuilding cache in Console or Drush
- ▶ Using Drush to interact with the database
- ▶ Using Drush to manage users
- ▶ Scaffolding code through Console
- ▶ Making a Drush command
- ▶ Making a Console command

Introduction

In the previous chapters of this book, there have been recipes that provide ways of using command-line tools to simplify working with Drupal. There are two contributed projects that provide Drupal with a command-line interface experience.

First, there is Drush. Drush was first created for Drupal 4.7 and has become an integral tool used for day-to-day Drupal operations. However, with Drupal 8 and its integration with Symfony, there came Drupal Console. Drupal Console is a Symfony Console-based application that allows it to reuse more components and integrate more easily with contributed modules.

This chapter contains recipes that will highlight operations that can be simplified by using Drush or Console. By the end of this chapter, you will be able to work with your Drupal sites through the command line.

At the time of writing, Drush was still the primary tool of choice for Drupal 8 as it had a larger feature set. However, Console is rapidly being developed and features are been added regularly. Due to this rapid development, the commands will still exist but the output may differ.

To get started, refer to the following installation guides for each tool:

▶ Drush: http://docs.drush.org/en/master/install/

▶ Console: https://hechoendrupal.gitbooks.io/drupal-console/content/en/getting/installer.html

Rebuilding cache in Console or Drush

Drupal utilizes caching to store plugin definitions, routes, and so on. When you add a new plugin definition or new route, you need to rebuild Drupal's cache for it to be recognized.

In this recipe, we will walk you through using both Drush and Console to clear various cache bins in Drupal. It is important to know how to clear specific cache bins so that you do not need to rebuild everything, if possible.

How to do it...

1. Open a terminal and navigate to an installed Drupal directory.

2. We use the `cache-rebuild` command in Drush to rebuild all of Drupal's caches, including routes:

```
$ drush cache-rebuild
Cache rebuild complete.
```

3. Drush will bootstrap Drupal to a full site and invoke a full cache clear.

4. In Console, we use the `cache:rebuild` command to clear specific cache bins:

```
$ drupal cache:rebuild
 Select cache. [all]:
 > all
 Rebuilding cache(s), wait a moment please.
 [OK] Done clearing cache(s).
```

5. If you select `all`, the same operation is run in Drush. However, Console is set up to allow distinct cache bins in future development.

6. If you only need to rebuild your routes in Drupal, you can use the `router:rebuild` command in Console:

   $ drupal router:rebuild

   Rebuilding routes, wait a moment please

   [OK] Done rebuilding route(s).

7. Instead of clearing all caches to rebuild routes, it can be done directly with this command.

8. Drush provides `twig-compile` to rebuild template changes without clearing all caches:

   $ drush twig-compile

How it works...

Both Drush and Console will load files off your Drupal site and bootstrap the application. This allows the commands to invoke functions and methods found in Drupal.

Currently, Drush does not implement the dependency injection container, and still needs to rely on procedural functions in Drupal. Console, however, harnesses the dependency injection container, allowing it to reuse Drupal's container and services.

Using Drush to interact with the database

When working with any application that utilizes a database, there are times when you will need to export a database and import it elsewhere. Most often, you would do this with a production site to work on it locally. This way, you can create a new configuration that can be exported and pushed to production, as discussed in *Chapter 9, Configuration Management – Deploying in Drupal 8*.

In this recipe, we will export a database dump from a production site in order to set up the local development. The database dump will be imported over the command line and sanitized. We will then execute an SQL query through Drush to verify sanitization.

Getting ready

Drush has the ability to use **site aliases**. Site aliases are configuration items that allow you to interact with a remote Drupal site. In this recipe, we will use the following alias to interact with a fictional remote site to show how a typical workflow will go to fetch a remote database.

Note that you do not need to use a Drush alias to download the database dump created in the recipe; you can use any method you are familiar with (manually, from the command line, use `mysqldump` or `phpMyAdmin`):

```
$aliases['drupal.production] = array(
  'uri' => 'example.com',
  'remote-host' => 'example.com',
  'remote-user' => 'someuser',
  'ssh-options' => '-p 2222',
);
```

 Read the Drush documentation for more information on site aliases at `http://docs.drush.org/en/master/usage/#site-aliases`. Site aliases allow you to interact with remote Drupal installations.

We will also assume that the local development site has not yet been configured to connect to the database.

How to do it...

1. We will use the `sql-dump` command to export the database into a file. The command returns the output that needs to be redirected to a file:

   ```
   $ drush @drupal.production sql-dump > ~/prod-dump.sql
   ```

   This will take the data from `sql-dump` and save it in `prod-dump.sql` in your home directory.

2. Navigate to your local Drupal site's directory and copy `sites/default/default.settings.php` to `sites/default/settings.php`.

3. Edit the new `settings.php` file and add a database configuration array at the end of the file:

   ```
   // Database configuration.
   $databases['default']['default'] = array(
     'driver' => 'mysql',
     'host' => 'localhost',
     'username' => 'mysql',
     'password' => 'mysql',
     'database' => 'data',
     'prefix' => '',
     'port' => 3306,
     'namespace' => 'Drupal\\Core\\Database\\Driver\\mysql',
   );
   ```

4. This will add our database connection information as the `default` database in the global `$databases` variable.

5. Using the `sql-cli` command, we can import the database dump that we created:

```
$ drush sql-cli < ~/prod-dump.sql
```

This will then run the SQL dump as a set of commands on the database, importing your data.

6. The `sql-sanitize` command allows you to obfuscate user e-mails and passwords in the database:

```
$ drush sql-sanitize
```

This will update all of the users in the user table by changing their usernames and passwords.

7. To verify that our information has been sanitized, we will use the `sql-query` command to run a query against the database:

```
$ drush sql-query "SELECT uid, name, mail FROM users_field_data;"
```

The command will return a list of the results.

How it works...

When working with Drush, we have the ability to use Drush aliases. A Drush alias contains a configuration that allows the tool to connect to a remote server and interact with that server's installation of Drush.

 You need to have Drush installed on your remote server in order to use a site alias for it.

The `sql-dump` command executes the proper dump command for the database driver, which is typically MySQL and the `mysqldump` command. It streams to the terminal and must be piped to a destination. When piped to a local SQL file, we can import it and execute the `create` commands to import our database schema and data.

With the `sql-cli` command, we are able to execute SQL commands to the database through Drush. This allows us to redirect the file contents to the `sql-cli` command and run the set of SQL commands. With the data imported, the `sql-sanitize` command replaces usernames and passwords.

Finally, the `sql-query` command allows us to pass an SQL command directly to the database and return its results. In our recipe, we query the `users_field_data` to verify that e-mails have been sanitized.

There's more...

Working with Drupal over the command line simplifies working with the database. We will explore this in more detail in the following sections.

Using gzip with sql-dump

Sometimes databases can be quite large. The `sql-dump` command has a `gzip` option that will output the SQL dump using the `gzip` command. In order to run the command, you would simply do:

```
$ drush sql-dump --gzip dump.sql.gz
```

The end result provides a reduction in the dump file:

```
-rw-r--r--    1 user    group   3058522 Jan 14 16:10 dump.sql
-rw-r--r--    1 user    group    285880 Jan 14 16:10 dump.sql.gz
```

 If you create a `gzipped` database dump, make sure that you unarchive it before attempting an import with the `sql-cli` command.

Using Console to interact with the database

At the time of writing this book, Console does not provide a command for sanitizing the database. There are the `database:connect` and `database:client` commands, which will launch a database client. This allows you to be logged into the database's command-line interface:

```
$ drupal database:client
$ drupal database:connect
```

These commands are similar to the `sql-cli` and `sql-connect` commands from Drush. The `client` command will bring you to the database's command-line tool, where `connect` shows the connection string.

Console also provides the `database:dump` command. Unlike Drush, this will write the database dump for you in the Drupal directory:

```
$ drupal database:dump
 [OK] Database exported to: /path/to/drupal/www/data.sql
```

See also

► *Chapter 9, Configuration Management – Deploying in Drupal 8*

> ▶ Refer to Dumping Data in SQL Format with `mysqldump` at `http://dev.mysql.com/doc/refman/5.7/en/mysqldump-sql-format.html`

Using Drush to manage users

When you need to add an account to Drupal, you will visit the People page and manually add a new user. Drush provides the complete user management for Drupal, from creation to role assignment, password recovery, and deletion. This workflow allows you to create users easily and provides them with a login without having to enter your Drupal site.

In this recipe, we will create a `staff` role with a `staffmember` user and log in as that user through Drush.

How to do it...

1. Use the `role-create` command to create a new role labeled `staff`:

   ```
   $ drush role-create staff
   Created "staff"
   ```

2. Use the `role-lists` command to verify that the role was created in Drupal:

   ```
   $ drush role-list
   ID              Role Label
   anonymous       Anonymous user
   authenticated   Authenticated user
   administrator   Administrator
   staff           Staff
   ```

3. The `user-create` command will create our user:

   ```
   $ drush user-create staffmember
   User ID      :   2
   User name    :   staffmember
   User roles   :   authenticated
   User status  :   1
   ```

4. In order to add the role, we need to use the `user-add-role` command:

   ```
   $ drush user-add-role staff staffmember
   Added role staff role to staffmember
   ```

5. We will now log in as the `staffmember` user using the `user-login` command:

   ```
   $ drush user-login staffmember --uri=http://example.com
   http://example.com/user/reset/2/1452810532/Ia1nJvbr2UQ3Pi_
   QnmITlVgcCWzDtnKmHxf-I2eAqPE
   ```

6. Provide the `uri` option to ensure that a correct URL points to a one time login link.

7. Copy the link and paste it in your browser to log in as that user.

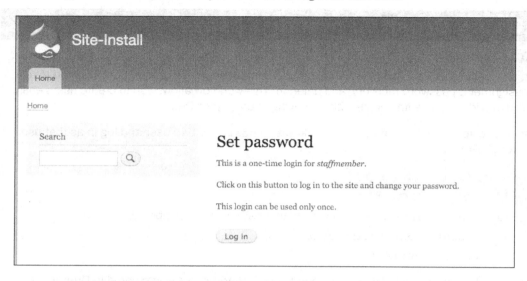

How it works...

When you reset a password in Drupal, a special one-time login link is generated. The login link is based on a generated hash. The Drush command validates the given user, which exists in the Drupal site and then passes it to the `user_pass_reset_url` function from the User module.

The URL is made up of the user's ID, the timestamp when the link was generated, and a hash based on the user's last login time, link generation, and e-mail. When the link is loaded, this hash is rebuilt and verified. For example, if the user has logged in since the time it was generated, the link will become invalid.

When used on a machine that has a web browser installed, Drush will make an attempt to launch the link in a web browser for you. The browser option allows you to specify which browser should be launched. Additionally, you can use `no-browser` to prevent one from being launched.

There's more...

The command line offers the ability to simplify user management and user administration. Next, we will explore more on this topic in detail.

Advanced user-login use cases

The `user-login` command is a useful tool that allows some advanced use cases. For instance, you can append a path after the username and be launched to that path. You can pass a UID or e-mail instead of a username in order to log in as a user.

You can use the `user-login` to secure your admin user account. In Drupal, the user with the identifier of 1 is treated as the root, and can bypass all permissions. Many times, this is the default maintenance account used to work on the Drupal site. Instead of logging in manually, you can set the account to a very robust passphrase and use the `user-login` command when you need to access your site. With this, the only users who should be able to log in as the administrator account are those with access to run Drush commands on the website.

Using Drupal Console

Console also provided commands to interact with users. While they do not allow the creation of users or roles, they provide basic user management.

The `user:login:url` command will generate a one time login link for the specified user ID . This uses the same methods as the Drush command:

```
$ drupal user:login:url 2
```

The `user:password:reset` command allows you to reset a user's password to the new provided password. You can provide the user ID and new password as arguments, but if missing, the values will be prompted for interactively:

```
$ drupal user:password:reset 2 newpassword
```

The `create:users` command provides an interactive way to generate bulk users, which are useful to debug. However, it cannot make individual users with specific passwords like Drush.

Scaffolding code through Console

When Drupal Console was first introduced, one of the biggest highlights was its ability to scaffold code. The project has turned into a much larger Drupal runner over the command-line interface, but much of its `resourcefulness` is code generation.

As you may have noticed in the previous chapters and recipes, there can be a few mundane tasks and a bit of boilerplate code. Drupal Console enables Drupal developers to create various components without having to write all of the boilerplate code.

In *Chapter 10, The Entity API* we covered the *creation of a custom entity type*. In this recipe, we will automate most of that process using Console to generate our content entity.

Getting ready

For this recipe, you need to have Drupal Console installed. The tool will generate everything else for us. You will need to have a Drupal 8 site installed. Many of Console's commands will not work (or be listed) unless they can access an installed Drupal site. This is because of the way it interacts with Drupal's service container.

How to do it...

1. From the root of your Drupal site, generate a module with the `generate:module` command and follow the interactive process. Use the defaults prompted besides giving it a module name:

```
$ drupal generate:module

Welcome to the Drupal module generator

Enter the new module name: My module
Enter the module machine name [my_module]:
Enter the module Path [/modules/custom]:
Enter module description [My Awesome Module]:
Enter package name [Other]:
Enter Drupal Core version [8.x]:
Do you want to generate a .module file (yes/no) [no]: no
Define module as feature [no]? no
Do you want to add a composer.json file to your module [yes]? yes
Would you like to add module dependencies [no]?
Do you confirm generation [yes]?

Generated or updated files

Site path: /path/to/drupal8/www
1 - modules/custom/my_module/my_module.info.yml
2 - modules/custom/my_module/composer.json
```

2. The command walks you through prompts to generate the `info.yml` and will output the path of the generated `info.yml` and `composer.json` files.

3. Next, we will generate our content entity. Provide a module name:

```
$ drupal generate:entity:content
```

```
Enter the module name: my_module
Enter the class of your new entity [DefaultEntity]:
CustomContentEntity
Enter the name of your new entity [custom_content_entity]:
Enter the label of your new entity [Custom content entity]:
Do you want this (content) entity to have bundles (yes/no) [no]:


 Generated or updated files


Site path: /Users/mglaman/Drupal/sites/drupal8/www
1 - modules/custom/my_module/my_module.routing.yml
2 - modules/custom/my_module/my_module.permissions.yml
3 - modules/custom/my_module/my_module.links.menu.yml
4 - modules/custom/my_module/my_module.links.task.yml
5 - modules/custom/my_module/my_module.links.action.yml
6 - modules/custom/my_module/src/CustomContentEntityInterface.php
7 - modules/custom/my_module/src/
CustomContentEntityAccessControlHandler.php
8 - modules/custom/my_module/src/Entity/CustomContentEntity.php
9 - modules/custom/my_module/src/Entity/
CustomContentEntityViewsData.php
10 - modules/custom/my_module/src/CustomContentEntityListBuilder.
php
11 - modules/custom/my_module/src/Entity/Form/
CustomContentEntitySettingsForm.php
12 - modules/custom/my_module/src/Entity/Form/
CustomContentEntityForm.php
13 - modules/custom/my_module/src/Entity/Form/
CustomContentEntityDeleteForm.php
14 - modules/custom/my_module/custom_content_entity.page.inc
15 - modules/custom/my_module/templates/custom_content_entity.
html.twig
```

4. When the command is finished executing, it will output all of the created files.

5. Install your `my module` using Console:

    `$ drupal module:install my_module`

    `[OK] The following module(s) were installed successfully: my_`
    `module`

    `Rebuilding cache(s), wait a moment please.`

    `[OK] Done clearing cache(s).`

6. View **Structure** and find your **Custom content entity settings**:

> **⊘ Contact forms**
> Create and manage contact forms.
>
> **⊘ Content types**
> Create content types and manage their default settings.
>
> **⊘ Custom content entity settings**
> Configure Custom content entity entities
>
> **⊘ Display modes**
> Configure what displays are available for your content and forms.
>
> **⊘ Menus**
> Manage menus and menu links.

How it works...

One of the biggest features of Console was its ability to reduce the time spent by developers to create code for Drupal 8. Console utilizes the Twig templating engine to provide code generation. These Twig templates contain variables and logic that are compiled into the end result code.

A set of generator classes receive specific parameters, which are received through the appropriate command, and pass them to Twig for rendering. This allows Console to easily stay up to date with changes in Drupal core and still provide valuable code generation.

Making a Drush command

Drush provides an API that allows developers to write their own commands. These commands can be part of a module and loaded through a Drupal installation, or they can be placed in the local user's Drush folder for general purposes.

Often, contributed modules create commands to automate user interface operations. However, creating a custom Drush command can be useful for specific operations. In this recipe, we will create a command that loads all the users who have not logged in in the last 10 days and resets their password.

Getting ready

For this recipe, you need to have Drush installed. We will be creating a command in a local user directory.

How to do it...

1. Create a file named `disable_users.drush.inc` in the `~/.drush` folder for your user:

```php
<?php

/**
 * @file
 * Loads all users who have not logged in within 10 days and
disables them.
 */
```

2. Add the Drush command hook that will allow Drush to discover our commands provided by the file:

```php
/**
 * Implements hook_drush_command().
 **/
function disable_users_drush_command() {
  $items = [];
  $items['disable-users'] = [
    'description' => 'Disables users after 10 days of inactivity',
  ];
  return $items;
}
```

3. This hook returns an array of command configurations; the hook should be prefixed with the part of the file before `.drush.inc`.

4. Next, we will create the command callback function, which will end up holding all of our logic:

```php
/**
 * Implements drush_hook_COMMAND().
 */
```

```
function drush_disable_users_disable_users() {

}
```

5. Since our filename is `disable_users.drush.inc` and our command is `disable-users`, the hook turns out to be `drush_disable_users_disable_users`.

6. Update the function to create a `DateTime` object, representing 10 days ago. We will use this to generate a timestamp for our query:

```
/**
 * Implements drush_hook_COMMAND().
 */
function drush_disable_users_disable_users() {
  // Get the default timezone and make a DateTime object for 10
  days ago.
  $system_date = \Drupal::config('system.date');
  $default_timezone = $system_date->get('timezone.default') ?:
  date_default_timezone_get();
  $now = new DateTime('now', new DateTimeZone($default_timezone));
  $now->modify('-10 days');
}
```

7. We load the `system.date` configuration object to get the default time zone and properly construct a `DateTime` object, modified 10 days ago.

8. Now, we will add our query, which will query all the user entities who have a login timestamp greater than 10 days:

```
/**
 * Implements drush_hook_COMMAND().
 */
function drush_disable_users_disable_users() {
  // Get the default timezone and make a DateTime object for 10
  days ago.
  $system_date = \Drupal::config('system.date');
  $default_timezone = $system_date->get('timezone.default') ?:
  date_default_timezone_get();
  $now = new DateTime('now', new DateTimeZone($default_timezone));
  $now->modify('-10 days');

  $query = \Drupal::entityQuery('user')
    ->condition('login', $now->getTimestamp(), '>');
  $results = $query->execute();

  if (empty($results)) {
    drush_print('No users to disable!');
  }
}
```

9. If there are no results, an empty array will be returned.

10. Next, we will iterate over the results and mark the user as disabled:

```
/**
 * Implements drush_hook_COMMAND().
 */
function drush_disable_users_disable_users() {
  // Get the default timezone and make a DateTime object for 10
days ago.
  $system_date = \Drupal::config('system.date');
  $default_timezone = $system_date->get('timezone.default') ?:
date_default_timezone_get();
  $now = new DateTime('now', new DateTimeZone($default_timezone));
  $now->modify('-10 days');

  $query = \Drupal::entityQuery('user')
    ->condition('login', $now->getTimestamp(), '>');
  $results = $query->execute();

  if (empty($results)) {
    drush_print('No users to disable!');
  }

  foreach ($results as $uid) {
    /** @var \Drupal\user\Entity\User $user */
    $user = \Drupal\user\Entity\User::load($uid);
    $user->block();
    $user->save();
  }

  drush_print(dt('Disabled !count users', ['!count' =>
count($results)]));
}
```

11. The result is an array of user IDs. We loop over them to load the user, mark them as disabled, and then save them to commit the changes.

12. Drush's cache will need to be cleared in order to discover your new command:

```
$ drush cache-clear drush
```

13. Check whether the command exists:

```
$ drush disable-users --help
Disables users after 10 days of inactivity
```

How it works...

Drush works by scanning specific directories for files that follow the COMMANDFILE.drush.inc pattern. You can think of COMMANDFILE for Drush as a representation of a module name in Drupal's hook system. When implementing a Drush hook, in the HOOK_drush format, you need to replace HOOK with your COMMANDFILE name, just as you would do in Drupal with a module name.

In this recipe, we created a disable_users.drush.inc file. This means that all hooks and commands in the file need to use disable_users for hook invocations. Drush uses this to load the hook_drush_command hook that returns our command information.

We then provide the functionality of our logic in the drush_hook_command hook. For this hook, we replace hook with our commandfile name. This was disable_users, giving us drush_disable_users_command. We replace command with the command that we defined in hook_drush_command, which was disable-users. We then have our final drush_disable_users_disable_users hook.

There's more...

Drush commands have additional options that can be specified in their definitions. We explore their abilities to control the required level of Drupal integration for a command.

Specifying the level of Drupal's bootstrap

Drush commands have the ability to specify the level of Drupal's bootstrap before being executed. Drupal has several bootstrap levels in which only specific parts of the system are loaded. By default, a command's bootstrap is at DRUSH_BOOTSTRAP_DRUPAL_LOGIN, which is at the same level as accessing Drupal over the web.

Commands, depending on their purpose, can choose to avoid bootstrapping Drupal at all or only until the database system is loaded. Drush commands that are utilities, such as the Git Release Notes module, provide a Drush command that does not interact with Drupal. It specifies a bootstrap of DRUSH_BOOTSTRAP_DRUSH, as it only interacts with repositories to generate change logs based on git tags and commits.

See also

- ▶ Refer to how to creating custom Drush commands at http://docs.drush.org/en/master/commands/
- ▶ Refer to how to installing Drush at http://docs.drush.org/en/master/install/
- ▶ Refer to the Drush Bootstrap process at http://docs.drush.org/en/master/bootstrap/

Making a Console command

Drupal Console makes use of the Symfony Console project and other third-party libraries to utilize modern PHP best practices. In doing so, it follows Drupal 8 practices as well. This allows Console to use namespaces for the command detection and interaction with Drupal by reading its class loader.

This allows developers to easily create a Console command by implementing a custom class in a module.

In this recipe, we will create a command that loads all the users who have not logged in in the last 10 days and resets their password. We will generate the base of our command using the scaffolding commands.

Getting ready

For this recipe, you need to have Drupal Console installed. The tool will generate everything else for us. You will need to have a Drupal 8 site installed.

How to do it...

1. Create a new module that will hold your Console command, such as `console_commands`:

    ```
    $ drupal generate:module

     // Welcome to the Drupal module generator

     Enter the new module name:
     > Console commands

     Enter the module machine name [console_commands]:
     >

     Enter the module Path [/modules/custom]:
     >

     Enter module description [My Awesome Module]:
     >

     Enter package name [Other]:
     >
    ```

```
        Enter Drupal Core version [8.x]:
        >


        Define module as feature (yes/no) [no]:
        >


        Do you want to add a composer.json file to your module (yes/no)
        [yes]:
        >


        Would you like to add module dependencies (yes/no) [no]:
        >


        Do you confirm generation? (yes/no) [yes]:
        >


        Generated or updated files
        Site path: /path/to/drupal8/www
        1 - modules/custom/console_commands/console_commands.info.yml
        2 - modules/custom/console_commands/console_commands.module
        3 - modules/custom/console_commands/composer.json
```

2. Next, we will generate the command's base files using the `generate:command`
    command. Call the `Disable Users` command:

    ```
    $ drupal generate:command

     // Welcome to the Drupal Command generator
     Enter the module name [console_commands]:
     > console_commands


     Enter the Command name. [console_commands:default]:
     > console_commands:disable_users


     Enter the Command Class. (Must end with the word 'Commmand').
     [DefaultCommand]:
     > DisableUsersCommand


     Is the command aware of the drupal site installation when
    executed?. (yes/no) [yes]:
     > yes


     Do you confirm generation? (yes/no) [yes]:
     > yes
    ```

```
Generated or updated files
Site path: /path/to/drupal8/www
1 - modules/custom/console_commands/src/Command/
DisableUsersCommand.php
```

3. Edit the created `DisableUsersCommand.php` file and remove the boilerplate example code from the `execute` method:

```
/**
 * {@inheritdoc}
 */
protected function execute(InputInterface $input,
OutputInterface $output) {
}
```

4. The `execute` method is invoked by Symfony Console and contains all the execution operations.

5. Update the function to create a DateTime object, representing 10 days ago. We will use this to generate a timestamp for our query:

```
/**
 * {@inheritdoc}
 */
protected function execute(InputInterface $input,
OutputInterface $output) {
  // Get the default timezone and make a DateTime object for 10
days ago.
  $system_date = \Drupal::config('system.date');
  $default_timezone = $system_date->get('timezone.default') ?:
date_default_timezone_get();
  $now = new \DateTime('now', new \DateTimeZone($default_
timezone));
  $now->modify('-10 days');
}
```

6. We load the `system.date` configuration object to get the default time zone and properly construct a `DateTime` object, modified for 10 days ago.

7. Now, we will add our query, which will query all the user entities who have a login timestamp greater than 10 days:

```
/**
 * {@inheritdoc}
 */
protected function execute(InputInterface $input,
OutputInterface $output) {
  // Get the default timezone and make a DateTime object for 10
days ago.
```

```
    $system_date = \Drupal::config('system.date');
    $default_timezone = $system_date->get('timezone.default') ?:
date_default_timezone_get();
    $now = new \DateTime('now', new \DateTimeZone($default_
timezone));
    $now->modify('-10 days');

    $query = \Drupal::entityQuery('user')
      ->condition('login', $now->getTimestamp(), '>');
    $results = $query->execute();

    if (empty($results)) {
      $output->writeln('<info>No users to disable!</info>');
    }
  }
```

8. To output to the terminal, you need to use the `write` or `writeln` functions from the `OutputInterface` object.

9. Next, we will iterate over the results and mark the user as disabled:

```
/**
 * {@inheritdoc}
 */
protected function execute(InputInterface $input,
OutputInterface $output) {
    // Get the default timezone and make a DateTime object for 10
days ago.
    $system_date = \Drupal::config('system.date');
    $default_timezone = $system_date->get('timezone.default') ?:
date_default_timezone_get();
    $now = new \DateTime('now', new \DateTimeZone($default_
timezone));
    $now->modify('-10 days');

    $query = \Drupal::entityQuery('user')
      ->condition('login', $now->getTimestamp(), '>');
    $results = $query->execute();

    if (empty($results)) {
      $output->writeln('<info>No users to disable!</info>');
    }

    foreach ($results as $uid) {
      /** @var \Drupal\user\Entity\User $user */
      $user = \Drupal\user\Entity\User::load($uid);
```

```
    $user->block();
    $user->save();
}

$total = count($results);
$output->writeln("Disabled $total users");
}
```

10. The result is an array of user IDs. We loop over them to load the user, mark them as disabled, and then save them to commit the changes.

11. Enable the module in order to access the command:

    ```
    $ drupal module:install console_commands
    ```

12. Run your command:

    ```
    $ drupal console_commands:disable_users
    Disabled 1 users
    ```

How it works...

Console provides integration with modules using namespace discovery methods. When Console is run in a Drupal installation, it will discover all the available projects. It then discovers any files in the `\Drupal\{ a module }\Command` namespace that implement `\Drupal\Console\Command\Command`.

Console will rescan the Drupal directory for available commands every time it is invoked, as it does not keep a cache of available commands.

There's more...

Drupal Console provides a much more intuitive developer experience, as it follows Drupal core's coding formats. We will touch on how Console can be used to create entities.

Using a Console command to create entities

A benefit of Console is its ability to utilize Symfony Console's question helpers for a robust interactive experience. Drupal Commerce utilizes Console to provide a `commerce:create:store` command to generate stores. The purpose of the command is to simplify the creation of a specific entity.

The `\Drupal\commerce_store\Command\CreateStoreCommand` class overrides the default `interact` method that is executed to prompt data from the user. It will prompt users to enter the store's name, e-mail, country, and currency.

Developers can implement similar commands to give advanced users a simpler way to work with modules and configuration.

See also

- ▸ Refer to how to create custom commands at `https://hechoendrupal.gitbooks.io/drupal-console/content/en/extending/creating-custom-commands.html`
- ▸ Refer to how to installing Drupal Console at `https://hechoendrupal.gitbooks.io/drupal-console/content/en/getting/installer.html`

Index

translations
  exporting 186
  flagging, as outdated 194
  providing, for custom module 187
translation server, Drupal
  reference link 188
translation status
  checking 186
Twig documentation
  reference link 112
Twig templating 109-111

U

Universally Unique Identifier (UUID) 207, 212
URL formatter
  adding, for image field 313
user-login command
  use cases 327
users
  managing, Drush used 325, 326

V

Vagrant
  about 16
  URL 16
VDC Initiative
  reference link 52
version control
  using 218
View
  about 28, 51
  block, creating from 55-57
  relationship, adding in 61-64
  routes, overriding with 55
  translating 191
  used, for providing custom
    data sources 310, 311
  using 65

View arguments field 68
Views, in Drupal Core Initiative 51
Views listing content
  listing 48-50
VirtualBox
  about 16
  URL 16

W

wikimedia/composer-merge-plugin library
  reference link 291
wikimedia/composer-merge-plugin manage
    contrib dependencies
  reference link 291
WYSIWYG editor
  configuring 24-26

X

XAMPP
  about 18
  URL 18
X-CSRF-Token header 306

Thank you for buying
Drupal 8 Development Cookbook

About Packt Publishing

Packt, pronounced 'packed', published its first book, *Mastering phpMyAdmin for Effective MySQL Management*, in April 2004, and subsequently continued to specialize in publishing highly focused books on specific technologies and solutions.

Our books and publications share the experiences of your fellow IT professionals in adapting and customizing today's systems, applications, and frameworks. Our solution-based books give you the knowledge and power to customize the software and technologies you're using to get the job done. Packt books are more specific and less general than the IT books you have seen in the past. Our unique business model allows us to bring you more focused information, giving you more of what you need to know, and less of what you don't.

Packt is a modern yet unique publishing company that focuses on producing quality, cutting-edge books for communities of developers, administrators, and newbies alike. For more information, please visit our website at www.packtpub.com.

About Packt Open Source

In 2010, Packt launched two new brands, Packt Open Source and Packt Enterprise, in order to continue its focus on specialization. This book is part of the Packt open source brand, home to books published on software built around open source licenses, and offering information to anybody from advanced developers to budding web designers. The Open Source brand also runs Packt's open source Royalty Scheme, by which Packt gives a royalty to each open source project about whose software a book is sold.

Writing for Packt

We welcome all inquiries from people who are interested in authoring. Book proposals should be sent to author@packtpub.com. If your book idea is still at an early stage and you would like to discuss it first before writing a formal book proposal, then please contact us; one of our commissioning editors will get in touch with you.

We're not just looking for published authors; if you have strong technical skills but no writing experience, our experienced editors can help you develop a writing career, or simply get some additional reward for your expertise.

Drupal 8 Configuration Management

ISBN: 978-1-78398-520-3   Paperback: 148 pages

Make the most of Drupal 8's coolest new feature—the Configuration Management system

1. Understand Configuration Management from a non-developer perspective.

2. Achieve a faster moving configuration between environments.

3. Create custom configuration inside your own modules.

Learning Drupal 8

ISBN: 978-1-78216-875-1   Paperback: 328 pages

Create complex websites quickly and easily using the building blocks of Drupal 8, the most powerful version of Drupal yet

1. Build complete, complex websites with no prior knowledge of web development entirely using the intuitive Drupal user interface.

2. Follow a practical case study chapter-by-chapter to construct a complete website as you progress.

3. Ensure your sites are modern, responsive and mobile-friendly through utilizing the full features available in Drupal 8.

Please check **www.PacktPub.com** for information on our titles

Learning Phalcon PHP

ISBN: 978-1-78355-509-3   Paperback: 328 pages

Learn Phalcon interactively and build high-performance web applications

1. Learn how to install and configure Phalcon PHP on your server.

2. Develop a fully functional multi-module application with Phalcon PHP.

3. A step-by-step guide with in-depth coverage of Phalcon and best practices.

Learning PHP 7 High Performance
Second Edition

ISBN: 978-1-78355-419-5   Paperback: 260 pages

Get up and running with the highly customizable and powerful e-commerce solution, Magento

1. Build your first Magento extension, step by step.

2. Extend the core Magento functionality, such as the API.

3. A practical and succinct guide to test your Magento code.

Please check **www.PacktPub.com** for information on our titles